THE EFFECT OF STRESS
ON DREAMS

P9-EMP-454

THE EFFECT OF STRESS ON DREAMS

LOUIS BREGER, IAN HUNTER, *and* RON W. LANE

Psychological Issues
Monograph 27

INTERNATIONAL UNIVERSITIES PRESS, INC.

New York

Manufactured in the United States of America

CONTENTS

THE EFFECT OF STRESS
ON DREAMS

To

Ingmar Bergman

Federico Fellini

Sigmund Freud

who have used the secrets of their dreams
to illuminate the dark side of man

PREFACE

The studies to be presented in this monograph were carried out as Ph.D. dissertation projects by Ian Hunter and Ron Lane. The work was done within the context of a group working on dream research at the Psychology Clinic of the University of Oregon from 1964 to 1966.

The theoretical conception of dream function discussed here was shaped by these studies and became clear only toward the end of this work. The research was carried out not to test any specific hypothesis or theory, but to observe dreams under conditions that might be informative. The theoretical ideas in their more structured form are the result of these observations; they represent the way our vague notions about dream function and our understanding of the ideas of Freud and others were clarified, modified, or changed by these observations.

While the two studies represent a great deal of individual effort and involvement—Dr. Hunter was both group therapist and dream experimenter, and Dr. Lane spent many nights awake with his surgery patients—nevertheless, it is fair to say that they are part of a group effort. The participation of Dr. Leslie A. Davison, a faculty colleague, in all phases of this work was invaluable.

We were fortunate to have a group of stimulating graduate students who helped make the research group a productive one. These included Steve Fahrion, Garold Collins, Shirley McNeal, and William Bergquist. A group of undergraduate students who also contributed a good deal of effort included Braddie Benson, Joyce Brothers, Terry Crow, Frank Lemons, Lynn Long, and John McInnis. We are greatly indebted to Dr. Mark Vetto, Chief of General

1

Surgery, and Dr. Vince Glaudin, Chief Psychologist, both of the Veterans Administration Hospital, Portland, Oregon, and Dr. John Bascom, Eugene, Oregon, whose cooperation made the Surgery Study possible.

Special thanks must be extended to the four subjects of the Group Therapy Study, and the five subjects of the Surgery Study, on whose personal involvement and courage the projects depended.

The final manuscript has greatly benefited from the careful editorial work of Suzette Annin.

Louis Breger
Ian Hunter
Ron W. Lane
Pasadena, 1971

INTRODUCTION

This monograph describes two studies in which the dreams of a small number of subjects were gathered, using the EEG and rapid eye-movement (REM) techniques of the dream laboratory, under conditions of high arousal and intense personal involvement. An examination of dream content under such conditions seemed an excellent way to study dream function, particularly the role of dreams in psychological adaptation, and to test various hypotheses derived from the dream theories of Freud and others.

Our work was guided, in a general way, by two ideas which emerged from a review of previous attempts to influence dream content and of the general findings with respect to psychological stress (see Lazarus, 1966). First, the more intense the arousing stimulus the more likely it is to have an impact on the subject and, therefore, the easier it should be to observe that impact in dreams. Second, it seemed essential that both the subject's reaction to the arousing experience and the dreams themselves be examined on an individual, subject-by-subject basis. With this procedure, the specific meaning of the experience to the person and his particular mode of coping with it can be taken into account.

Intensely arousing experiences can be experimentally created or observed as they occur in nature. Experimental situations allow for greater control—the situation can be kept relatively constant for all subjects, and observations and measurements can be systematically carried out—but the inevitably artificial nature of most laboratory situations, as well as ethical considerations, limit the degree to which subjects can be aroused or subjected to stress. Naturally occurring situations, on the other hand, may be much more arousing and stressful but cannot easily be controlled, and frequently present obstacles to systematic measurement. Since we wanted to observe dreams under intensely arousing conditions we favored real situations, a strategy which seems appropriate to research in a hypothesis-seeking or discovery-oriented phase.

In a study of the effects of presleep group psychotherapy on subsequent dream content (hereafter called the *Group Therapy Study*) we created a situation in the laboratory and then allowed it to take its natural course. In a study of the effect of preoperative stress on dreams (hereafter called the *Surgery Study*) we took advantage of a naturally occurring event—having a surgical operation—and examined subjects' dreams in connection with it.

In the Group Therapy Study, four nights of dreams were collected in the dream laboratory from each of six subjects. Four of the subjects were then brought together with a therapist to form a "sensitivity-therapy" group. After four warm-up sessions, each subject in turn served as the focus of the group interaction for two sessions, his dreams being collected in the laboratory after each session. The postgroup dream reports were then analyzed on a subject-by-subject basis, and were related to the material that had emerged in the group sessions, as well as to the subject's style of dealing with that experience. In addition, three other procedures were carried out: the dream reports were scored on a number of formal and content dimensions; the pre- and postgroup dreams were compared; and the postgroup dreams of the group-therapy subjects were compared with those of the two control subjects who spent two additional nights in the dream laboratory with no systematic arousal.

In the Surgery Study, the dreams of five subjects were collected on four nights before surgery and on three nights after. Each of the subjects was individually studied before surgery to assess his degree of arousal, the particular meaning of the surgery to him, and the degree and form of psychological preparation that he was engaged in. A subject-by-subject analysis was performed in which the preoperative dreams were analyzed in the light of each subject's conception of his operation and his mode of coping with it. Three other procedures were also carried out: the dreams were rated on the same scales used in the Group Therapy Study; the pre- and postoperative dreams were compared; and the dreams of the surgery subjects were compared with those of two control subjects, whose dreams were collected during the same time period but who had no intervening experience of arousal.

As we shall see, being the focus of a therapy group and anticipating surgery both proved to be highly arousing experiences which were significantly reflected in dream content. Both studies, therefore, bore out our belief that a highly arousing experience would have a strong effect on dreams. In addition, the results of both studies confirmed the value of analyzing the dreams on a subject-by-subject basis in which special attention was paid to the meaning and degree of the arousing experience for each person.

In the next two chapters, material pertinent to both studies will be presented. In Chapter 1, we will discuss the theoretical ideas that guided our work. Freud's theory of dreams will be discussed, certain problems noted, and the outline of a cognitive or information-processing model of dreams presented. In Chapter 2, we review the literature, with special emphasis on studies of the effects of presleep experience on dream content. In Chapter 3, the methods common to the two studies will be presented, including descriptions and reliabilities of the rating scales. Subsequent chapters will present the methods and results of the two studies in detail, including a discussion of the findings specific to each. In the final chapter, the results of both studies will be discussed and a theoretical interpretation attempted.

1

THEORETICAL CONSIDERATIONS

The central ideas and hypotheses concerning dream function that have guided and emerged from the present work constitute a cognitive or information-processing interpretation of Freud's (1900) dream theory. In many ways this interpretation is similar to the clinically based views of Erikson (1954), French and Fromm (1964), and Bonime (1962). Elsewhere, one of us (Breger, 1967) has discussed this cognitive model, the relations between dream function and the function of REM sleep, and the particular problems of Freud's energy concept. Rather than repeating that material, we will here adopt another course. We will describe Freud's several views of dream function and briefly present the cognitive model. Then, certain of Freud's central ideas about dreams—sleep preservation, wish fulfillment, disguise and censorship, manifest and latent content, and dreams as the royal road to the unconscious—will be discussed in terms of their compatibility with such a cognitive model and with recent evidence from REM studies of sleep and dreams.

FREUD'S DREAM THEORIES

As was true of so much of psychoanalytic theory, Freud held several views of dreams, some compatible and some not, at different points in the development of his theories. It is probably also fair to say that one view—that dreams serve to discharge drives or gratify unconscious impulses—remained dominant throughout the changing course of his theory.

In *The Interpretation of Dreams* (1900) Freud initially assumes that dreams function to preserve sleep; the dreamer is motivated by a wish to sleep, and stimuli which would disturb him, such as external noises or bladder pressure, are incorporated into the dream in such a way as to allow sleep to continue. This view then becomes broadened to the more general one that dreams are "wish fulfillments"—that they are a means by which the dreamer gratifies aspirations and fantasies that may not be realizable during waking life. But a consideration of anxiety dreams poses a contradiction to this view—why should one "wish" to dream about something unpleasant?—and, along with other considerations, leads Freud to a further modification, in which the concept of "wish" is redefined as unconscious impulse.

"Wish fulfillment"—an idea easily understandable from everyday experience—becomes "the discharge of unconscious impulses"—an idea embedded in a complex model of the mind that Freud presents in the final chapter of *The Interpretation of Dreams*, a chapter containing many concepts which remain central to psychoanalytic theory.

According to Freud, the wish to sleep coincides with a withdrawal of interest from the external world. This occasions a return to primitive mental processes—the primary-process mode of thought—which predominated at early stages of development. At the time when Freud formulated his theory of dreaming, he conceived of the sleeping psyche as divided into two main systems: the unconscious, which contains the instinctual impulses, and the preconscious, which consists of a censoring agency or barrier of repression guarding against the direct discharge of impulses. With the reduction of the energy available to the preconscious during sleep, the censoring process is weakened and an intrusion of unconscious forces into the preconscious can more readily occur. Even so, to bypass the repressive barrier and obtain entry into the preconscious, the unconscious impulse or wish must attach itself to a day residue—what is left over in the preconscious from the previous day. Day residues are thoughts which persist in sleep and act as convenient "covers" to which the repressed wish can be transferred. If the dreamer were awake, the transferred latent wish would ordinarily seek gratification through motor discharge. However, since the avenues to motility are blocked during sleep, the wish must regress to the memory of a previous gratification. This process results in the reactivation of memory images which were once linked with the satisfaction of the need, and impulse gratification is achieved in the form of a hallucination. That is, the reactivated images take the form of an actual perception which attracts consciousness and results in a dream.

During this process of dream development, the plasticity of unconscious modes of thought, combined with the influence of the reduced but still active repressive barrier of the preconscious, succeeds in altering and disguising the wish and its object of gratification. This disguising process often forces the latent wish to be condensed, displaced, symbolized, or represented as its opposite before it is finally expressed in a distorted, unrecognizable form in the manifest content of the dream. This process Freud calls the dream work and it is what gives the dream its unique form. The preconscious, however, has a final influence which Freud terms secondary revision, and which consists of a relatively minor revision of the dream content with the aim of increasing its organization and coherence.

In sum, the primary function of the dreaming process is to accommodate the demands of the unconscious; an unconscious that "knows no other aim than the fulfilment of wishes."

Thus Freud attributes two roles to the dream: wish fulfillment or impulse gratification—which is what provides the motive force—and sleep protection. The persistence of this model is illustrated by the following quotations—the first from 1900 and the second from 1933.

Dreaming has taken on the task of bringing back under control of the preconscious the excitation in the *Ucs.* which has been left free; in so doing, it discharges the *Ucs.* excitation, serves it as a safety valve and at the same time preserves the sleep of the preconscious in return for a small expenditure of waking activity. Thus, like all the other psychical structures in the series of which it is a member, it constitutes a compromise; it is in the service of both of the two systems, since it fulfils the two wishes in so far as they are compatible with each other [1900, p. 579].

The dream which originates in this way is already a compromise-structure. It has a double function; on the one hand it is ego-syntonic, since, by getting rid of the stimuli which are interfering with sleep, it serves the wish to sleep; on the other hand it allows a repressed instinctual impulse to obtain ... satisfaction ... in the form of hallucinated fulfilment of a wish [1933, p. 19].

The model involving a compromise expression of an unconscious impulse and what is essentially an ego-defensive attempt to avoid anxiety is the basic one that Freud subsequently employs to explain a large array of phenomena, including neurotic symptoms, slips of the tongue, wit and humor, and character structure itself.

A rather different model of dream function is hinted at in Freud's 1920 essay, *Beyond the Pleasure Principle*. Confronted with the evidence that experiences of psychological trauma may lead a person to dream continually about the anxiety-provoking traumatic event, Freud postulated a separate function for dreaming. This function consists of binding the tensions that arise from the trauma; he speaks of it as antedating wish fulfillment. This view of traumatic dreams is embedded in a discussion of the repetition compulsion in which Freud suggests a common underlying principle for certain repetitive neurotic symptoms, traumatic dreams, and the repetitive play of children. All are attempts at mastering, under one's own control, events that one could not deal with originally. As Loevinger (1969) points out, Freud here suggests a central principle of ego function and ego development: that one actively repeats what one has passively suffered and, in the process, is continuously impelled into new situations to master. In this view, ego development may proceed independently of drive discharge.

Freud's suggestion that dreams may play a role in such experiences of mastery is congruent with the view of such ego psychologists as Erikson and French and Fromm, as well as with the model that we will present. However, Freud never gave this idea as central a position as he gave the drive-discharge theory.

Evidence from a variety of sources now urges an extensive modification of the drive-discharge theory (see White, 1963; Holt, 1967a, especially the chapters by Holt, 1967b, Klein, 1967, and Wolff, 1967; Loevinger, 1969; Breger, 1967). The observations and ideas that this theory covers can be placed within a different model—one which does them justice, is closer to the clinical data that was the basis of the original theory, and avoids certain ambiguities and inconsistencies of the drive-discharge model.[1]

---

[1] Such a cognitive reformulation of psychoanalytic theory has been presented, in one form or another, in a number of recent sources. Klein (in preparation), for example, attempts explicitly to restate psychoanalytic clinical theory as a theory of *meaning*. Loevinger (1969) presents a clear discussion of the differences between drive-derivitive and intrinsic motivation theories of ego development, and argues strongly for the latter. Wolff (1967) discusses ways in which psychoanalytic theory can be integrated with Piaget's sensorimotor theory.

AN INFORMATION-PROCESSING MODEL OF DREAMING

We can begin constructing an alternative model of the mind using a unit of psychological structure termed the "memory system," after Freud's usage in *The Interpretation of Dreams*. (This might alternatively be called a "schema," following Piaget, an "ideomotor system," following Klein [1967], or a "cognitive map," "program," or "plan" in the words of other cognitive theorists.) The mind is made up of *interrelated* memory systems, which determine: (1) *perception*—the organization, interpretation, and processing of incoming information from the world of external stimuli and from within one's own body; (2) *psychological transformations* of such perceived information, as in thinking, fantasy, dreaming, and various related conscious, semiconscious, and unconscious processes; and (3) *action*, as in motor activity, speech, and the like. The substance of such memory systems can be thought of as stored information or content, and the programs or plans by which the content is retrieved and utilized. It should be noted that content and programs are probably intertwined with each other, though artificially separated for purposes of discussion. That is, while there is no doubt a certain degree of flexibility or fluidity, by and large certain classes of information are tied to certain programs.

Related models are presented by Dewan (1967), who emphasizes the feedback-control aspects of information processing, and Shapiro (1967).

Motivation—the problem of the dominance or persistence of some plans and actions rather than others—can be accounted for by two hypotheses: (1) The initial structuring or programming of the memory systems determines their subsequent functioning, and (2) the major "need" areas—the processes most important to the person—are tied to emotional-affective feedback systems which amplify or potentiate the thoughts and actions associated with them. A prime example of the motivational importance of initial structuring is the way in which the child's early experiences with core family members determine his later relations of love and hate; of the way in which "interpersonal schemas" become "intrapersonal schemas," in Loevinger's (1969) terms. This principle makes it possible to encompass much of the data which Freud

deals with as "vicissitudes of the libido," "psychosexual development," the centrality of early "object relations," and the like,
with a model closer to the clinical facts and to phenomenological
experience.

The intensity of highly motivated processes—their drivelike quality—seems best accounted for by the involvement of strong affects. These are initially associated with the earliest social interactions of love, separation anxiety, curiosity, and aggression.
These "interpersonal drives" are extremely plastic, undergoing a
number of transformations in the course of development. The
persistence of affective amplification through these transformations accounts for the intensity with which one may be "driven
toward" or "repelled from" particular relationships. These are, in
effect, symbolic transformations of early relationships which still
contain the original affective charge. Piaget views this aspect of
psychoanalytic theory in essentially the same fashion, as the following quotation illustrates:

> Day to day observation and psychoanalytic experience show that the first
> personal schemas are afterward generalized and applied to many other
> people. Accordingly as the first inter-individual experiences of the child
> who is just learning to speak are connected with a father who is under-
> standing or dominating, loving or cruel, etc., the child will tend (even
> throughout life if these relationships have influenced his whole youth) to
> assimilate all other individuals to this father schema. On the other hand,
> the type of feelings he has for his mother will tend to make him love in a
> certain way, sometimes all through his life, because here again he partially
> assimilates his successive loves to this first love which shapes his innermost
> feelings and behaviors [1945, p. 207].

Piaget refers to these personal schemas as "affective schemas,"
stressing that while they are cognitive—operating according to the
same principles of assimilation and accommodation that are involved in intellectual functioning—they are also characterized by
the participation of strong feelings. Translated into present terms,
this would be the affective amplification of interpersonal memory
systems.

Within this model dreams can be viewed as pure *psychological
transformations* which occur during a period when little or no new
information is coming in and little or no action is possible. In fact,

evidence from the sleep laboratory indicates that the person is quite unresponsive to external and internal bodily stimuli during REM sleep and that motor acts are, to all intents, actively blocked during that time. Dreams, then, are creatively constructed from stored information—from memories—and this fact gives rise to two questions: (1) Why some memories rather than others? (in other words, what principle determines the selection of content?), and (2) Why are dreams dreamlike? What determines their unusual form? In answer to the first question it can be hypothesized that before sleep particular memory systems have been *affectively activated* and that these are the ones that provide the material for the night's dreams. This is another way of stating Freud's view that certain day residues enter dreams because of their connection with unconscious themes.

The form taken by dreams is determined by the operation of those programs unique to periods of pure transformation, including programs characteristic of developmentally early modes of thought. In this respect, several points need brief discussion.

First, it is worth noting that, as recent work from the sleep and dream laboratory has shown, much of what goes on in dreams is not very different from waking thought. Bizarre and fantastic dreams do occur and assume prominence because of their unusual nature. Nevertheless, there is an essential continuity of mental processes. Dreams, as well as the activities that take place during non-REM sleep (Foulkes, 1962) and when falling asleep (Foulkes and Vogel, 1965), are often similar to waking thought. Conversely, certain kinds of waking activity may be quite dreamlike: e.g., daydreaming (Singer, 1966), and activities during relative stimulus deprivation (Bertini, Lewis, and Witkin, 1964), in certain drug states (Cartwright, 1966), and states of psychological disturbance such as acute psychosis. Sleep per se is not, therefore, sufficient to account for the quality of dreams; rather, the principles which account for their form and content must be assumed to be active during these other periods as well.

We have suggested two general conceptions—the connection of information with affect and the operation of particular early programs—and can now consider the conditions which bring about their operation. Dreams occur during a time when there is little or no interchange with the external world. What is more, they have existed in this form from earliest infancy. Apart from such special circumstances as those of the sleep laboratory or psychotherapy, dreams are not communicated to others. In fact, the majority of dreams are not even recalled in the morning. Periods of intense fantasy during sleep therefore provide the occasion for a singularly *unsocialized* form of mental activity. That is to say, since dreams are ordinarily not communicated nor is there any *anticipation* that they will be communicated (or even remembered), they need not be subjected to critical processing. They need not be logical or make sense, nor must certain of the dreamer's own characteristics (e.g., his fears or feelings of inferiority, his aggressiveness or sexual desires) be kept hidden. Daydreaming and childhood play have these same qualities, but with the important difference that such waking fantasies stand in proximity to the world of social demands: while one's attention may drift away from ongoing events into a daydream, there is usually a continuing sampling of reality—if there is not, the daydreamer falls asleep and into a real dream!—and it is this checking with reality which places the daydream closer to psychological processes of a critical nature, i.e., those which impose the rules and conventions of society on our thoughts. In this regard, it is interesting to note that the earliest dreams of the night are most like waking thought and that with each successive REM period they become more dreamlike; more bizarre and more remote from the present (Rechtschaffen, Verdone, and Wheaton, 1963).

Freud is speaking of the same phenomena when he discusses the "relaxation of censorship" during dreams. An information-processing model allows one to treat the problem without seeming to talk as if there were a little man in the mind—the dream censor—who is fooled by some other part of the mind into letting something slip by. But there is also another and more important respect in which the present model differs from Freud's.

In psychoanalytic theory, the form taken by dreams is accounted for by positing a regression to the primary-process mode of thought, in which the pleasure principle predominates over the reality principle. It is assumed that the earliest form of mental activity consists of attempts to seek the immediate gratification of impulses, not by interchange with reality, but by a hallucination

of the memory image associated with previous experiences of gratification. Attempts to act on the world—to reach goals realistical-
ly—develop only out of the inevitable frustration of such "hallucinatory wish fulfillments." The primary-process mode remains available in later life, after the development of secondary-process
thought, and, according to psychoanalytic theory, its operation
accounts for the form taken by dreams. Several serious difficulties
are involved in this model.

The problems and complications in the underlying energy model
have been extensively treated elsewhere (Holt, 1965, 1967b) and
need not be detailed here. Suffice it to say that neither neurologi-
cal nor psychological evidence supports the view of a passive or-
ganism which acts only when prodded by the build-up of stimulus
energy. Such a mechanistic energy model, most clearly seen in
libido and cathexis theory, is an anachronistic carry-over from
nineteenth-century science. It has long lived a life separate from
Freud's clinical theory, which is based more directly on the data
of psychoanalysis—free association, dreams, and the human relationships that develop in psychoanalytic therapy. Similarly, the
pleasure-principle account of motivation, if interpreted at all
strictly, is incompatible with the evidence from developmental
studies. Infants do not act only to obtain pleasure through oral
gratification or otherwise. Rather, they are stimulus-seeking organ-
isms that engage in a wide array of active interchanges with the
environment. They practice reflex actions, explore, babble, become angry, imitate people, and persist in attempting to master
new situations, all without any direct impetus from the pleasure
principle, the need for oral gratification, or the like.

A second difficulty with the hallucinatory wish-fulfillment
model arises from the attribution to the young infant of conceptual abilities that he does not possess. The hallucination of the
memory of a previous gratification is a complex mental operation,
involving the conservation of a permanent object and its construction in memory in coordination with some drive information such
as hunger pains. While all models of thought in infants are speculative, it seems more consistent with evidence such as Piaget's to
assume that "imaginary thought" of the hallucinatory wish-fulfillment sort does not appear until the second year of life at the

earliest. The ability to engage in such "imaginary thought," according to Piaget, must be preceded by a sequence of sensorimotor stages. For Piaget, therefore, *action precedes the image* in early development, whereas for Freud the image (in the form of a primary-process hallucination) precedes action (in the form of secondary-process interchanges with the world). Piaget's work is based on the observation of infants and children, whereas Freud's involves a reconstruction of infant thought from the memories of adults. For this and other reasons (see Holt, 1967b; Wolff, 1967; and Piaget and Inhelder, 1969), Piaget's model seems superior. It seems more likely that schemas associated with sensorimotor actions are the primary forms of mental activity, and that imaginative thought emerges later, in conjunction with developing linguistic and conceptual capacities.

A final difficulty concerns what is essentially the trace, as opposed to reconstruction, theory of memory implied in Freud's model of the primary process. This, too, is a complicated issue which can be only briefly touched on here. In his early work, Freud followed the associationists in assuming that memories were both stored and retrieved as traces. This assumption is implied in the model of hallucinatory wish fulfillment and is seen most clearly in Freud's early "trauma" theory of neurosis, i.e., neurosis due to the memory of an actual childhood seduction. Most, if not all, modern writers on memory, including Bartlett (1932), Piaget, and contemporary information theorists, hold to a schema model. Information is not stored and retrieved as memory traces. Rather, it is encoded according to certain schemas or programs, and decoded according to others.

Memory is essentially reconstructive; it involves a psychological creation of the past from stored information organized by currently available schemas. (Such a model fits better with Freud's later ideas about the role of childhood seductions in neurosis, i.e., that they are fantasies or, in present terms, reconstructions of the past created in the mind of the neurotic with his currently active programs.) In general, a schema theory seems to fit better with psychoanalysis as a theory concerned with meaning (Klein, in preparation).

We can dispense with the drive-discharge view, assume that action precedes image, and substitute a schema for a trace theory of memory, but still retain the essence of Freud's model regarding the importance of early forms of mental operation in the construction of dreams. This essence is the idea that certain memory systems or schemas which are characteristic of *early symbolic thought* remain available to the person and become operative when conditions are appropriate. The memory systems would stem from a later period in childhood than does primary-process thinking; they would be those involved in the child's fantasies and play and not in his supposed hallucination of the breast. They would be a set of memory systems operative throughout life in a variety of fantasy situations such as daydreaming, identification with fictional characters, hallucinatory states, and, of course, dreaming itself. Fantasy and play are not exclusively concerned with the seeking of pleasure in the "pleasure-principle" sense. Rather, they are involved in a whole range of activities including preparation for mastery, the magical overcoming of fears and obstacles, identification, the winning of aggressive victories, and the like.

What is common to these activities is that they consist of psychological transformations of stored information with a relative lack of attention to input and a relative lack of externally directed actions. As we have noted before, dreams provide the conditions par excellence for pure psychological transformations. This, then, accounts for why the schemas or memory systems associated with these early forms of mental activity are likely to operate during the REM periods of sleep. Other memory systems, such as those characteristic of waking thought, may also operate, particularly if they involve strong affect. Fantasy schemas may also be in operation during periods other than REM sleep insofar as conditions are conducive to internal transformation. To state the point in another way, the "regression" characteristic of dreams consists of the utilization of memory systems that developed initially during childhood play and fantasy. These systems have remained available throughout life as a means of manipulating symbols when conditions permit the relative suspension of social demands. When thought is guided by such memory systems there may be a much freer combination of elements, including association by shape, color, common sound, or function, as well as along idiosyncratic psychological dimensions. In Freud's terms, there is a suspension of logic and the use of displacement, condensation, and symbolization.

We have posited that their intrinsically private character is a central condition in the utilization of such creative, unsocialized modes of thought. An additional condition stems from the fact that dreams are primarily composed of visual images. Unlike spoken or written productions, visual images are directly available only to the person having them, although, of course, they may be communicated to others by translating them into verbal or written reports or pictures. Since by their nature visual images cannot be directly communicated, they are less subject to the social rules and demands that apply to communicative modes such as speech. They may thus be less constricted, more egocentric, and free from a variety of restrictions ordinarily observed in communicative modes. The force of such social restrictions is illustrated when one attempts to speak as one dreams; that is, to free associate. Resistances immediately become apparent which make this extremely difficult, as anyone involved with psychoanalytic psychotherapy can testify.

A final factor bearing on the form of dreams concerns the curious role of the self or ego. One of the striking features of dreams is that they are typically experienced as "unwilled"; as happening to the dreamer in a way that he cannot control. This fact presents a very difficult conceptual problem, and here we shall merely mention that the unwilled character of dreams is another factor related to the utilization of memory systems which stem from early developmental stages.

A CRITICAL REVIEW OF FREUD'S HYPOTHESIS

Let us now return to certain of Freud's well-known ideas about dreams.

Dreams protect sleep. Of all Freud's hypotheses, this one seems most clearly contradicted by the evidence from the sleep and dream laboratory. REM periods during sleep—the periods when dreaming typically takes place—occur in accordance with a biological cycle of great regularity. This cycle is found in all mammals and occurs, with modifications, throughout the human life span beginning at birth, if not in utero (Roffwarg, Muzio, and Dement,

1966). It seem unnecessary, therefore, to posit exogenous stimuli as initiators of the dream which then "preserves sleep" by assimilating such stimuli into a fantasy. Experience in the sleep laboratory shows that occasionally an external stimulus that might awaken the sleeper is incorporated into a dream, allowing sleep to be temporarily prolonged. But such instances are infrequent and lend no general support to the sleep-protection hypothesis. In any case, sleep protection is a peripheral aspect of Freud's theory.

Wish fulfillment. As we noted earlier, Freud used the term "wish" in two ways: first, in the common-sense meaning of a desire or aspiration, and second, as a theoretical term referring to unconscious impulses which can be, but are usually not, the same as conscious desires. The hypothesis that dreams are wish fulfillments is Freud's way of accounting for dream content—for why some memories and day residues find a place in dreams instead of others. The redefinition of "wish" as unconscious impulse then ties the problem of dream content to his central theory of motivation.

It is interesting to note that in all of the dreams that Freud presents as examples in *The Interpretation of Dreams* it is a wish in the everyday sense, and not an "infantile impulse," that emerges (Jones, 1968). For example, in the dream of "Irma's Injection" (pp. 106-121), Freud, by his own account, gratifies his wish for revenge on unappreciative colleagues and patients and obtains reassurance for his anxiety and concern about his new method of treatment. Such wishes might perhaps be reproached in polite society, and their intensity might be a surprise to the dreamer, but they hardly seem to fit the notion of an "infantile impulse." The infantile-impulse hypothesis seems better described in terms of affective amplification and the transformation of interpersonal patterns. The intensity of feeling—the drivelike quality—stems from the involvement of strong affect. And it is the affective arousal of particular presleep events which determines their selection as dream elements. The "infantile" nature of the dream refers to the interpersonal antecedents of the symbolic dream relationships. For example, in the Irma dream Freud finds himself in a vaguely illicit, sexualized relation with a young woman in the presence of an older man. The dream may be seen, then, as a very complicated symbolic transformation of the oedipal situation, discovered by Freud from an analysis of just such dreams (Erikson, 1954).

The affective amplification of interpersonal schemas is more accurate, both clinically and theoretically, than the concept of "impulse gratification," which refers, in psychoanalytic theory, to the affect of pleasure only. Pleasure is one affect that can amplify the memory systems prior to dreaming, but it is not the only one. Anger, fear, excitement, and others can all serve as dream motives. "Wish fulfillment" can therefore be retained in its original sense and broadened to include a variety of strongly felt desires, aspirations, fears, and purposes—some clearly known to the dreamer, others socially reprehensible and therefore likely to be disowned.

Disguise and censorship. That dreams are frequently not comprehensible to the dreamer according to ordinary standards of logic is accounted for by the fact that different modes of symbolic transformations are possible during the dream state. "Transformation" is a more general term that seems preferable to "disguise" or "censorship," which imply an intent to hide something and also lend themselves to the "little-man-in-the-head" analogy. The symbolic transformations that occur in dreams, like those in art and literature, may be extremely creative. It is therefore perhaps more meaningful to focus on their expressive character than on their censored or disguised nature.

Manifest and latent content. The distinction between the manifest content of the dream and the so-called latent content is central to dream interpretation within psychoanalytic therapy, in which the uncovering of latent content may be a central part of "making the unconscious conscious." In our view, a serious theoretical confusion exists here. There is, in fact, only one form of dream content, and that is the visual dream as it is experienced by the dreamer. To be communicated to others the visual dream must be remembered and transformed into a verbal or written report. It is typically such a dream report that is referred to as the manifest dream content. Additional information may be gathered in the form of associations and memories related to the events and affects from the presleep period. Using the dream report and such additional information, one may make inferences about the underlying structure—the memory system—from which dreams, associations, and so forth, arose. This inferred structure is what psychoanalysts typically have in mind when they speak of "latent content" or the "latent dream thoughts." It is a mistake to refer to such inferences about structure as "content" or "thoughts," however: this confuses a scientific inference with the data on which the inference is based. In part, this mistake arises from the trace theory of memory, discussed earlier.

Within the trace theory, it is difficult to speak of the relationship between structure and content without falling into confusions of the "latent content" sort. From the way the idea of latent content—as well as the broader concept of the unconscious—is used clinically, it seems clear that it refers to inferred structures. "Making the unconscious conscious" is thus a case of the patient's coming to understand the way his own mind operates from a different perspective—it is akin to a "paradigm shift" in science (Kuhn, 1962). The next section may clarify this point further.

WHY DREAMS ARE THE ROYAL ROAD
TO THE UNCONSCIOUS

As we have stressed, a cognitive or information-processing theory posits internal structures such as memory systems or schemas which give rise to the experiences (images, thoughts, fantasies, etc.) central to interchange with the world. Such interchange may be conceived of as a process of feedback-controlled matching of stimulus input with inner experience. As Klein (in preparation) points out, during active, waking periods most interchanges go on "unnoticed"—that is to say, one attends only to discrepancies. What is essentially unattended is the internal-image portion of the matching process, which is too embedded in the total action to be perceived independently.

Dreams consist of internally generated images in the relative absence of external input. What replaces input are the memories generated by systems activated from the presleep period—though these become increasingly distant in the course of the night. An examination of dreams therefore allows one to attend more directly to the internal image portion of what, during waking periods, is a matching procedure. By examining these internal images one can make inferences about the structures which generate them, the memory systems; inferences based on a purer form of data. As we have seen, such internal structures are another way of describing the unconscious and, therefore, discovering the nature of memory systems from dreams may be a "royal road" to the understanding of such guiding structures.

A HYPOTHESIS CONCERNING DREAM FUNCTION

A central idea that emerges from the cognitive view just discussed is that dreams may serve a unique function in the integration or assimilation of affectively aroused information into the "solutions" embodied in existing memory systems. Let us consider an example:

A young man goes to sleep after an argument with an authority which has aroused a good deal of anger and fear. The initial arousal of these feelings is determined by the structure of his memory systems which cause him to perceive the authority in a particular way, produce the angry behavior, and bring about a fear of retaliation. This structure is, of course, a function of his previous experience with a variety of people going back to those important early authorities, the parents. He goes to sleep with these conflicts aroused, and the memory systems related to them are those activated during the cyclic REM periods. During these periods the current situation is displayed, but the memory systems are "opened up" and the related earlier information is also made available. That is, the present authority and the theme of fighting and fear may be played out with a number of related characters including the important early figures. Here, the "solutions" worked out earlier (whether defensive, magical, or realistic) may be incorporated into the theme. For example, a symbolic fight may be won, or the young man (or a symbolic substitute) may intellectually surpass a father figure, etc. *The present conflict is blended with its historical roots* (which are what make it a conflict), *and solutions, frequently of a symbolic nature, are displayed.* It is in this way that the aroused conflict is integrated into existing solutions—this is the integrative function of dreams.

The specific ways in which the integration occurs, as well as the relations between arousing presleep events and dream content, vary from person to person. It is our hope that the data to be presented will shed some light on the specific forms of this integrative or "assimilative" function of dreams.

2

REVIEW OF THE LITERATURE

Our review of the literature will be confined to studies which deal with the effects of various conditions on dream content collected from REM periods. We will not attempt to cover the extensive clinical literature, nor will we deal with research based on retrospective dream reports. (A review of research on psychological reactions to surgery is presented in Chapter 5.) Various methods have been shown to influence the reported content of laboratory dreams, including: (1) the experimental situation itself; (2) the application of presleep stimuli; (3) the application of stimuli during sleep; (4) interference, deprivation, or interruption of REM sleep; (5) drugs.

EFFECTS OF THE EXPERIMENTAL SITUATION

Being a subject in the dream laboratory has proved to be one of the most potent, albeit unintentional, influences on dream content. A laboratory subject is connected to an impressive electrical apparatus and sleeps in an unfamiliar setting. He is in the hands of an experimenter who remains awake and in control of the situation. Perhaps most important, the laboratory situation involves having one's mind probed, and exposing a large amount of dream material that one is normally unaware of. References to the experimental situation (to the equipment, the experimenter, etc.) have been noted in a number of investigations. Dement, Kahn, and Roffwarg (1965) and Hall (1967) provide the most detailed data, summarizing findings from several studies with different conditions and experimenters. Dement et al. found some reference to the experimental situation in 33% of dream reports from the first night in the laboratory. The figure then dropped to 18.7%, where it remained on subsequent nights. Subjects with more "personal involvement" had a higher incidence of incorporation; when these subjects were excluded, references to the experimental situation dropped to 13%.

Hall essentially confirmed these findings, and added some important clarification. His subjects were studied in a situation designed to minimize the "laboratory" aspects and were given much more time to adapt. He found 14% incorporation over-all (similar to the 18.7% reported by Dement et al.), but large individual differences, ranging from 2.5 to 41% across 15 subjects. Four psychologist-experimenters who served as subjects tended to show the highest degree of incorporation, presumably because of their more intense involvement. Hall then examined the *degree* of incorporation, and found that in only 6.2% of dream reports did the experimental situation have a major or dominant influence. In the others, stimuli from the laboratory situation appeared as minor elements, much like other recently encountered material.

Other investigators (Whitman et al., 1962; Domhoff and Kamiya, 1964) have reported higher percentages of incorporation, which may have been due to the conditions under which the dreams were gathered and the methods used to score incorporation. Hall showed that as the conditions became less threatening or less directly involving, the amount of incorporation diminished. The large differences among individual subjects may have been a function of their differential reaction to the situation—a point we will return to later.

APPLICATION OF PRESLEEP STIMULI

A number of investigators have attempted to influence dream content with a range of presleep conditions. Dement and Wolpert (1958) deprived subjects of fluids for 24 hours before sleep and found only minimal effects on REM dream content. Bokert (1967) also deprived subjects of fluids and found increases in themes of general frustration and/or consummation. Subjects whose dreams contained conspicuous themes of gratification were less thirsty and drank less water in the morning than subjects whose dreams were primarily frustrating. A comparison of the

Bokert with the Dement and Wolpert study indicates that their different results are probably due to differences in the way dream content was scored for thirst-related material; Bokert employed a much more inclusive scoring procedure which included themes of consummation and frustration not obviously related to thirst or drinking. A discussion of Bokert's findings (see Klein, 1967, fn. 17) indicates that the idiosyncratic meaning of "thirst" is central to understanding its impact on a subject's dreams (i.e., how this "deprivation" is perceived and what processes this perception sets into motion).

Several studies report the effects of viewing films before sleep. Foulkes and Rechtschaffen (1964) exposed college students to either a violent or a nonviolent film. While the dreams following the violent film tended to be longer, more imaginative, vivid, and emotional, there were no differences on dimensions specific to the film content, such as violence or hostility. Over-all, the effects were significant but small. In a similar study, Foulkes et al. (1967) exposed young boys to either a violent Western or a relatively neutral baseball film before sleep. Here the results were the opposite of the Foulkes and Rechtschaffen study: more vivid, hostile, and frightening reports occurred on nights following the baseball film. Again, the differences were small. Foulkes et al. interpret these findings as being due to the "cathartic" effect of viewing the Western film. As an alternative explanation we would suggest that the baseball film, while lacking aggressive content, might touch themes closer to the life concerns of young boys. Neither explanation can be tested from the available data, however, since there was no assessment of the specific meaning of the film to, or its arousing effect on, each subject.

In these two studies, the presleep films may have been "exciting" but they were not particularly threatening; i.e., they were of a type familiar to the subjects, and the violence in the Western was of a sort to which most American subjects are well adapted. In the following studies, films of a more unusual and threatening nature were used.

Collins, Davison, and Breger (1967) used the film "Subincision," a documentary which depicts a crude operation on the penises of adolescent boys in an aboriginal culture. Each subject's reaction to the film was assessed before sleep. Significant correlations were found between the subject's own rating of how emotionally aroused he was by the film and independent ratings of the incorporation of film-related content in the REM dream reports. The subjects who were aroused by viewing the film tended to dream about it (almost invariably in a symbolized fashion) whereas those who were not aroused did not. These findings illustrate the importance of assessing the degree of individual subject arousal.

Witkin (1969a, 1969b) and his colleagues have reported a large-scale study of the effects of presleep films on REM dream content. Twenty-eight subjects have been shown four films—two neutral and two arousing-threatening ("Subincision" and a medical film depicting the birth of a baby) before sleep. Subjects' reactions to the film before sleep and after each REM awakening are assessed physiologically and by self-report. Additional dream-recall data, dream associations, and further reports of reactions to the film are gathered after the final awakening. A biographical interview is conducted at the conclusion of the four film nights. The findings indicate that the arousing films do indeed influence dream content (e.g., more rated anxiety dream reports following the threat as compared to the neutral films). Two general features of the Witkin study are worth stressing. First, the presleep stimuli are of a more arousing-threatening nature than the films used in some of the previously mentioned studies. Second, the reactions of the individual subjects are studied in detail, permitting the assessment of the particular *meaning* of the arousal experience. This is subsequently coordinated with information from associations and, still later, from the biographical interview. Witkin reports the role of early fantasies in the dream assimilation of aroused material, a finding which appears to support the present approach.

Several experimenters have studied the effects of other presleep conditions on dream content. Wood (1962) kept subjects socially isolated for a day (they read, studied, and so on, in a room by themselves) and found an increase in social activity in subsequent dream content. This is interpreted as "compensation" for the deprivation of social interactions. Hauri (1967) had different groups of subjects engage in six hours of strenuous physical exercise, six hours of intensive studying and test taking, or six hours of relaxation (watching TV, reading, etc.) before sleep. Less dream content concerned with thinking or problem solving followed the intensive study condition, and less dream content concerned with physical activity followed the exercise condition. In order to assess physiological reactions Hauri did not awaken his subjects during the first three and one-half hours of the night and therefore did not sample the REM periods most likely to reflect the impact of recent experience. His results are nevertheless of interest because they suggest a sort of "compensation" similar to that observed by Wood. For example, one subject, after pedaling a stationary bicycle for six hours, dreamt that he was lying in a hammock on a tropical isle while a gentle breeze turned the pages of a book he was reading. "Compensation" or the obvious "wish fulfillment" in this example may be interpreted as a special case of the principle that affective arousal of particular memory systems during the presleep period determines the selection of the dream "problem" which is contained in the system. Similarly, when loneliness was aroused by social isolation, subjects created symbolic situations from their stored memories in which they interacted with people.

Two investigators (Stoyva, 1965; Tart, 1963) report the effect of hypnotic suggestion on REM dream content. In both cases, hypnotic suggestion was an effective influence on dream content, although the effect varied widely among subjects. Highly suggestible or hypnotizable subjects dreamed of the induced content as much as 100% of the time, whereas some others showed no apparent effects.

APPLICATION OF STIMULI DURING SLEEP

Several studies have demonstrated the effects on dream content of stimuli applied during sleep. It is clear that such stimuli neither initiate dreaming nor determine the major thematic dream content (which would have pleased Freud, no doubt). Dement and Wolpert (1958) applied a tone, a flashing light, and a spray of cold water, and found incorporation of these stimuli in 9, 24, and 47% of the subsequent REM dream reports. The incorporations were almost never direct; the stimulus, if incorporated at all, seems to have been symbolically blended into the ongoing dream.

Berger (1963) played recordings of neutral and emotionally meaningful names to subjects during REM sleep and found that the more meaningful ones appeared in about 50% of the subsequently reported dreams. As in the Dement and Wolpert study, the stimuli neither initiated nor determined the dream, but were symbolically assimilated into it. Assonance—the production of a sound-related element—was the most frequent form of incorporation. For example, the name "Gillian" was associated with a dream about a woman from Chile ("Chilean"). Berger's findings suggest that the "programs" which determine the symbolism characteristic of the visual dream transform incoming auditory messages.

In a similar study, Castaldo and Holzman (1967) compared the effects on REM dream content of their own and another person's voice, played to subjects during sleep. Hearing one's own voice was associated with greater activity, assertiveness, and independence on the part of the dreamer, whereas hearing another person's voice was followed by dreams in which the dreamer was in a passive position. The same differences were reflected in the subject's associations and drawings of their dreams. These findings seem to reflect the more pervasive or thematic influence of an external stimulus on dream content which may be due to the centrally meaningful nature of the stimulus. The active-passive dimension is an important one with respect to dreams. The completely passive position of the sleeper (there is even evidence of an active blocking of motor output during REM sleep) may contribute to the experience of dreams as "unwilled," inasmuch as the experience of self as active agent is related to active interchange with the world. Hearing one's own voice is the feedback normally associated with one form of active interchange—speech—and it is therefore interesting to find it associated with dreams in which the dreamer is in a more active, assertive, and independent role. Such an interpretation (which is ours, though it does not contradict that of the authors) is speculative, even though the reported relationships are quite striking and the study itself has been replicated (Castaldo and Holzman, 1968).

Among other studies of the effects of stimuli applied during sleep are that of Foulkes, Swanson, and Larson (1968), who found some minimal incorporation of stimuli in the dreams of preschool children, and that of Rechtschaffen and Foulkes (1965), who found that visual stimuli presented to sleeping subjects whose eyes were taped open did not influence dream content.

Internal or organismic stimuli are another class of factors that have been hypothesized as influencing dream content. Such hypotheses range from popular notions about the effect on dreams of rich meals to ideas about the effects of various autonomic activities, penile erections, and the eye movements themselves. It is clear that many response systems of the body are variably active during the REM periods of sleep; the evidence (see Foulkes, 1966, pp. 164-168, for a summary), however, does not provide much support for any of the hypotheses that such internal stimuli are determinants of dream content. For example, the Dement and Wolpert and Bokert findings concerning the effects of thirst show that it is not the internal organismic feedback of thirst that affects dreams but the psychological meaning to the subject of being "deprived."

A regularly occurring cycle of penile erections has been found to accompany REM sleep (Fisher, Gross, and Zuch, 1965) and was initially interpreted as support for the "sexual" determination of dream content (presumably due to feedback of genital stimulation). Fisher et al. found some correspondence of erection and detumescence with erotic and anxious content in dreams. Several lines of evidence make it seem unlikely that it is the genital stimuli which determine the dream content, however. The REM erection cycle is present in neonates, elderly men, and monkeys (Fisher, 1966). Moreover, the fact that by no means are all or even most dreams concerned with sexual content (unless "sexual" is stretched beyond all recognizable meaning) puts a good deal of strain on this view. The fact that genital stimulation is not necessary for the production of sexual dream content has been demonstrated by Money (1960), who observed dreams with orgasm imagery in quadriplegic patients whose spinal cord transection prevented the experience of genital-pelvic sensations. It seems more reasonable, therefore, to view the sexual content of the dream as "centrally" determined and capable, in some instances, of affecting the ongoing penile erections themselves. That is, the usually regular erection cycle may be disturbed by extremely anxious dreams.

This point can be extended to other internal, visceral, or organismic sources of stimulation as well. As Hauri (1967) concludes, dreaming is largely a matter of the brain. We can agree with Foulkes's (1966) statement that:

> Dreams do not seem to be the brain's interpretation of eye movements, as the nature of these movements is conveyed to the brain by way of *proprioceptive* feedback from extrinsic ocular muscles. Dreams do not seem to be the brain's interpretation of patterns of excitation of the light-sensitive retina . . . of impulses arising in the viscera . . . [nor] of autonomic nervous system arousal. Where some influence of peripheral organismic arousal can be demonstrated, it is mediated rather than direct, and where possibilities remain for demonstrating some influence, this influence is insufficient to explain more than certain very crude parameters of dream content [p. 168].

DREAM DEPRIVATION OR INTERRUPTION

One of the earliest approaches to understanding the function of REM sleep used the method of deprivation. Dement's (1960) initial findings about the effects of REM or dream deprivation have been confirmed by others (Kales et al., 1964; Sampson, 1965). These studies have shown that when REM sleep is interfered with or prevented there is an increase in the number of REM attempts, shorter latency to first REM, and a compensatory increase of REM time on postdeprivation nights. A great deal of interesting work has been done in this area, but little of it bears on our present concerns as most deprivation studies do not examine dream content. Of those studies which have, several (Kales et al., 1964; Pivik and Foulkes, 1966; Collins, Davison, and Breger, 1967) found that the content that is retrievable from REM-deprivation awakenings seems to be more concentrated or intense—as if the subject, anticipating the deprivation, attempts to squeeze in as much dreaming as possible.

A series of studies carried out by Fiss and his colleagues is perhaps the most pertinent. Their general strategy has been to compare the effects of REM deprivation (awakenings at the beginning of an REM period), REM interruption (awakenings somewhere around the middle), and REM completion (awakenings at the end). They have found that interruption leads to a carry-over of dreamlike activity into a waking fantasy task, TAT stories (Fiss, Klein, and Bokert, 1966), and that subjects adjust their REM cycles to this anticipated interruption, having purer (by EEG criteria) REM periods with a greater density of eye movements (Fiss and Ellman, 1967). These findings are interpreted as indicating the subject's need to complete a particular kind of dream experience. In confirmation of this hypothesis they found that content was repeated far more frequently in the reports from REM interruptions than from REM-completion awakenings (Fiss et al., 1968). In an intensive study of two subjects via dream content, Fiss et al. found that the interruption procedure seemed to "accelerate the sharpness and speed" with which the subjects' central conflicts were brought into focus. This general conception of dream function in terms of a need to complete a certain amount and type of psychological "work" is quite close to our own position.

Two recent studies by Cartwright and her collaborators (Cartwright, Monroe, and Palmer, 1967; Cartwright and Monroe, 1968) have yielded results which are consonant with the Fiss studies. Discussion of this research will be deferred until later as it bears only indirectly on dream content.

EFFECTS OF DRUGS

A fair amount of work has been devoted to the effects of various drugs on REM sleep. Like the work on REM deprivation, most of this research has focused on such variables as REM time, and little on dream content. Whitman and Kramer and their co-workers have carried out several studies in which barbiturates, tranquilizers, and an antidepressant (Imipramine) were administered before sleep, and dream reports obtained from REM awakenings. The only finding of substance (Kramer et al., 1968) followed the administration of Imipramine to hospitalized depressed patients. Their dreams showed increased hostility and anxiety during the first week of Imipramine treatment, followed by decreased hostility and anxiety and a rise in heterosexuality and motility during subsequent weeks, paralleling their clinical improvement. The methods and interpretations of results are not always of the most rigorous nature, so these findings should be viewed with caution.

A study by Cartwright (1966) represents a very different approach to drug-dream relationships. The responses of subjects to an LSD-like hallucinogen (piperidyl benzilate) and during REM sleep were compared. The fantasy material produced by the drug was similar to the dream reports obtained from REM awakenings, as indicated by the subjects' own reports and by blind matching of REM-dream and drug-state reports by independent judges. In addition, the percentage of sleep time spent in REM was reduced by almost half following the day of the hallucinatory experience—a kind of reverse dream-deprivation effect—indicating that if subjects get their dreaming done in advance (i.e., if they process aroused information with primary-process programs) they have less need to dream later. This general interpretation is consistent with the Fiss results, though it should be stressed that this conclusion rests on REM-time, and not dream-content, indicators.

In summary, the work reviewed in this chapter indicates that a number of conditions have some influence on the dream content reported from REM awakenings. At the same time, it is clear that most of this influence is peripheral. When presleep events or sleep stimuli are incorporated into a dream, they most frequently appear in symbolic form and seem to be assimilated into the ongoing dream. As Foulkes puts it, "The dreamer does not generally depend upon pre-sleep experience to give him his dream topics, rather he takes bits and pieces of his daytime impressions out of their original context and turns them to some other purpose" (1966, p. 153).

The central question is, then, what is the "other purpose"? What does determine the principal thematic content of dreams? The work just reviewed provides some evidence that the principal thematic content stems from the ongoing—typically interpersonal—events that the dreamer is most "involved" in (which we interpret as affectively aroused). Such a hypothesis is suggested by the large individual differences in incorporation of the experimental situation; by the Fiss et al. (1968) finding, on the basis of intensive study of two subjects, that more than 50% of their dreams concerned specific sexual-identity conflict themes; and by Witkin's work.

The two studies to be reported in this monograph were designed with the above considerations in mind. We selected presleep situations which seemed to be the kind of highly involving events most likely to appear in dream content. In addition, we studied the dream material in the context of enough personal information about each subject so that the specific meaning of the presleep experience could be determined and followed into the dream. We will turn now to a description of the methods common to the two studies.

3

THE GENERAL METHOD

In this chapter we will discuss our general approach and present the methods common to the Group Therapy and the Surgery Studies. Methods specific to each will be described in Chapters 4 and 5. As we have already mentioned, our intention was either to arrange, or to take advantage of, situations of high arousal and great personal involvement, and then to observe dreams, using the EEG-REM methods of collection, under these conditions. It was our belief that a number of advantages accrue from the use of reports obtained from REM sleep. One of the central purposes of this monograph is to present REM dream reports in enough detail to familiarize the reader, who may be acquainted with retrospective dream reports or projective-test material, with this unique and singularly rich form of data.

THE REM DREAM REPORT

It is clear that the methods used to obtain dream reports from REM sleep influence the dream data. Sleeping in a laboratory environment, being wired to an EEG recording machine, having one's sleep interrupted, and the like, have all been shown to affect dream content. While the effects of such methods can be reduced by allowing enough time for adaptation, making the laboratory more homelike, and establishing a good working relationship between experimenter and subject, laboratory influences can never be completely removed. A Heisenberglike effect is at work here: one cannot observe dreams without to some degree influencing them by the very process of observation. A similar effect is also operative in the translation of the visual dream into a verbal report

within the person and is, of course, an inherent problem of introspective data that psychologists have long struggled with. Given
these difficulties, REM dream reports still have a number of advantages: (a) the possibility of a superior sample, (b) the nature of
reports obtained immediately after the dream occurs, and (c) the
availability of dream sequences.

Perhaps the greatest advantage of dream reports obtained from
REM-period awakenings is that they provide a far more extensive
sample of dream data than is available by any other known method. This enables the experimenter to observe dreams much more
completely and in much greater detail—it is akin to the advantage
that biologists gain by using a microscope. Work in the dream
laboratory demonstrates the ephemeral quality of dreams. De-
laying report by just a few minutes beyond the end of a REM
period typically results in much poorer recall. In addition, we have
become convinced, as have others who work with REM methods,
that the only dreams likely to be recalled in the morning are from
REM periods during which the dreamer has awakened. That is, the
dreams that occur during the REM periods of a normal, sound
night's sleep are probably never recalled. Dreams from the REM
period in progress at the point of final awakening are therefore
likely to be heavily overrepresented in retrospective dream reports,
and it has been shown that these last dreams are qualitatively
different from those of the early part of the night (Verdone,
1965). Moreover, Goodenough et al. (1959) have shown that the
large individual differences in ability to recall and report dreams
retrospectively are markedly reduced when such "dreamers" and
"nondreamers" (i.e., good and poor recallers) are put in the laboratory and reports are obtained from REM awakenings. This too
means the elimination of an important source of bias, and demonstrates that the REM report can produce a more complete and
representative dream sample than any other method of dream collection.

Another advantage stems from the quality of the verbal reports
obtained directly from REM-period awakenings. Subjects vary in
this respect, but in general reports tend to be more "dreamlike"
than are retrospective reports of dreams. The associations may
be looser, the imagery freer, and certain considerations of logic
and social acceptability of communication partially abandoned.

Some of the subjects that we have observed seem to slip back and forth among reporting, additional dreaming, and associative activity, as the following example illustrates.

The subject, a female college student, is reporting a dream of several episodes from a 28-minute REM period. She has described being in a kitchen while some people are conversing in another room. She pauses, and the following dialogue with the experimenter takes place:

E: Then what happened?
S: Okay, just saw a little man. I just asked this other guy where "I" street was. Anyway, they . . . got the name right. Paloa.
E: What was the name?
S: A groundwash.
E: Okay, what else do you get there?
S: What about a wash? Can you change continuity in form when you use a wash; you know, turpentine with your paints. That was one of their big discussions . . .

She then resumed the description of the kitchen where she is overhearing a discussion.

The "little man" seems to be from an additional, associatively connected dream fragment that occurs during the reporting procedure. Also, she responds oddly to the experimenter's question, seeming to assimilate it into the dream process. This sort of carry-over from the dream to the waking state is exactly what Fiss, Klein, and Bokert (1966) demonstrated in the TAT stories their subjects produced following REM (as compared to non-REM) awakenings. The stories following the REM awakenings were more vivid, bizarre, complex, visual, and emotional—in short, more dreamlike—and the authors attribute these characteristics to the persistence of dream properties into the waking state. In the terms of our own conception, we would say that "primary-process" types of programs, which in part determine the form of dream thought, continue beyond the REM stage into the waking or semi-waking state. Temporal proximity to the REM stage, as well as the type of intervening activity, would affect the amount of carry-over. To put it another way, as the subject wakes up and directs his attention to the various tasks of waking reality, a different set of programs is activated which precludes those involved in the creation of dreams. The dream report obtained directly from a REM awakening is therefore more likely to be characterized by those psychological processes involved in the dream and less likely to be contaminated by other, nondream modes of thought and reporting.

A final advantage of the REM report is that it enables one to collect entire sequences of dreams from a single night, and from several nights in succession. It is probably impossible ever to get a complete series; sleep onset, non-REM activity, and even some REM activity will not be reported even when awakenings are attempted for each REM period. The matter is relative—but a sample of four to seven detailed, sequential dream reports from a single night is a great deal more than has heretofore been available. If the hypothesis of an integrative or "problem-solving" function of dreams has any validity, we might expect a sequential processing of the aroused information over the course of the night's dreams. Only REM dream reports can shed light on this matter. When the particular arousing events are known for a subject, the sequence of his REM dreams from a single night should all relate to them, since no new input occurs in between (except for the awakening and report of the previous dream). Insofar as this is the case, a night's sequence of dreams allows one to examine several subsamples of the subject's attempts to cope with a particular experience, and thus broadens the base on which to make inferences concerning the characteristic workings of his mind.

THE METHOD OF DREAM
COLLECTION AND PRESENTATION

The sleep of each of our subjects was monitored throughout the night using EEG and EOG (electro-oculogram) recordings. (The details of the procedures are reported separately in Chapters 4 and 5.) Subjects were awakened near the anticipated conclusion of each REM period and asked to report what was going through their minds. The schedule of awakenings used was intended both to maximize REM length and to minimize the disruptions of dream recall caused by bodily movements. This schedule (see Appendix A) was based on the known characteristics of the sleep-dream cycle (increasing length of REM periods through the night) adjusted for any individual peculiarities observed on the subjects' adaptation nights.

A semistandardized interview was used, which permitted comparisons among subjects while still allowing each the freedom to describe dream experiences spontaneously, in his own terms. After the subject's initial reactions had been obtained, he was asked at least two general questions: e.g., "Is there anything else?"; "Can you tell me some more about that?" The interviewer then inquired about the people, feelings, locations, and subject's own role in the dream if these were not clear from the report.

All dream-report interviews were tape-recorded and subsequently transcribed verbatim; the typescripts were used in all subsequent data analyses. These typescripts contain a certain amount of superfluous and redundant information, such as the experimenter's questions, subject's response that he "doesn't know," and the like, which has been eliminated from the protocols presented below (a series of periods indicates an omission). In editing the material we took a conservative stance, leaving in all material that might possibly be relevant, in an effort to guard against bias in the editing process.

RATING SCALES

The major presentation of results will take the form of individual case studies in which the dream reports of each subject are analyzed in the context of his presleep experience. In addition to these case analyses, it seemed advisable to perform some independent content analyses, as a check on the subjective nature of the case studies as well as to facilitate comparisons with other studies which have used similar methods. Three sorts of content ratings were performed: (1) Incorporation of stress-related content; (2) Thematic dimensions; and (3) Formal qualities.

Incorporation

The purpose of this rating was to test for the kinds of effects reported in Chapter 2 in the section on "Application of Presleep Stimuli." *Incorporation* was scored differently in the two studies. In the Group Therapy Study, the dreams of the "focus" subject were examined for the incorporation of material dealt with during the preceding group meeting. A judge (not the therapist) reviewed tape recordings of the group sessions and rated the subsequent dreams for (1) incorporation of group members, (2) incorporation of physical surroundings (therapy room, clinic building, etc.), and (3) incorporation of important content dealt with during the session. With respect to the last category, we attempted to guard against "overinterpretation" by having the judge score incorporation only when fairly prominent themes from the group session appeared.

In the Surgery Study, the nature and meaning of the stress of surgery was defined for each subject, and his dreams were then scored independently by two judges for incorporation of elements pertaining to his perception of the stress. Such incorporation was scored as *Direct* or *Indirect* (i.e., symbolic). Both *Direct* and *Indirect incorporations* were scored 1 (one element present), 2 (more than one element present), or 3 (if the rated elements were prominent enough to qualify as the major theme of the dream). For the 96 dreams rated in this way, the two judges achieved 90% agreement on the *Direct incorporation* scale and 65% on the *Indirect incorporation* scale. The details of these incorporation scoring procedures will be presented in Chapter 5.

Thematic Dimensions

The dream reports were scored on four dimensions: (1) the quality of the interactions between the dream characters; (2) the types of role assumed by the dreamer; (3) the types of role played by the other persons in the dream; and (4) the thematic outcome of the dream.

Interactions. It is our belief that the quality of the interpersonal interactions that take place in a person's dreams is one of the keys to his character. While this dimension might be rated in a variety of ways, we used just two ratings—one of the general affective tone of the interactions, and the other of the roles assumed by the dreamer and others. Each major interpersonal interaction in each dream was rated as "pleasant" (score of 1), "neutral" (score of 2), or "unpleasant" (score of 3). Two judges rated 50 dreams on this dimension and, on the basis of only the interactions which were scored by both, a reliability of .86 was obtained.

Roles. Like interactions, the roles assumed by the dreamer and attributed to others are central variables that might be categorized in a number of ways. In the present studies we scored roles as "inadequate or unsuccessful," as when a character fails at a task, etc. (score of 1); "neutral," e.g., a character walking around talking to people, etc. (score of 2); and "adequate-successful," e.g., a character wins a game, does something well, etc. (score of 3). The roles of the dreamer and those played by others were each scored in this fashion. Independent ratings of 50 dreams by two judges yielded a reliability of .84.

Outcome. This scale represents the desirability of the outcome of the dream viewed as a whole. The major activities of the dream are determined and their desirability estimated, on the basis of an explicit reference where possible (e.g., "I was traveling to New Orleans to attend a Mardi Gras, which I always enjoy"). Where no explicit reference is made, the judgment is based on what would be generally true for the activity; if that is not clear, it is rated as "neutral." Dreams were rated "desirable outcome" (score of 1), "neutral" (score of 2), and "undesirable outcome" (score of 3). Independent ratings by two judges yielded a reliability of .84.

Formal Qualities

The dream protocols were scored for six categories of content on rating scales similar to those used in a number of previous studies. Since these scales are fairly well-known, they will not be described in detail here. The dreams were rated on five-point scales for: *Anxiety* (1 = complete absence of anxiety, 5 = extremely anxiety-provoking); *Cognitive disturbance* (1 = none, 5 = very high); *Implausibility* (1 = quite plausible, 5 = bizarre); *Involvement* (1 = no involvement, 5 = intense involvement); *Primitivity* (1 = extremely socialized expression of impulses, 5 = extremely primitive or unsocialized expression of impulses); and *Recall* (1 = no report, 5 = exceptionally well-recalled dream). (The complete rating scales are presented in Appendix B.) A sample of 50 dreams independently scored by two judges yielded the following reliability coefficients: *Anxiety*, r = .90; *Cognitive disturbance*, r = .69; *Implausibility*, r = .86; *Involvement*, r = .89; *Primitivity*, r = .82; and *Recall*, r = .90. These were considered adequate, and all subsequent analyses were based either on averaged scores or on the ratings of a single judge.

4

THE GROUP THERAPY STUDY

The purpose of this study was to observe the dreams of a small group of persons after an intense therapy experience. Each of the subjects was in turn the focus of a therapy-group interaction which constituted a stress or arousal experience. Dreams were collected immediately afterward and subsequently examined for signs of the experience.

Subjects

The subjects were undergraduate students who volunteered after hearing a brief description of the experiment in class. Prospective subjects were given the MMPI and seen in a brief screening interview, to determine their willingness to participate in such a demanding project and to eliminate anyone who appeared to be seriously disturbed. One subject from the first seven was eliminated; of the remaining six, four (two male and two female) were randomly assigned to the experimental condition (group therapy), and two (one male and one female) to a control condition (no therapy). No attempt was made to match the subjects for personality variables; all, however, were college students of generally similar background. A detailed description of the four experimental subjects is presented below.

Baseline Dream Collection

Each subject spent five nights in the sleep laboratory for baseline dream collection. The first night (Sunday) was an adaptation night: the subject slept with EEG and EOG electrodes in place, but no awakenings were attempted. On the four subsequent nights (Monday through Thursday), he was awakened toward the end of each REM period, according to the prearranged schedule (see Appendix A), and his dream reports were collected. Two experimenters, Dr. Hunter and a female assistant, always performed the initial electrode placements; two other experimenters worked the two later shifts.

Group Formation

After the collection of baseline dreams from the four experimental subjects, they were brought together with the therapist (Dr. Hunter) to form a therapy or "sensitivity" group. The group met for two hours a night, four times a week (Monday through Thursday) for three weeks; all sessions were tape-recorded.

During the first week they were encouraged to talk openly about themselves, to express emotions, and to interact honestly with one another. The therapist emphasized the value of self-exploration and understanding, and the group members were encouraged to share their feelings and memories. During this period the therapist attempted to encourage group cohesion—he tried to keep the group moving toward the stated goals while maintaining tension at a tolerable level. Despite the experimental nature of the group, it was surprising how rapidly frank communication developed and how intense—and frequently upsetting—the experience became. In other words, the subjects acted much like members of any psychotherapy group.

The Focus Sessions

During the second and third weeks, a different procedure was followed: each subject in turn served as the focus of the group for two consecutive sessions. The focus subject was prompted by the therapist and the other group members to express, as openly as he could, his feelings, fears, conflicts, and memories. The group reacted with questions, feelings, interpretations, and support. The therapist encouraged frankness on all sides, and provided a model for appropriate behavior—listening intently, questioning, making interpretive remarks, expressing his own reactions, and the like.

Collection of Posttherapy Dreams

After the two sessions in which the subject served as the focus of the group, he spent the night in the sleep laboratory, where dream reports were collected from each REM period in the same manner as during the baseline period. The subject was awakened during REM periods according to the same schedule that was used for baseline dream collection, and the same interview was used to obtain dream reports.

The two control subjects were brought back for two nights of dream collection four weeks after the collection of their baseline dreams.

The data consisted, therefore, of: (a) tape recordings of the 12 group sessions; (b) four nights of baseline dream reports from all subjects; (c) two nights of dream reports following focus sessions from each of the four experimental subjects; and (d) two nights of follow-up dream reports from the two control subjects. Also available were the personality data about each experimental subject derived from the brief initial interview and the MMPI.

Using the available personality information as a context, we attempted to integrate the subject's experience during the focus sessions with the dreams that followed these sessions. Each dream report was also independently scored according to the rating scales previously described. The scores obtained in this way were then used to assess the differences between baseline and postfocus-session dreams for the four experimental subjects, and between the experimental and control groups. The results of these comparisons will be presented after the case studies.

THE CASE STUDIES

The therapy group was made up of four college students whom we shall call Hal, Roger, Pam, and Jackie, and the therapist, Dr. Hunter. Each case study will begin with a brief personality description, followed by a synopsis of the subject's first focus session and the dream reports obtained immediately afterward. A synopsis of the second focus session will then be presented, followed by the ensuing dream reports. We will then attempt a brief qualitative analysis of the subject's total response to the focus group experience.

HAL

Hal is a markedly obese 19-year-old sophomore whose outward appearance is one of joviality and naïveté. On first questioning he stated that he had "no problems," felt "great," and looked forward to the group experience. He is the youngest of four sons, raised in a small, rural town, and is the first of his family to attend college. His older brothers were successful athletes in high school who have now all left the family. Hal, however, remains tied to his parents, especially his mother. He spoke eagerly of his desire to "take care of her" and is proud when she "confides her troubles" to him. He spoke respectfully of his father but the picture that emerged was of a cold, stern disciplinarian toward whom he harbors considerable resentment.

His ties to his parents are intensified by the lack of any satisfactory peer relationships. He has never dated girls, for which he tends to blame his obesity. He described having "buddies" in the dorm where he lives with whom he likes to wrestle, an activity that serves to express several sides of his feelings toward them. The over-all picture that emerged was of an isolated young man who hides his conflicts behind a mask of good humor, denial, and rather massive repression. Underneath, he is childish and dependent, harboring resentment toward authorities who would force him to be an adult and toward women who represent the heterosexual relationship he feels incapable of attaining.

The First Focus Session

Hal naïvely volunteered to be the first focus subject and then arrived late and asked if someone else would do it. He seemed quite resentful when no one would. At the suggestion of the therapist he began to speak of areas of personal importance. He spoke, initially, about the importance of friends, about the "good old days" in high school, and of his "old buddies" who are now getting married and leaving him behind, which leaves him with a lost feeling. He spoke of being the "baby" in the family, of having gotten his own way, particularly with his mother, who pampers him. He is afraid of leaving home, of change, and of his parents and brothers leaving him. He came to the university to prove himself to his father, who is very controlling. He expressed the wish for "greater companionship" with his father, who, he feels, will never regard him as grown up. The older brothers have broken away but Hal is still afraid of his father and must deny his anger by constantly emphasizing what a "great guy" his father is. He spoke of his difficulties with girls; he has had only one date in his life, and his parents prohibited him from going out in high school. He is frequently preoccupied with sex, dreams of conquering girls, and masturbates frequently with subsequent guilt feelings. He said he gets jealous of other guys who date, and his friendships cool if dorm-mates go out with girls. He fears that he now prefers masturbation to intercourse and said he really doesn't want to go out with girls but feels forced to by society. He was visibly anxious when he talked about sex. He seemed ambivalent about his obesity, feeling that it gives him real "individuality" yet knowing that it interferes with his ability to date.

The initial reaction of the other group members was to his defensiveness. They talked about his denial and how he passes off as trivial things which are really vital to him. He was asked if he ever had "homosexual fantasies" and he said no, but spoke of his concern that others could consider him "queer" because of his "joking around" and lack of dates. The other group members focused on his shallowness, lack of interest in their feelings, immaturity, and lack of courage to change himself. The reaction from the two girls was essentially negative, Pam saying that she felt he was "too shallow" and Jackie that he made her uncomfortable because he was so self-conscious. Throughout this, Hal's anxiety grew and he became more depressed. He said, "I feel like everything's dropped out underneath me," that everyone disliked him, and now he "didn't give a hang about anything." He felt like crying but didn't want their sympathy; he was "ticked off" at everyone and didn't want to hear any more.

Immediately after the group session, during the presleep period in the laboratory, he expressed his anger, confusion, and depression. He was flushed and breathing heavily, and felt a strong urge to return to the dorm and talk to the boys. He was very agitated, said he felt like wrestling, and that he would have trouble falling asleep. Nevertheless, he did fall asleep and produced the following dreams.

Dream 1: I was in a swimming pool . . . all the water dripped out . . . I was swimming along . . . then there was nothing left . . . everything disappeared . . . I was alone in the pool . . . no lifeguard . . . no nothing. Everything just dropped out right underneath me. Roger and the two girls [Pam and Jackie] were there . . . we were having a great time and suddenly the water and the people disappeared . . . I was just wallowing on the bottom . . . crying out. It scared me . . . I could feel myself falling. Not hurt physically . . . I just felt damaged or bruised . . . I wasn't bleeding or anything.

Dream 2: A couple of friends were with me listening to these sort of weird records, some deal on dreams. The record was Roger's voice; he was screaming and talked about the fever, "Fever take me with you," as if he wanted to die. It sounded so real it really scared me . . . Roger kept yelling "Goodbye, goodbye—no, no, let me go with you" . . . Roger was having all sorts of trouble . . . "No, no, don't leave me" . . . He talked about his mother . . . something about "Don't leave me" and then he talked about the fever . . . the fever was leaving and he wanted to go with the fever . . . After the record was done my friends were going to plaster my dreams up on a board and show them to everybody. My feelings toward Roger were very emotional . . . it really tore me up. I was kind of mad at the other fellows because they were doing this. They got to hear somebody else's dreams and they were going to do this to me and put my dreams up.

Dream 3: I was talking to some friends in the dorm about some experiences up here . . . some of the dreams and some of the people. They tried to get me not to come any more because it was bothering me too much— the things that I found out in the group-therapy session. Well, it really didn't make any difference . . . I'd come anyway. One of the guys attacks me . . . these guys get me down . . . one guy on each appendage. I wasn't sure if it was in fun or whether they really meant it . . . what strikes me funny is that they turned against me, which they never have. I felt like I was being persecuted. They didn't want me to come up here any more. They could tell the therapy was bothering me because I was particularly uncomfortable. I had mixed emotions, at one point I felt kind of hurt and at another point I wasn't mad. Things were really bothering me. They felt I wouldn't really have anything left to believe in and that everything would be shot out from underneath me. I was feeling really depressed, I'm usually not that way to other people.

Dream 4: I was on a basketball team . . . we had just beat the heck out of the U. of X . . . 106 to 43. I scored about 63 points, a new school record, and it was really a great feeling. My parents were there. I felt pretty good about it. I used to be a pretty good shot when I was a small kid . . . but my weight has always kept me from participating in basketball. I was the main player on the floor . . . everything centered around me.

Dream 5: It was in the past. We were building our old basement in our house . . . laying the foundation. I was helping my dad to work along with my other three brothers. It was just a great time, just such a good time of fellowship . . . just getting together and meeting and working together . . . just helping my dad . . . to perform his job. It was very satisfying. I got a great feeling out of a dream like this just like I was working with the rest of the family. It was sort of a general project. My role was the main role. Everything centered around me. It was almost as if everybody else was helping me build this. I felt glad and privileged to help my dad. I like working with him. It was sort of a family affair, everybody in the family pitched in and helped.

The relationship of these five dreams to the immediately preceding group experience—the impact of this very upsetting experience on Hal's dreams—is almost too obvious to mention. Dream 1 portrays, in interesting symbolic form, his experience of lack of support and gratification from the group. ("All the water dripped out of the pool" just the way "Everything's dropped out underneath me," his actual remark toward the end of the group session.) We see various attempts to deal with this upsetting experience in the subsequent dreams, which at the same time portray some of the basic dimensions of his memory systems and reveal some of the roots of the conflict. For example, in dream 2 he displaces his conflict and the accompanying intense emotion onto Roger, the other male in the group. The fear of lack of support is also, in this dream, tied to a fear of his mother leaving. In the second half of dream 2 and in dream 3 he projects his own concerns onto his "friends" in the dorm. It is they, not the therapist-experimenter, who are revealing his inner thoughts to the world and it is they, not himself, who do not want to come to group therapy. "They" are an interesting symbolic fusion here, since the homosexual aspects of his relationship with them were approached in the group (note the ambiguous term "appendage" in dream 3). In dreams 4 and 5 he finally overcomes the discomfort that arose from being at the center of attention, that is, from being the focus subject, by integrating the experience into a well-established fantasy in which he is the center of adulation of a supporting family. In dream 4 he assumes his brother's athletic powers; in dream 5 he clearly experiences the emotion appropriate to being the adored "baby-leader" of the family. These ideas probably resemble well-established fantasies that he engaged in during the lonely years of his youth and adolescence.

The Second Focus Session

Hal began by expressing some anger at the group for the previous session. He brought up the dream he had had about Roger. Jackie said it was actually he who didn't want to leave his mother. He resisted this idea, as he did the group's efforts to make him react, get him to change, to lose weight, etc. The therapist asked about his feelings toward the two girls in the group. Initially, Hal was cold and said he thought Jackie an "introvert" and Pam a "campus babe" and that he wouldn't want to sleep with them because "he now knew them personally." Later, his challenging stance toward the group weakened, and he admitted that he felt the girls were "better" and smarter than he and probably wouldn't want to go out with him. He said he is attracted to short, "heavy," "dumb" girls ("Mom is short and heavy") because he feels that is the only kind of girl he could get. Pam said he put too much emphasis on appearance and suggested that he look at it from the girl's point of view. The therapist suggested that he was looking for a girl who was an embodiment of his own inadequacies. At about this point Hal looked visibly upset and depressed. He said that the bottom had been cut out from under him again and he felt insignificant and like a "nothing." Roger said he thought Hal used his obesity as a crutch, believing that if he lost weight he could do many things, but being afraid to lose it and put these beliefs to the test. At this point Hal's defenses seemed to be penetrated. He talked about his inadequacies and obesity and felt the need to make a decision about himself right then and there. He said he felt like a "nothing" and realized that much of his life was a way of keeping these feelings at a distance. Then an amazing reversal took place. He began to pull himself together, denied that he cared if the others felt frustrated—even said it was pleasing to him—and that he had made up his mind to remain as he was; not date girls, not lose weight, not change friendship patterns, etc. He said that nothing they could say could affect him and he "really was happy."

During the presleep period in the laboratory he kept reassuring Dr. Hunter, in a driven manner, that he really was very happy the way he was, that he really had very good relations with his friends, that he only needed a couple of years to mature, and that he would be all right. He hoped Dr. Hunter was not angry with him.

Dream 6: I was in a small group . . . talking about air pollution. I wasn't the leader of the group but the people did take into concern what I said and I felt they were very understanding toward me. The people in the dream were the people in the therapy group. The person that would get material through against me . . . he wasn't really against me . . . was the therapist and I really did nothing to stop him. I like the therapist because it seemed like he supported me and almost everything I did he at least agreed with me once or twice—which helps one hell of a lot. It was in this sleeping room sitting around a table. I was the administrator but what was actually accomplished was left quite as much to the therapist. Whereas one of the other group would make a point or put forth a paper with some ideas on it the rest of us would really tear it down. When the therapist would present something . . . it would be accepted by the group and the fact that he was accepted made me feel like he was sort of on my side because of the fact that they were all against me in trying to get anything done. I felt sort of an affection toward him . . . as if he was playing a supportive role. I don't know if he realized it, but he was helping me.

Dream 7: I was out on a beach at Bikini atoll. I had found possibilities of a very precious mineral . . . something virtually unknown to the U.S. I was going through the process of setting up an interview to start production but I ran into organizational and administrative trouble. One of the biggest problems was a food problem with the natives. One of the biggest problems of reaction of the natives was increased need for food. I had gotten quite a ways in this when I realized it would be nonprofitable and I realized I was wrong from the very start. I lost money on it. I was alone except for natives. I was the person that actually discovered the mineral and was using it by exploiting the mineral as much as I could. I had no feelings about the natives and I mainly thought about myself . . . what I got out of it and I realized I'd done the wrong thing . . . caused human misery. I had been thinking more of wealth than human beings as individuals and I wasn't making enough money. If there were any feelings against me I didn't want to think of them. So it would just go out of my mind and it wasn't a big concern.

Dream 8: I was out in the ocean on a raft. I was alone with no one to help me. I was taking correspondence courses somehow. Although I was running into a few difficulties, I somehow always found something to eat. There was always food there, sort of like it came from heaven. I was feeling lost and lonely but I'd learned to cope with this by myself.

Dream 9: I was dreaming about when I was four years old. I used to think of all the times I used to walk away from home—I guess you'd call it that. I used to be in a little world all my own. Even at that age I used to just walk off. I know my parents were concerned about me and my older brothers would just have a fit. I don't know if I was really running away from home. I walked down to a bridge—not too far from the house—lay on the bridge and watched water go by. I had no concern for anybody else, just myself. I felt pretty good, like I was doing the right thing. I was the one that was doing all the action. I felt very lonely and wished somebody would come after me and bring me back. I know for sure they did come after me after a while. In my own little world I was actually escaping, but I was in sight of the house.

Analysis of Hal's Dreams

The emotional impact of the group experience on Hal was striking, both during and after the two focus sessions. He felt very threatened, his characteristic defenses were not capable of warding off this threat and gave way, resulting in the awareness of conflict (his loneliness, his use of obesity as an excuse) and feelings of anxiety and depression. As a part of this same process, however, additional defensive efforts were mobilized, and at the end of the second session were dominant.

These processes are rather strikingly portrayed in the postgroup dreams which, through the operations of dream programs, also open up the relevant memory systems. In the process, they reveal some of the background memories and "solutions." Dream 6, like dream 1 after the first focus session, portrays fairly directly the threatening aspects of the therapy experience. Group members "tear down" the ideas presented by others (much as his defenses were "torn down"). The general topic is "air pollution," probably a symbolic fusion of his own bad qualities and the unpleasant reactions of the other group members. Defensive efforts include the shift to an impersonal topic and the rather exaggerated attempt to neutralize the powerful therapist.

Let us attempt to analyze the sequential working through of the material aroused in the group session. Dreams 7, 8, and 9 deal with a core difficulty—dependency gratification versus frustration—and attempt to integrate the present aroused material into a solution of a longstanding nature. The potential desolation of his loneliness is symbolized by "Bikini atoll," being alone on a raft in the middle of the ocean, and the last dream in which he is alone as a child. The symbolic substitution of food for love as a solution to the problem of his isolation (which is intimately tied to his feeling that people don't gratify his childish wishes to be taken care of, to be at the center of attention, etc.) is hinted at in dream 7 as the "precious mineral" that would solve Hal's problems and is somehow associated with solving the "food problem" of the natives. The "organizational and administrative difficulties" referred to in the dream seem to represent his intellectual understanding (brought out in the group) of the "magical" nature of food as a solution to the dependency conflict. In dream 8 these obstacles are overcome, and an unambivalent, magical solution re-emerges. In this dream people are abolished and he is supported by an endless ocean and a bountiful supply of food from heaven. He remains connected to the university (probably a symbolic fusion of the place he had to leave home for and the place where the group sessions and dream collections take place) only indirectly— via "correspondence courses." In this dream the present threat (i.e., his lack of closeness with others, his heterosexual failure, feelings of worthlessness, and the stress of being alone at the university away from home and mother) is symbolically integrated into an existing solution; one in which food is substituted for people. The last dream shows some of the earlier memory material and affect related to this same issue—his desire to be close to and taken care of within the family and his essential loneliness. "Escaping while still in sight of the house" well sums up Hal's style of life: one in which the childish gratification of eating is substituted for close human relationships; one in which he partly satisfies his childhood desires (with the attention that obesity brings, the pleasure of eating, and the focus on his own body) but remains ultimately frustrated in a world of adult demands.

The qualitative differences between these nine dreams and the baseline dreams from the pregroup period are striking. The pregroup dreams are predominantly pleasant in affect, and reflect little of the loneliness and isolation that characterize the post-group dreams. In the pregroup dreams, interactions with other people are both more frequent and likely to be more pleasant. At least two deal with heterosexual approach: in one he has a long talk with a girl on a date, and in another he follows a sexy Negro woman around town. Interestingly, although a main topic in the group was his unsatisfactory relations with women, that subject never appears directly in the postgroup dreams. Our hypothesis is that his difficulties with women are a current manifestation of the conflictual family relationships that do appear in the dreams.

ROGER

Roger is a 23-year-old psychology student of pleasant appearance. He is anxious and immediately gives the impression of being helpless and inadequate. He tends to berate himself, and his background contains several instances in which he attempted to gain some objective, almost succeeded, did something to insure his own failure, and then blamed others. This pattern has been evident in both his academic work and his personal relations.

Roger was raised in a small city. When he was 10 his father died of a heart attack, and he feels that he was forced into assuming the role of father to his younger brothers, then four and seven. He feels this forced premature responsibility on him and prevented a "normal, carefree adolescence." His relationship with his mother has been very intense since his father's death. He feels she has "always wanted to keep me as her little Roger and not allow me to grow up." This seems related to a pattern—apparent in his life style—in which he seeks strong, dominant women and assumes a dependent-submissive role in relation to them. While he is anxious much of the time, he does use the defenses of projection, intellectualization, and rationalization to good effect. His interest in psychology enables him to take an intellectual approach to his problems. In the group this led him to take the role of "therapist" in relation to the other members, though he remained basically quite anxious and involved.

The First Focus Session

Roger came prepared to talk about himself and initially seemed quite comfortable as he outlined his basic problems. He spoke of feelings of inferiority, of difficulty in trusting people, and of problems with girls and homosexuality. He said he feels embarrassed when his mother talks about sex to his younger brothers. He is now afraid of getting into close relationships with girls. He described his fear of becoming a homosexual and an upsetting fellatio experience with playmates when he was six. He then spoke of the death of his father and how it forced him to grow up too fast. While at times he felt that he had his mother "wrapped around his finger" as the favorite son, he secretly hoped that she would deny him something. He felt responsibility for his younger brothers but inadequate to the father role. He then talked of feeling that he frequently "plays roles," and that he feels he doesn't fulfill the "masculine role." He also spoke of feeling that he has the power to "fight dirty" psychologically and has done so with his brothers, and that at times he tries to make people feel inferior and wretched.

As had been the case in Hal's focus sessions, the group's reaction was initially directed at Roger's defensive style. The therapist said he felt competition from him, a statement which brought forth agreement from Roger, and a highly intellectualized monologue on psychological theory. Hal said this made him feel inferior and that he would like to see Roger crawl. Jackie said he made her feel cut off, and the therapist suggested that perhaps he tries too hard to impress and needs to have everything figured out ahead of time to protect himself from the possible attack of others. Roger said he was afraid to let out feelings because he wanted to impress the therapist and was afraid the therapist would be condescending. Pam said she couldn't trust him because she felt he was capable of doing something mean. She said sometimes he seemed to want protection and at other times to impress her, but that most of his communication was words, not feelings. Roger became visibly upset and shouted, "Well what do you want me to do, man?" He said he felt "locked in" and upset; that he couldn't get past the words and express the feelings that were there. When the therapist said he saw Roger as an anxious, insecure guy who needs protection he responded that he didn't want protection but honesty, and that people don't know when they hurt him.

Roger had some difficulty in getting to sleep. Twice he got up to go to the bathroom, and twice called out for paper and pencil so he could write rebuttals to the group's comments to bring to the next session. He was obviously preoccupied with the group session.

Dream 1: Conscious content . . . something dealing with sensitivity . . . dreaming about myself and about the way I'd been dreaming . . . I was apart from me and yet I knew I was thinking. You're different and you're the same because you could look at it from a different point of view . . . something, it dealt with the group because of the fact or whatever it was I was thinking about . . . I disagreed what my sensitivity to myself or whatever this thing was with the other people in the group . . . other person might have been a girl . . . I had the role of explainer or interpreter . . . it seemed pretty important to me to explain to this other person the way I felt . . . I was trying to explain why I thought the other people in the group had gotten the wrong idea . . .

Dream 2: Something very similar to the one that was going on before . . . some clarifications . . . it dealt with dreaming and clarity of perception . . . self-sensitivity . . . change in sensitivity over time . . . interest in explaining to the other person what I felt about . . . looking at different aspects of it . . . sort of like watching a movie . . . I didn't have any control over the movie, I was just watching it to see what it was about and what was happening.

Dream 3: There were some little girls and all these people I know . . . my mother and younger brother and he was a little girl—it seemed natural in the dream. And there were a couple of his little boyfriends or girlfriends—I couldn't tell which. They were about his age except he was a lot younger at the time, and they were the same sex he was—they were all female. We were all lying on the bed in sort of a big heap . . . I had been talking to another woman and she thought that another man was sexually going after her but she was going to show me something she could do. I don't know what. She went downstairs and a little bit later she came back up and he came up with her and they went up to the third floor and both of them got drunk. And then she started playing all these little games. She jumped into bed and soon she started playing peekaboo games where she would look at people's genital organs. I was embarrassed more than anything, especially when she started to look at mine. She wasn't really looking, just pretending. She would attempt to look at mine and I would attempt to show it didn't make any difference to me . . . I felt I wasn't supposed to show embarrassment although I felt it. Then my mother started to do the same thing and I really got upset and angry. I told her to "cut it out." Then the other gal got up and went upstairs with this other guy. I don't know what was going on up there. Then I shifted attention to the other little kids who were reading comic books or *Mad* magazine. I got involved in the game they were playing. Except there was one little kid they didn't like. He wasn't popular and he was the one who lived there so he must have been my brother earlier because he wasn't then. They ended up saying, "Oh, he's always that way." I said, "Well, don't you like that other little . . . what's the other little kid doing over there?" He said, "Reading a magazine," and they said, "He's always like that." I said, "Well, why doesn't he come over and play," and they said, "Oh, I don't know, he's always like that." There was something in the air that they didn't get along well. Something happened, they were all playing together and the other two left and left the other one sitting there.

The first two dreams seem to be continuations of Roger's attempts to master the experience intellectually, evident both in the group and during the long period in bed before falling asleep: the themes of his role as "explainer," his own sensitivity, and his concern over not having control are all represented. Dream 3 presents several of the key topics from the group session, including his homosexual fears and his isolation from other children. Of perhaps greater interest is the symbolic portrayal of his sexualized relationship with his mother and how this relates to his embarrassment about sex and his distance from the other children.

The Second Focus Session

Jackie was absent because she was sick. Roger appeared to be more anxious than on the previous night. Using his last dream, he talked of his sexual conflicts and, with some prompting, said it probably reflected "an unresolved Oedipus complex" but that he didn't believe in dream interpretation. He talked primarily about sex and his feelings of inferiority, citing his embarrassment, hesitancy with girls, and lack of confidence. He has had satisfactory intercourse with his current girlfriend, but feels "mothered" by her. He then talked about having cheated on tests and about how his mother used to write all his papers for him and helped him to rationalize his failures. When Pam said, "You're actually quite bright," he got mad because he felt she was trying to mother and protect him. Returning to sex, he said that he found sex revolting with a promiscuous girl, but is nevertheless excited by discussions of other guys' experiences. He fears becoming homosexual although he has not had any experiences or fantasies since the fellatio experience as a child. He perceives himself as a sensitive, understanding, nonaggressive, nonmasculine person, and added that he doesn't like the extremely masculine role. The therapist said he felt that Roger put him in a fatherly position, and Pam said she felt motherly toward him. Roger spoke of his fear that he might be using his girlfriend as a crutch as he did his mother. The therapist interpreted his mother's implicit contract: "You display your weaknesses for me, and I'll take care of you and protect you." Roger gave a set of supporting memories and then wondered if his mother's motives weren't selfish. The therapist continued the interpretation, pointing out how Roger had insured his own failure in several specific instances, concluding, "It seems you have been your entire life living out the role of the tragic hero—almost succeeding, failing, and blaming others," and that his mother encouraged this pattern. Pam agreed, and Hal said he thought it had been a great session. Roger seemed intense and shaken. He said he felt confused and wanted to change, but didn't know how and felt it was hopeless.

Dream 4: I get the picture of some powerful object. Sort of a very sensitive stimulus object in the fact that you have to be very careful what you do and the way you present stimuli because that determines the effect of the way they are perceived. The perception is to some extent determined by the person's feelings. I've forgotten the dream more or less. The only thing left is the general idea of . . . inefficiency of people and in the way I perceive myself as stimuli . . . of inefficiency of people . . . in the way I perceive it and my perceiving myself as seeing it. I perceived myself as inefficient that way . . . inefficient because of the way I get involved in relationships. It puts me in a certain type of situational pattern or something. Different stimuli help put me in a relationship with other people in which I am the submissive individual or type.

Dream 5: In the first part of the dream I was in my brother's room and he came in because it was time for him to go to bed and he found me with his little toy animal. I guess I wasn't supposed to have it. I was sort of looking at it or playing with it and trying to fix the head because it was broken and held down with a rubber band, and little elastic type thing . . . Seemed like someone was helping me with it . . . I made a hypothesis for the best way to have the head on tight and then I had another hypothesis for why the head stayed on better than the way I used it. I've forgotten the hypothesis. I couldn't figure out the hypothesis and my mother might have come in at the end and been the person who did it right. The wires came loose and I didn't get the relationship but she did and explained it to me . . . I had a feeling of slight frustration that I couldn't figure out the second part of the problem . . . I felt sorry for my brother, but I also really felt good that I was really doing him a favor by helping him get those heads tight back on those animals so he could have them to play with . . . I was just trying to get those heads so they'd stay back on and my mother found a way. She said, "Here, let me show you how to do it."

Dream 6: I had a dream and an analyzer . . . I don't know who this person was or why I was going to them. It was sort of like they were a quack type. One was sort of a temporary one. She was either working for someone else or her technique was quite a bit different . . . In this dream building I'd walk into a room which was empty . . . and I'd get the feeling that things were being watched . . . by somebody for the Communist party. Then someone else was analyzing for me. I went to him one time . . . because he was a professional dream analyzer. The second dream analyzer [female] wanted one person to come in at a time and I don't know what she was going to do. There was one person ahead of me . . . this person went in the room and she said, "Nope, I've changed my mind, I want all three of you." There was myself and two other people. One might have been my brother. She said she was going to dream analyze us all together . . . You never saw the dream analyzer. They were talking over an intercom or something. There was something about . . . she was giving threats and everything. I mean, she said, "If you try to leave this place or try to do this, man, I'll do this." . . . They were all female . . . She was a member of the Communist party and I guess they were using this as sort of a threat . . . I felt fear . . . The dream analyzer got excited and said, "Ah-ha, get those other two people in here and we're going to start something." . . . Like she had really devised something very wicked and very clever that she was going to perform on all three of us.

Dream 7: I had a dream about my girl except in the dream I didn't love her . . . I joined a sorority and was a member of the same one that she belonged to. I wasn't a girl but I joined the same sorority. It was time for me to graduate from school so we were sitting at some group meeting with the whole university. We were talking and everyone is listening. These people she knows are sitting next to us and there are some snoopy people out front . . . and then I just bit her . . . I didn't pull up her dress or anything but I just bit her underwear. She looked around and saw it . . .

about right on the hip or something and when she put her hand down there she found there was saliva and she was upset. She said something. Everybody started making jokes about what she said . . . I had feelings of fear and embarrassment . . . afraid of losing my girl. It was a sexual-type bite . . . sexual urge probably. I got embarrassed about these people turning around and watching when she got upset about finding saliva on her underwear. There were all these comments that people had written on a piece of paper . . . guys in the row in front of us. They were watching and giggling. They handed us a note and one of the comments was "State Police." The girls behind us were members of the sorority and they got up and made comments. I might have had feelings of guilt because my girl was putting up a fuss and others were looking. The fact that I had done it didn't bother me a bit. She looked down, saw it and said, "Oh, my God," and goes on about how she's got saliva on her underpants . . . There was a lot of stuff that went on in between somewhere. At one point I was going up to Portland to . . . interview at graduate school . . . and I remember sort of a tape recorder . . . in front of your eyes where you could see all the words.

Analysis of Roger's Dreams

It is really not possible, in the available space, to do justice to the rich content revealed in this small sample of dreams; we can only touch on certain themes. We will try to keep our hypotheses close to the data and to avoid the temptation to speculate about provocative subjects, such as the meaning to Roger of his father's death. What is immediately apparent, as was the case with Hal, is the close correspondence between the content of the dreams and the material dealt with in the group session.

The dreams can be seen as a sequence in which the conflicts aroused in the group session are represented and successive attempts are made to deal with them. These attempts consist of an integration of the aroused material into the matrix of solutions that exist in the memory systems and that exemplify "character structure." The integration is facilitated by the "loose" symbolic processes that characterize dreaming and that permit the fusion of one situation with another (as in dream 5, where the group and the family situations are fused); substitution of one character for another (the "woman" and his mother in dream 3); and the creation of new situations which represent many aspects of "conflict" and "solution" (i.e., his membership in a sorority in dream 7, and the bite on his girlfriend's underpants which symbolizes the several sides of his relationship with women—the orality and childishness, the sexuality, the aggressiveness, and his embarrassment).

The conflicts aroused in Roger center on the question of how to be a man—a conflict evident in his attempts to achieve and succeed, academically and otherwise, and in the area of sexuality; how to be a man with women. His characteristic solution is to make an exaggerated attempt at success, followed by failure. He then assumes the position of a child who can be helped by a mother figure. A persistent effort is made to handle the aroused conflicts intellectually. Dreams 1 and 2 in which he is the "explainer"; his attempts to fix the doll's "head" in dream 5; "reading" as an escape from the embarrassing sexuality in dream 3; or the way the obviously sexual dream 7 is tied to graduating from the university—all exemplify this intellectual approach. And in almost every case it does not work—he cannot fix the doll and his mother must step in to help; the reading is of *Mad* magazine (a symbol for the failure of this intellectual pursuit to lead to sanity); etc. The later dreams (and his current life relationships) depict him in the position of the "child who is not a man." This solution is not very satisfactory, and Roger is in a state of much more turmoil than is Hal. He remains anxious, embarrassed, and questioning of his characteristic relationships. The negative affect is as apparent in his dreams as in his waking life.

Comparing these postgroup dreams with those from the pregroup period, we find that they are essentially similar in intellectual quality and general level of anxiety. The content is quite different, however; the postgroup dreams are much more specifically related to the material, and particularly the major conflict areas, discussed in the focus sessions.

PAM

Pam is an attractive 20-year-old junior who volunteered for the group to help "further psychological knowledge." This seemed to be a way of indirectly seeking help for her problems. During the past year she had been very much upset about her 19-year-old brother, who had been sent to a psychiatric hospital and diagnosed as schizophrenic. She felt intense guilt whenever she spoke of this matter, feeling that she had played a major role in precipitating his psychosis. An additional current stress was the breaking up of a longstanding relationship with a boyfriend. He had decided to date other girls for a while to see if they were "really right" for each other. As with her brother's breakdown, Pam blamed herself for the difficulty with her boyfriend, and kept torturing herself with self-accusations.

Pam comes from a family with strong ambitions. Her father is a lawyer and all the children are either attending college or have already finished (in addition to the younger brother there are two older sisters, 27 and 24). Pam describes herself as appearing outwarding aggressive and independent but feeling very dependent inside. She was probably the most openly upset of the subjects: she used the focus sessions for confession and catharsis, wept a good deal, and, at one point, described a temporary, though apparently severe, experience of depersonalization.

The First Focus Session

Pam contacted the therapist before her first focus session to say she had been very much upset during the past few days and was apprehensive about the meeting. She asked if Roger and she might speak to him before the session. When they met, Roger said that Pam had come to see him the previous night and that they had had sexual intercourse. Pam had been much upset, had gone to talk with him, and was surprised that it had happened. Roger felt guilty for having "taken advantage of her mental condition," but Pam said she didn't feel guilty and liked him more today because of it.

During the focus session she appeared visibly upset, repeatedly fighting back tears and frequently getting so carried away with emotion and memories that she sounded very much like a little girl. She spoke first about her feelings of depression, her lack of organization, and the feeling that she was continually searching for something she could not find. She then talked about her relationship with her boyfriend. They have been going together since high school, initially because of his persistent attention and idolization of her. She found security in this relationship, but resisted his wish to get married. Recently she decided that they should get married and, at this point, he became uncertain and suggested that they break up so he could separate his "identity" from hers. She denied any anger and took all the blame for the breakup, saying that now she feels that her whole world has collapsed. She did express some resentment that after she had devoted three years of her life to him some "silly fluff might grab him off."

She spoke of her family, describing her mother as a flighty woman who closes her eyes to bad things. She added, "We don't have much of a relationship." She described her father as "strict—too strict," a judge who accepts "no excuses" and demands honesty. She has always been close to him, feels that she is like him, and is certain that she has stolen him away from the younger brother and is thus responsible for their lack of closeness. Her brother has turned out to be a "spoiled bully" who has had difficulty with the law and, last year, was hospitalized in a catatonic state. She feels that she is largely responsible for this situation, and described an incident that occurred when she and her father visited her brother in the hospital. Even there she felt she had interfered with their closeness because, although they both needed to cry for emotional release, she couldn't stand to see her father cry and interrupted the scene.

She remembered being a tomboy in her youth; she feels that she has always identified herself very closely with her father and, consistent with his judicial values, has never made excuses for her actions and always attempts to control her emotions. She recalled how he would make the children "confess" their shortcomings.

She described an incident that had occurred a month previously, when she made a "great discovery" about herself and got very excited about finding her boyfriend and telling him. She got so excited that she went into a "daze" in which she felt weightless, as though she were rising from the ground. She fears that she may go into such a "daze" permanently sometime, and that she may be "going crazy." The group reaction was primarily supportive, though toward the end it was pointed out that she attempts to carry the world on her shoulders. She was also asked why she continually picks "weaker males," and she said she felt that femininity and sex were related to her problems. The only time she really feels relaxed is after intercourse; she feels that she relied too much on it with her boyfriend as a substitute for confronting their problems.

During the presleep period she said she felt frustrated and that "nothing had really come of the group." She seemed subdued and slightly depressed, though she reported feeling "a little bit better" before going to bed.

Dream 1: I was sort of analyzing myself. I must have been trying to tell somebody something and I was kind of at a barrier where I was really frustrated. I wanted to find out something about myself and I was talking to someone and they couldn't help me. I can't remember who the person was except that my feelings for them were very mixed up. Some of the things we talked about in therapy tonight were all mixed up into one situation. It confused me to the point that this person was part everybody I know. It was everybody that's important to me all mixed up into one. It's too frustrating, I was trying hard to tell someone something or figure out the way I felt about myself. And it was just impossible, it just reminded me of a great big thick glass and just scratching on it because you wanted to get through it or something and just being helpless . . . They were kind of objective . . . about wondering about me and wanted me to tell them about the way I felt. It was almost like a curiosity, just wanting me to tell them what my problems were . . . just sort of like in our therapy. In another way they were much closer and I was involved with them just as much. I was just to try to get close to somebody or to try to explain something to somebody. It was very frustrating . . . it's sad . . . I just couldn't get anywhere.

Dream 2: I remember sitting in a classroom and the teacher had the therapist's personality partly and partly the personality of a creative writing teacher that I used to have . . . I put on my reading glasses . . . It made everything blurry and hurt my eyes. It was a psychology class. Someone told me you had to take a great big long test that took a whole bunch of hours. It was supposed to be done this week and I found I had five tests in one week that I didn't even know about and I got panicked . . . When I put my glasses on my desk was kind of moving. I said, "Gee, I feel funny here." It was sort of as if I had mental telepathy with the instructor and I told him, "I don't want to spend all those hours doing that thing . . ." Sometimes some of the students seemed like children to me and I was degrading some of them sitting around me . . . I felt like there was a distance between us . . . I asked some silly boys, younger than myself, sitting around me, "What happens if you don't do it?" They said it was very important and you had to do it or you'd fail. One said he'd never dream of not doing it. Another boy said, "Actually, this is just a student's experiment and there are just four categories down here they're looking

for on the back side of your test . . . all you do is tabulate the thing
yourself and then hand it in so that they'd think it was already tabulated
and not look for an answer sheet." I said, "How would I choose which of
the brackets to fill in? I really don't know what those initials stand for and
I really would like to do it accurately. I don't want to misrepresent myself.
I want them to know the right one." He said, "Look around . . . when they
get theirs tabulated find someone with similar opinions to you and then
you'll know which ones you should blacken out." I decided it wouldn't
work and I couldn't do it and now I'd have to take the test. There was
something else . . . about the way I put on my reading glasses that had
meaning . . . like it was a front . . . so that they couldn't really see what I
was like. It was to confuse whoever was looking at me. I don't need to
wear them . . . It was as if I was trying to look intellectual for the instructor . . . kind of phony or something. I really wanted to let this instructor
know how I felt. I don't know if the instructor understood. Sometimes the
instructor was a man, sometimes a woman.

Dream 3 (Like several of Pam's dream reports, this one consists of fragments. We will present it in three sections.):
    a: I went to a house and my roommate and her boyfriend were there. I
had a date. Part of the time he was Roger and part of the time the guy I'm
going with. My roommate wasn't ready and we had to wait on her . . . She
really bugged me . . . She was putting on make-up in front of everyone and
she put a great big streak of eye shadow across her eyelid . . . and I saw the
guy that I was with had a streak of eye shadow across his eye too. When I
went to the place I felt very uncomfortable because I didn't know the
people. On my way in from the yard I found my doorbell that hangs on a
string with a bunch of rocks. It was broken. I was with Roger and I
stopped to try to fix it. I thought I didn't have time so I laid it down.
Roger said, "These people are real particular about things in their yard and
they probably wouldn't like that." So I said, "Okay, we'll have to pick up
all the pieces." So he helped me pick up the pieces and put it inside of a
pickup. On the last part of the double date I wasn't with Roger any more,
I was with Bill [the boyfriend] and we were walking over real old streets
that were real sad and real gray and crumbly. I didn't want to be with the
others. I just wandered around and didn't like it very much. I was kind of
confused and sort of going along with things.
    b: I was at my apartment house and it was a really big, funny-shaped
building made out of . . . funny old gray stone with lots of mortar holding
it together . . . There were numbers all over it for apartments—just crummy
little apartments, and one of them was mine. I remember crawling in the
grass and it seemed like everything at the apartment was too short . . . not
high enough. The doors were five feet high. I was crawling around on the
grass and I felt like I couldn't stand up. I saw . . . this little, tiny . . . evelike
thing . . . down low . . . coming out from the house. And underneath it I
saw a little tiny nest with cobwebs and stuff surrounding it. In the nest

there was a bunch of food that was real old and hard. I thought that some child had a little pet, like a chipmunk or some little pet, but they didn't have it anymore. It was just a little deserted nest like for a pet or mice or guinea pigs. In this apartment place there was a girl or lady . . . and it was a therapy-type deal because I was telling her a lot of stuff. At first we got along real well and then she said I bugged her because I seemed like a person who was always looking back at the past. It made me feel funny because I didn't want to think it was true. She was an actress in that she could just turn things on . . . and put on funny little shows. I told her she manipulated people and got herself out of situations and that she was dishonest because she would always snap into some act. Then it was sort of a group . . . first like a real serious therapy group. I had feelings I trusted her and then all of a sudden I didn't like her and she didn't like me.

c: I was in a huge gymnasium. I was with a friend. The therapist was there. This friend and I climbed up these ladders way up high. I think it was a girlfriend. We were watching a boy's P.E. class and we felt funny. Sometimes we didn't feel funny and sometimes we did. There was just a bunch of boys doing a bunch of things. Whoever I was with swung down on a rope and we were going to take turns swinging down on it but they just hung there for a long, long time. I felt kind of funny just way up there in the air just watching. I was afraid to hang from the rope because I was getting kind of dizzy being up that high . . . I was kind of embarrassed by the situation but this person just kept hanging and hanging and finally she dropped and and everyone applauded like she'd done a really neat thing. I was afraid to hang from the rope and I was trying to think of some way to get out of it.

Once again, almost all of these dreams clearly reveal the impact of the group experience. Dream 1 portrays the group rather directly; dream 2 fuses the therapist with an instructor, and her own focus-subject position with that of a student who must perform a difficult task about which she feels ambivalent. More generally, two themes appear in these dreams. First, there is her view of the group situation as a difficult task in which she must reveal her emotions, much as her father made her confess. Although she does this, she senses that the emotional display, like the sexual promiscuity, may be in part "phony"—hence the glasses that blur her vision (a symbol of her tearful performance) hide something. Her use of sexuality to neutralize Roger is probably related to her relationship to both her father and her brother. The symbolism in dream 3a is too rich to pass over without comment. She goes to Roger to help "pick up the pieces" of her broken doorbell which is made of rocks (her emotionally disturbed state, fear of "cracking up"?), and his help ends "inside of a pickup," that is, her offering herself to him sexually. Like her use of emotional display both to reveal and to conceal, the promiscuity is in danger of getting out of hand: in dream 3c she outdoes the boys, is way high up, but runs the risk of going crazy (represented by the dizziness, which is like her depersonalization experience).

The Second Focus Session

This session developed into the most intense so far. Pam spoke of placing too much stress on sex in her relationship with her boyfriend. Roger said he didn't think she was talking honestly and said he felt the need to speak about their relationship outside the group. After a little hesitation, Pam agreed, and Roger said he had "been going through hell" since having had intercourse with her, feeling guilty and worried about losing his girlfriend. He was afraid Pam would tell her. Pam broke into tears, saying, "You don't trust anyone, do you? I'm sorry I haven't been able to convince you that I'm really your friend." The therapist said he thought she kept people away by crying and by playing the "poor defenseless female," which made others feel guilty. The other group members were upset by this discussion. Roger wondered why "it" had happened and Pam said maybe she did it to spite her boyfriend. She said she felt Roger needed it to prove his masculinity and that she was trying to help him. The therapist commented on her great need to help others and the repetition of this pattern with her boyfriend, Roger, her brother, etc. This comment stimulated a number of memories, after which the therapist suggested that she might be trying to "make up for her wrongs" to her brother by helping out unfortunate males. She denied this at first, but then cried profusely, left the room and then returned. For several minutes she described with intense emotion memories of occasions when she had not let her brother speak for himself and her guilt about having done this. She also felt she had always cut off her boyfriend during their relationship whenever he wanted to speak, and that she had driven him away. She recalled having done the same with childhood friends, and described how she always had to be right about everything—even when she was wrong. When Roger sat next to her in a gesture of sympathy, she said that she couldn't stand for him to be objective about her. At the end of the session, she said she felt relieved and relaxed for the first time in weeks.

Dream 4: It was like Bill [boyfriend] and I had kind of a vicious cycle that we had sort of let our relationship get into. It wasn't hopeless feelings. It was a big question of being selfish or thinking of the other and it was very confused for both of us ... It was sexual but I can't remember exactly how. I think both of us were really trying to find out what was going on. We thought it was a problem that we were really selfish or something. It could have been supervised by the therapist. It was in the therapy room and we were really working at something. I can't remember what this sex thing was ... but there was something really important about it. I was frustrated but I had adapted my personality to this sort of thing ... I was a little bit comfortable in it [the relationship] because I was used to it ... It was like a habit. Even though I was frustrated about making it better, there was a certain amount of being at home and in the situation. Either the therapist or part of the group was there. I felt somebody was supporting me in what I was trying to do. The relationship was in a rut. It had something to do with sex or selfishness. I was trying to find out what was going on and kind of pushing and the analytical side of it or something more than Bill was ... Maybe one of us wished we could be more like a child. It felt like a rubber band kept snapping me back into the same problems and it would just wave back and forth in kind of a funny way. I think he cried and he had a little bit of Roger in him.

Dream 5: I asked someone who was really close to me to be very patient ... It was really hard ... It seemed like it was just a struggle for me to humble myself and like I knew it was a struggle and so I really tried and it was pretty good too ... the person I was talking to was sort of a cross between friend and lover. I'm perspiring and everything. All I remember is that it was good.

Dream 6: I was just thinking about everything I've learned in therapy ... Thinking about changing myself. My dreams are so vague tonight. I was thinking how possible a change is ... I can't remember any details. Like before, someone really important to me was with me. I think it was Bill. I was just trying to do something ... I felt like I was getting somewhere a little bit ... That I had something now to work with or something. I just kept having the same dream. I felt much less frustrated than in the others. Everything was kind of slowed down a little bit and kind of relaxed.

Dream 7: I was with my roommate in an art store buying some prints. She said she had to have one print because it set her mind at ease. She went on about how it was her very favorite picture. She was just giving me a bunch of phony crap . . . She was giving the dealer a whole bunch of b.s. and it really bothered me . . . Then I was moving . . . I went back to check if I'd missed anything and I found a prophylactic on the sidewalk in front of the apartment . . . I picked it up to throw it away and associated it with myself. I started to take it inside to throw it away . . . I said to myself, "Why am I throwing this away?" . . . Because someone who didn't understand what it was might find it and make a big deal out of it or be embarrassed by asking someone what it is . . . I was going back to the apartment because I missed my little tiny candle holders . . . I saw my roommate in the apartment and didn't like her very much . . . Those two little candle holders were the only things I wanted to save.

Then I was at the house of a Catholic priest who served wine and gave everyone lots and lots. Next . . . I remember a marriage scene. The two people were absurd-looking. They had funny costumes, scary faces, and were degenerate-looking . . . it was almost like a mockery of marriage. I remember then that an old man I don't like wanted to hug me . . . He came to see me and said a bunch of junk . . . I tolerated him and talked to him a little and he started to leave . . . I was a Catholic [in the dream] . . . He came back and said he wanted to hug me as an old friend . . . He said, "It's really hard to do with you Catholics because you don't show your affection." . . . I just tolerated him and he hugged me and I hated it. Then I was in the neighborhood where I grew up . . . I was sitting in the yard with a playmate from two houses down and next door there was a lady who never could have any children . . . It really bothered her. She drove up in a big long Cadillac . . . There was a bunch of children inside her house in desks . . . She was making a play school for them. I felt sorry that she had to have that nursery because she didn't have children of her own . . . I wanted to relax so I lay down in my back yard and a puppy dog came up and went to sleep right next to me. It was summery and I just lay down on the grass and just was limp . . . Then Roger drove by looking for me. I could see him but he couldn't see me . . . I was tired and wanted to be away from people . . . I kind of wanted to see him but I decided just to rest so I let him drive by. Then I was on campus . . . and I ran into a teacher who actually had his house burn down . . . I started walking and talking to him . . . I didn't know if I should bring it up . . . He looked sad and I touched his arm and he just started crying and sobbing on my shoulder. Next, I remember being at a great big table with a cousin and aunt and uncle . . . my brother was there and some kids my age. My brother was being real inconsiderate and snotty and offending everybody. They asked him what he was going to do that night and he said he was going to so-and-so's house . . . I thought he was just a "hood" and I was trying to soften everything he said so it wouldn't appear to others that he was that much of a brat, because I was embarrassed that he was my brother. In the last part, I was at a river with a guy I used to know. I used to idolize him. He was stiff . . . this part is more about letting down barriers . . . The guy studied more than most in high school and never went out with girls . . . He seemed mature and responsible but was socially retarded. We were at a picnic talking about letting down barriers . . . like the teacher crying . . . and he said he wished he could have a healthier attitude toward saying what he felt like or doing what he felt like . . . He also said he had a problem approaching girls and that he was afraid of sex . . . I felt like I'd heard it before and I felt like cutting him off when he started talking of his barriers and that he couldn't talk of sex. That's what the whole thing was about [the many fragments of the dream] . . . letting down barriers . . . It came out in a hundred different ways . . . letting down barriers and doing and saying what you like.

Analysis of Pam's Dreams

Like the dreams of the previous subjects, Pam's contain a number of instances of the impact of the group experience: such specific elements as the therapist, the room, etc.; symbols such as the "test" that took a "whole bunch of hours" in dream 2, which probably refers to the MMPI and the therapy group; and central themes which parallel the themes discussed during her focus sessions. These latter include: trying hard to perform at something difficult (dreams 2 and 3c); the sexual conflict with her boyfriend (dreams 4 and 7); and the general theme of the "phoniness" of a surface emotion, "letting down barriers," etc.

Let us consider some hypotheses about the central themes of these dreams and their relation to Pam's personality as revealed in the focus sessions. Pam presents a contradiction. She volunteers for the experiment and, perhaps more than any other subject, becomes intensely involved, almost to the point of torturing herself. She is extremely cooperative, giving long, involved dream reports and even waking herself up to report additional material. In the group sessions she attempts to reveal the most upsetting "bad" aspects of herself and cries a great deal. All of this behavior, however, stands in contradiction to what she presents as her central problem: her ability to ruin men, specifically the damage she has caused her brother and her boyfriend. Her guilt about her own destructiveness seems contradicted by her lack of overt aggression, and by the fact that she seems to suffer at least as much as the men.

Her characteristic mode of interpersonal operation, as revealed in the group sessions and by her outside contact with Roger, gives a first clue to this contradiction. She tends to play a "weak" feminine role with men who either are, or soon become, weak and childish in comparison to her. In other words, her feminine "weakness" becomes a source of strength, and her guilt arises from the underlying aggressiveness that is a part of her solicitous concern for men. (See dream 2, "degrading" the childish, "silly boys.") As a part of this interpersonal pattern she uses her own sexuality as an aggressive tool, one with which she can hurt men in the very act of "giving" to them. This maneuver is revealed very clearly in her pregroup sexual contact with Roger, which made him feel intensely guilty and also "cut off" any attacks he might have made on her in the ensuing group meeting. The use of sex for aggressive purposes is suggested at several points in the dreams: for example, the confusion of "sex" and "selfishness" in dream 4 (in which the boyfriend "cried and he had a little bit of Roger in him") indicates that sex, for her, has aggressive as well as loving components. This "sex-selfish" reference occurs in a dream context that also contains reference to "phony" emotional displays, which was also central in dream 2, in which her crying is symbolized as something that conceals rather than reveals. Again, what is hinted at here is the aggressive component of her "weakness" (i.e., crying as a way of maintaining control of the group).

Combining the ideas of phoniness and control with what we know about her history leads to the following hypotheses. She reports identifying closely with her father, having been a "tomboy," and having been very openly competitive with and aggressive toward her brother. Out of this experience, she internalized the father's "judicial" standards, the guilt and the need to perform. And yet she is a woman and sees herself, in fact, as always weaker in relation to men. Homosexuality, a possible resolution of her conflict, she rejects in several dreams in which the roommate's feminine qualities are seen as unattractive. Rather, she has evolved a life style in which her femininity, her "weakness" (as in just those qualities that the father disapproved of, such as crying), can be used to achieve the strength that her identification drives her toward. At the same time, this style allows her to express her anger and competitiveness, though the indirectness serves to perpetuate the guilt.

Dream 7 reveals some of the basic dimensions of this particular conflict. It also shows how she is able to control the aroused stress of the group and dream situations by integrating them into the symbolic world of earlier solutions. The earlier dream 5 gives a clue: she is having a "struggle to humble herself"; she really tries, and achieves a good feeling. Dream 7 is all about "letting down barriers" which, on the surface, means being a good girl in group therapy, doing what the therapist asks, i.e., making a great emotional display of self-revelation. But it is also all about taking men's erections away from them (she has the prophylactic to throw away, going "limp," Roger as a "puppy dog," the instructor whom she gets to cry; the boy who is "stiff" and afraid of sex whom she induces to "let down barriers"; and other elements, e.g., the "tiny little candle holders"). The dream reveals, in a series of relationships, how the hostility to her father (the Catholic priest and the distasteful "old man" who appear in the dream) is transformed into a sexualized "mothering" which effects, in part, a hostile aim. Her actions can then be perceived as good, helpful, enjoyable (and sometimes associated with pleasure and "tension-relieving" sexual intercourse). The dream fuses this basic life "solution" with the solution to the immediate stress of being a subject. She ultimately pleases the therapist by being the most "giving," emotional subject while maintaining a position of strength and accomplishment.

JACKIE

Jackie is a tall, attractive 19-year-old sophomore. She describes herself as a "nonconformist" and this is partly reflected in her appearance: very long hair, sweatshirt, denims, and high-heeled boots. She is outwardly friendly and vivacious although with a certain superficiality. From the beginning, her relationship with the therapist had a childish seductiveness and at times she pouted or adopted the role of a little girl. In these and other ways, she tried to keep things on a light, humorous plane. Jackie is proud of her conscious control of her feelings and her ability to control her involvement and to remain unaffected by others. She says that her only problems are some minor fears and occasional psychosomatic reactions, for example, headaches, stomach cramps, and diarrhea.

She comes from a large family—she has three older brothers, two younger brothers, and two younger sisters. The father is a government official whom she describes as "completely devoted to his job." She says he is "cold and efficient" and rarely had time to spend with the children. During her early childhood the family lived on an Indian reservation, and she describes this as a period of almost complete isolation from other children which, she now feels, contributed to the estrangement she now feels from most people. She describes her mother as childlike and happy.

The First Focus Session

Jackie was the fourth focus subject and, after witnessing the experiences of the other three, she had come to view the group sessions as a hostile, destructive experience. She apparently saw the situation as a challenge to her defenses, and approached her focus sessions in an extremely controlled, intellectual manner. She admitted to having rehearsed a good deal beforehand. At the outset of the session she said she had no "psychological problems" other than a strong fear of dogs and the dark. She then went on to her major topic—her lack of emotional involvement. She said she is afraid of being tied down to the raising of children and therefore never goes into any relationship thinking it might be permanent. She described her father, saying that she had received little affection from him but that, after seeing other fathers, she could appreciate his stability. Pam suggested that she saw herself as similar to her father and was afraid to have children for fear she would treat them as he treated her. Jackie went on with the topic of emotional control, saying that she feels strong all the time, has never loved, never cries, and places great value on controlling her feelings. She spoke of her first "emotional experience," which had occurred the previous summer. She was attracted to a professor, got involved with him, and went to a rented room one night. However, they did not have intercourse, presumably because of the lack of time and the fact that she has a small vagina which, she subsequently discovered, will have to be incised before intercourse. She denied any strong fear of sex. When her boyfriend uncovered the relationship with the professor he told her she would have to choose between them, and at this point she developed severe headaches and stomach cramps. She began to live with her boyfriend then, but still refrained from sexual intercourse. The therapist commented on the surprising lack of sexuality in these relations, and she said that physical attraction was not important and that her attraction to the professor was primarily an intellectual one.

The group members reacted strongly to the planned and intellectual quality of her presentation. Pam told her she sounded like a philosophy book; Roger said that it was all "bullshit," no spontaneity, just words; Hal said that he just "couldn't believe it." She went on talking about her ambivalance toward men, saying she felt antagonistic to Hal because of his superficiality and that she didn't like Roger either sometimes. She said she liked the therapist because he was personable. She mentioned that she has recurrent dreams of killing and maiming men and of being maimed herself. She is usually attracted to older men who are more mature. By this time, the group was reacting with a good deal of anger. The therapist commented on her use of seductiveness to hurt men. He observed that in her relationship with men (professor, boyfriend) she seemed to be a sexual tease. She admitted that she was sadistic in these seductive actions and felt she gained power and strength through them. There were more angry interchanges with the other members, Hal and Jackie each accusing the other of having a "sex problem."

Dream 1: It was something about taxes . . . about how much you're going to pay . . . something about paying what we owed . . . the "we" was the therapist and I. There was some other man . . . just someone I know. Everyone was fairly happy and we were sitting around. Someone was writing. He wanted to know something about filing his tax return so he could get some money back. I was trying to help him with it . . . I was just kind of standing there figuring it out . . . It didn't seem very important. I was just kind of casually answering. It was kind of like we were friends or something.

Dream 2: I had just come back from dream research and one of the persons who was recording the dreams was a friend who lived next door. I wanted to know how he'd gotten interested in dream research and he said he kept dreaming that his adrenalin glands were secreting too much and that his psychologist told him that he had to limit it or something. So that's why he started coming here ... I was at my old apartment ... I can't seem to come to grips with anything ... I was a little irritated that this friend was one of the people in dream research ... I felt a little funny when I found out he was my neighbor.

Dream 3: When you woke me up the therapist was running real fast and I was lying on my bed in the Psychology Clinic and waiting for him to stop running and come back. I was afraid to be by myself in the dark ... There were all these rooms and he snuck away. I knew that he was doing it so that I would have to be by myself. I decided to just sit and wait ... so I chose a room and waited for him to come back ... because I was kind of mad at him. I was very calm and not much afraid ... I just sat and waited ... I ran away one time ... then I tried to sneak back in, but I was still clinging because he was there ... So then he decided it would be a good idea if he left. Then I was trying to decide if I should hide and if he came back what should I do ... These are my mildest dreams ever ... We were in these buildings [Clinic] ... I was doing something here and I guess the therapist was also doing something. For some reason he made me mad ... I don't remember why. I ran away or snuck away and then I kind of came back and I got in a room and he ran away ... real fast. It was scary but I wasn't very scared. I decided just to wait and then he came running back ... It was just the two of us. I didn't like to be left ... I thought it was a little bit mean. I think he was doing it for some reason ... The last thing I remember, he was running back and he was going to come in the door ... I was just waiting ... I was going to have my eyes open. I wasn't going to be asleep or hiding. He didn't know what room I was going to be in.

Unlike the first dreams of the other three subjects, Jackie's is not thematically dominated by the preceding therapy session, although the therapist appears as a central figure. The next two dreams are more easily interpretable as reflecting the session, however, so perhaps the first one does also. We might view it as a continuation of the defensive efforts that Jackie so successfully employed at the session. It has an intellectual quality (paying taxes; "writing"; figuring something out) and reverses the actual affective quality of the group session, i.e., it "didn't seem very important," she was just "casually answering," everyone was "fairly happy," etc. Dream 2 seems to represent her fear that her emotions will get out of control. This fear is symbolized by "adrenalin" glands that secrete too much, an interesting choice for one who relies on psychosomatic channels for the expression of conflict. Dream 3 indicates the special nature of her feelings about the therapist. He abandons her (which, as she later stated, she felt he did in the group) and she expectantly awaits his return. (In fact, as the tension of the project grew, Jackie began dropping by to see the therapist during the day, became more seductive toward him, and eventually indicated that she would like to "get to know him better" on an informal basis. This behavior is of course consistent with her character as revealed, for example, in the relationship with the professor.)

The Second Focus Session

Jackie began by saying that she was sorry everyone had to come because not much would happen—no defenses would be torn down, she was happy and had no incentive for changing herself, she had few problems and probably wasn't going to break down and cry. She saw the group members as trying to get a rise out of her and was determined to ward them off, maintaining a noticeable aloofness and coolness interspersed with some sarcastic humor. Roger began an intellectual discussion with her and she talked about her "problems" of emotional commitment and difficulty with "love" with little apparent involvement. When Roger said he saw her as a little girl playing a game she retorted that she just isn't used to relating on an emotional plane, works on an intellectual level, and has, in the past, lost friends through being "weak" and emotional. The group members reacted with increasing hostility to her stance of noninvolvement. Hal said he thought she was emotionally ill and felt sorry for her. Pam added that she used the things that happened in the group only to reinforce her already preformed ideas. Jackie answered that the group members really didn't care about her, and continued her rejecting, aloof stance. The therapist spoke of his feelings of frustration, sadness, and irritation, wondering why she might make him feel this way. Her responses included a smile and occasional sarcastic remarks which further provoked the other group members. Hal called her names—"bitch," "repulsive"—but she only smiled. Pam asked if she was afraid of finding out that she was not human.

Jackie spoke of having enjoyed the previous session and added that she was strong and that people couldn't get to her. She said she had no real feelings during the previous summer—for either the professor or her boyfriend. She said that only feelings can make her ill, not logic, and that emotional happiness will come to her only through intellect. She was amused and saddened by the fact that she has no feelings, but was sure that she is happy. Pam suggested that she was playing hard to get and punishing the group. The therapist added that she seemed to need to frustrate them and that everyone was involved and upset except her. Pam said if she doesn't change she will eventually be totally alienated. Jackie admitted that she wants some emotional life and would like someone with whom she could be weak and who would love her anyway. The therapist commented on the conflicting feelings she provoked in him: he liked some of her little-girl qualities but was surprised at the irritation he felt toward her. She responded with flippancy and sarcasm. The group members expressed their anger at her further. Pam said she would like to hurt her just to get a rise out of her, and Hal exploded, "I'd just love to get her."

While she maintained her posture of exaggerated aloofness throughout the group meeting, she immediately left the therapy room and cried violently for 10 minutes before preparing for sleep.

> *Dream 4:* I was lost and it was so vivid . . . I was measuring . . . I really didn't think that you could measure so much of the emotional . . . and even though I agreed with it somehow, I really didn't think you could just shift over onto an emotional plane. I was sending something. I had to wrap it and send it . . . It was some kind of package and the therapist and Hal were going to help me, I didn't want to completely abandon any rationality . . . about the course this package would take. So I was kind of arguing, I was reluctant to say . . . well, you know, "Just don't worry about anything, just respond to it emotionally." . . . And now neither of their judgments on the course of this package has anything to do with the address . . . It's just purely emotional . . . Maybe how the package was wrapped . . . it's just how they feel it should be without any regard to logical rationale. And even though I kind of want them to help me, I am not willing to abandon all rationale. I am still concerned about the character and nature and direction and all these kind of things with the package. It was a good dream . . . The package was something I had to fix . . . oh, God, incriminating . . . but I had to do something, alter it and pack it or wrap it or something . . . I wanted to do something but I was reluctant to just let them have free rein or just to do what they thought. I was still leary of just being open to them . . . It seemed like they were taking my role away,

because I felt like I was giving in to this emotional and nonrational thing. And yet, I was trying to cling to some fragments of structured decisions and things.

Dream 5: I was trying to find a deck of cards and I kept going to all these tables and everybody would quickly grab their deck or else only gave me an incomplete deck ... I couldn't get a deck ... There were lots of people and I kept going to their tables. I wanted to have a deck of cards sitting on the table for some reason. I was looking for something but I don't know what I was doing ... It was just frustrating not being able to ... It was some kind of communication problem. I wasn't able to get any cards. I just felt isolated. All these people were obviously not responding or else withdrawing or being belligerent or something by making it impossible for me to get the cards. I felt a little bit mad towards them. They didn't want me to have them. I remember one boy who used to live upstairs, I could have had one deck they had at their table but it was filled with miscellaneous cards from other decks, and I didn't want it ... When I woke up I was going through letters ... sifting ... thumbing through and looking for something. The mail was empty too, like it wasn't a complete set either. I felt that it was kind of futile.

Dream 6 (The only fragmented report given by Jackie during either pre- or postgroup periods):
a: I was in the hall talking to the therapist. He was saying how much he liked to drink and saying that when he was younger he used to drink all the time. In fact, he said he still loved to drink but now that he was married and Jerry had come he had too many other responsibilities ... I was trying to figure out who Jerry was ... if it was one of his kids. He seemed irritated when I asked who it was ... He was just talking about different times when he had gotten absolutely stoned ... It was a long conversation ... He was saying he used to drink a lot until Jerry came and I assumed it was his kid, but then he said, "Before I was married I was waiting for Jerry." ... And then I said, "Who is Jerry?" and he got all upset and told me, "It's none of your business, you know who he is," and kind of dropped the subject. Then he started telling about some of his exploits of wild drinking times ... of different capacities for drinks he's had ... kind of reminiscing, like it sure was fun. I was saying that I really like to drink too. I felt like we were friends ... mostly small talking ... Mostly about drinking and the fact that he didn't do it any more since he got older and more responsible and was married. It disturbed him very much when I alluded that Jerry must be his kid and he snapped at me, "Well, you didn't have any reason to think that." I didn't know how to act. We were drinking at a water fountain at first ... taking turns ... It was very dark ... I felt a little bit shy because I didn't know him well ... and apprehensive. I liked him and it was kind of nice.

b: Then the scene changed suddenly and there were three go-go girls at a night club where I was drinking. It disturbed me because they were hor-rifying—they were real tall, way above me and fairly unclothed. They had just expressionless faces and they seemed startling . . . I just remember these bodies violently dancing. I couldn't see their faces. It was extremely unpleasant. They seemed so hard, so unreal . . . I just felt bad. It was real ugly and horrible. There were blaring noises and ugly colors . . . Their bodies were repulsive . . . I almost seemed like a little kid in a way just thrown into it . . . I started thinking of my roommate because it was so ugly. They were standing way above me with their feet in my face. Their bodies were almost completely naked and they were kind of distorted . . . It just seems that I was standing there with my mouth open . . . I was just kind of amazed at them. They were just moving very hard . . . They didn't even seem human. I felt horrible and disgusted. One of the dancers wasn't even partially clothed . . . I was amazed at her vagina. It seemed like a little tiny, tiny hole. That's when I was most disturbed, I made it go away.

c: I started dreaming of my roommate . . . we were in some kind of apartment . . . I was waiting for her to come out of the bathroom . . . Right when I woke up it was 8:30 and she said she had to hurry to get to her church service because it started at 9 or 9:15 and she said it was 68 blocks. I couldn't imagine walking 68 blocks for anything. Her boyfriend was in the living room. I disliked her for her contrived attitude toward the church . . . she seemed so martyrlike that she was faithfully going to the church. It was kind of irritating. I don't like her boyfriend and I don't like her very well either, I guess.

Analysis of Jackie's Dreams

Two days after her last night in the laboratory, Jackie tele-phoned the therapist. She was extremely angry and went on at great length about how "sadistic" he had been in letting the group go on the way it did. She described being sick with stomach aches, headaches, and diarrhea the day after the group meeting. The therapist saw her in two supportive interviews which seemed bene-ficial to her, and during which she offered some interesting addi-tional material relating to the dreams.

Jackie's dreams differ from those of the other three subjects. The impact of the group experience is apparent in a number of elements, but the themes discussed in the group do not pre-dominate as they do in the dreams of the others. In addition, except for dream 6b, her dreams are not intensely emotional—they are, in fact, less emotional than her dreams in the baseline period.

A further difference is a lack of regressive or childhood material—elements which have been generally found in the dreams of most subjects studied, and which certainly appear in the dreams of the other subjects in this study. How can these differences be explained?

We can see in Jackie's dreams a number of parallels to the defensive stance she took in the group sessions. Her dreams are primarily intellectual, and even symbolize this defensive effort (as in dream 2 on limiting the oversecretion of "adrenalin" glands, and the "measuring" of "the emotional" in dream 4). When an intensely emotional dream does occur (6b), she reports willfully changing it to something less troubling. In these dreams, as in the group itself, she controls the threat of "the emotional" by confronting it and intellectually overcoming it. In this way she "gains strength," to use her words. One further point should be mentioned. Jackie attempted to establish a "special" kind of relationship with the therapist-experimenter and, in fact, was the only subject who eventually saw him for some individual sessions. In her dreams he seems a more central character than the other group members, especially in the very important first two parts of dream 6.

Let us turn now to some hypotheses about the conflicts that underlie Jackie's dreams and her actions in the group sessions. Briefly, one can describe her as a girl who puts herself in situations which are simultaneously emotionally (sexually) arousing and anxiety provoking, and then controls these situations by *not giving*. With the use of a little unconscious seductiveness, she establishes a relationship with a father figure (the professor) and finds herself with him in a motel room. But she does not have intercourse. The same pattern is repeated with her boyfriend. Similarly, she volunteers for the group, but when she gets to be the focus subject she does not "give" emotionally to the others. In each situation she gains strength by maintaining control. Dream 4 ties the idea of "opening up" emotionally (by talking to the men in the group) to "opening up" sexually, which she perceives as dangerous. The three parts of dream 6 are particularly revealing of the dimensions underlying this pattern. In 6a we see the sexualized interaction with the therapist (father figure), symbolized by his excessive drinking, their drinking together where it was very dark, feeling a little bit shy and apprehensive, liking him, its being nice, etc.—all affects appropriate to a sexual encounter. (She subsequently reported that this part had had a strongly sexual tone.) Dream 6b reveals, in a complex, symbolic way, her underlying feelings about sex. It is both exciting and horrible, wild and aggressive, it contains homosexual (her open mouth, the feet almost in her face) and heterosexual elements. The central "go-go dancer" can easily be seen as a symbol for herself: the "expressionless face" (her lack of overt emotion) atop the wildly sexual body with the tiny vagina. Turning to the roommate as a homosexual solution is suggested and carried further in 6c, but this too is unsatisfying. In fact, in the postgroup interviews, she did report several unsatisfying homosexual experiences.

In sum, Jackie's character structure is most like that of a classical hysterical neurotic. The seductive behavior toward older, father-figure males, the tremendous underlying anxiety about sexuality, the somatic symptoms, the almost counterphobic exposure of herself to just those situations that she most fears and, unconsciously, desires, are all apparent. The dreams, like her behavior in the group and the other interpersonal relations she described, provide evidence of the way her whole life is centered on attempts to deal with this core conflict.

RATING-SCALE RESULTS

A total of 147 dream reports were collected from the four experimental and two control subjects during the baseline and postgroup periods. The dream reports were rated on each of the scales previously described.

Incorporation

Each postgroup dream of the four experimental subjects was examined by an independent judge who first listened to the tape recording of the preceding focus session. The judge then rated the dream for incorporation of (1) group members (including the therapist), (2) elements from the group setting (the clinic room, furniture, etc.), and (3) the central content discussed during the group meeting. The results of this analysis are presented in Table 1.

TABLE 1

INCORPORATION OF ELEMENTS FROM THE GROUP SESSIONS
IN THE POSTGROUP DREAMS

Subject	N of Dreams	Elements		
		Group members	Group setting	Central content
Hal	9	3	2	9
Roger	7	0	0	7
Pam	7	4	0	7
Jackie	6	3	1	6

Thematic-Dimension and Formal-Quality Ratings

All dream reports were rated on four thematic-content dimensions (*Quality of interactions, Roles of dreamer, Roles of others,* and *Dream outcome*) and on six formal-quality scales (*Anxiety, Cognitive disturbance, Implausibility, Involvement, Primitivity,* and *Recall*). Tables 2-5 present the mean scores of the experimental and control subjects, and of each experimental subject, on these 10 dimensions and qualities.

There are two reasons for presenting these results in the way that we will. First, it could be argued that the subjects' dreams following their focus-session experience are merely samples of their typical dreams—that is, that the dreams do not necessarily show effects of being a focus subject. The baseline dreams were collected to check this possibility and the case analyses were carried out with the baseline dreams in mind. However, none of the baseline dreams are presented in the case studies. The rating-scale results are thus of value because they present an explicit comparison of the baseline and postgroup dreams. Second, it might be argued that the dream conflicts, affects, and defenses that we assume result from the focus-session experience are not necessarily a result of that experience. They might result from other factors, such as sleeping in the laboratory, being awakened throughout the night, and so on. Dream reports were collected from two control subjects under conditions that matched those of the experimental subjects in all respects except for participation in the therapy group. Comparison of the rating-scale results from the two groups in the baseline and postgroup conditions thus provides a check on the assumption that the sorts of dream conflicts and affects we attribute to the group experience do, indeed, stem from it and not from other factors.

To assess the statistical significance of the various rating-scale results, two analysis of variance tests were carried out on each of the 10 rated dimensions and qualities. One tested the differences between experimental and control groups, the other the differences between the four experimental subjects. These analyses of variance will not be described here; the interested reader is referred to the original study (Hunter, 1966) for a detailed description, including the complete analysis of variance tables. In the discussion to follow, we have simply noted those findings that were significant.

Thematic Dimensions. Table 2 presents the mean ratings of the experimental and control groups on the four thematic dimensions, for baseline and postgroup dream reports. The *Quality of interactions* among the characters in the dream (rated: pleasant = 1, neutral = 2, unpleasant = 3) is more unpleasant for the experimental group in the postgroup condition, whereas for the control group it is more pleasant. This interaction effect (group x conditions) was significant ($p < .01$). The ratings of *Roles of dreamer* (rated: inadequate = 1, neutral = 2, adequate-successful = 3) and *Thematic outcome* (rated: desirable = 1, neutral = 2, undesirable = 3) show comparable interaction effects: in both cases, the dreams of the experimental subjects change in the direction of less adequate-successful roles of the dreamer and less desirable thematic outcome from the baseline to the postgroup condition, whereas the dreams of the control subjects change in the opposite direction (more adequate roles of the dreamer and more desirable outcomes). These two interaction effects were significant (*Roles of dreamer*, $p < .05$; *Thematic outcome*, $p < .01$). The ratings of *Roles of others* (rated: inadequate = 1, neutral = 2, adequate-successful = 3) do not show a comparable contrast: for both groups, the *Roles of others* becomes slightly more adequate from the baseline to the postgroup condition.

TABLE 2

MEAN RATINGS OF EXPERIMENTAL AND CONTROL GROUPS ON THEMATIC-CONTENT DIMENSIONS

Groups	Quality of Interactions		Roles of Dreamer		Roles of Others		Thematic Outcome	
	Baseline	Postgroup	Baseline	Postgroup	Baseline	Postgroup	Baseline	Postgroup
Experimental (N=4)	2.26	2.45	2.04	1.56	1.86	2.03	2.26	2.35
Control (N=2)	2.20	1.84	2.00	2.17	1.77	1.85	2.23	1.83

Other significant differences among the ratings presented in Table 2 are the over-all group differences in *Quality of interactions* ($p < .01$) and *Roles of dreamer* ($p < .05$). These findings indicate that both the baseline and postgroup dreams of the experimental group were characterized by less pleasant interaction and less adequate roles of the dreamer. None of the other group or condition comparisons were significant.

Table 3 presents the thematic-dimension ratings of the experimental group subject by subject. Only one finding was statistically significant: the significant drop in the *Roles of dreamer* ratings from baseline to postgroup ($p < .01$) shows that the roles of all four subjects were less adequate-successful in the postgroup dreams.

Formal qualities. Each of the six formal qualities was rated from 1 to 5; the higher the rating the greater the amount of the variable in question. Table 4 presents the mean ratings of baseline and postgroup dreams for the two groups on each quality. The ratings of the experimental group tend to be higher on all the scales. The differences reached significance on *Anxiety* ($p < .05$); *Cognitive disturbance* ($p < .05$); *Involvement* ($p < .01$); and *Recall* ($p < .01$). For both groups the ratings on all scales tended to be higher in the postgroup condition, but only on the *Recall* scale was the increase significant ($p < .01$, for both groups). There were no significant group x condition interactions.

Table 5 presents the formal-quality findings for the experimental group subject by subject. The subjects differed significantly on *Cognitive disturbance, Involvement,* and *Recall* (all $p < .01$). Roger reported the most cognitively disturbed or fragmented dreams, followed by Pam, Jackie, and Hal. Pam's reports showed the greatest amount of involvement. Both of these findings are consistent with the personalities and styles of reaction described in the case studies of Roger and Pam. *Involvement* also increased significantly from the baseline to the postgroup condition ($p < .05$): all subjects show greater involvement after their focus sessions except Jackie, who, as we saw, made great efforts to control her emotional reactions.

Recall was significantly higher ($p < .05$) for all subjects in the postgroup condition. The *Recall* ratings (Tables 4 and 5) indicate

TABLE 3

MEAN RATINGS OF FOUR EXPERIMENTAL SUBJECTS ON THEMATIC-CONTENT DIMENSIONS

Experimental Subjects	Quality of Interactions		Roles of Dreamer		Roles of Others		Thematic Outcome	
	Baseline	Postgroup	Baseline	Postgroup	Baseline	Postgroup	Baseline	Postgroup
Hal	2.40	2.27	2.19	1.44	1.96	2.10	2.20	2.33
Roger	2.31	2.61	1.87	1.28	2.17	2.35	2.13	2.43
Pam	2.21	2.47	1.74	1.69	1.75	1.84	2.24	2.25
Jackie	2.23	2.33	2.37	1.70	1.85	1.93	2.44	2.44

TABLE 4

MEAN RATINGS OF EXPERIMENTAL AND CONTROL GROUPS ON FORMAL-QUALITY SCALES

	Anxiety		Cognitive Disturbance		Implausibility		Involvement		Primitivity		Recall	
	Baseline	Postgroup	Baseline	Postgroup	Baseline	Postgroup	Baseline	Postgroup	Baseline	Postgroup	Baseline	Postgroup
Experimental (N=4)	2.28	2.34	2.17	2.07	2.26	2.39	2.64	2.99	2.22	2.29	3.02	3.44
Control (N=2)	1.69	1.94	1.46	1.77	2.01	2.10	2.27	2.39	2.16	2.18	2.37	3.15

TABLE 5

MEAN RATINGS OF FOUR EXPERIMENTAL SUBJECTS ON FORMAL-QUALITY SCALES

	Anxiety		Cognitive Disturbance		Implausibility		Involvement		Primitivity		Recall	
	Baseline	Postgroup	Baseline	Postgroup	Baseline	Postgroup	Baseline	Postgroup	Baseline	Postgroup	Baseline	Postgroup
Hal	2.03	2.61	1.75	1.80	2.33	2.77	2.41	2.94	2.23	2.92	3.56	3.83
Roger	1.85	2.57	2.44	2.79	1.75	2.71	2.16	2.82	1.80	2.32	2.38	3.18
Pam	2.78	2.06	2.35	2.23	2.56	2.04	3.10	3.42	2.13	2.06	3.20	3.23
Jackie	2.29	2.28	2.14	1.62	2.29	2.25	2.69	2.62	2.69	1.94	3.05	3.52

that the experimental subjects, as a group, were better dream reporters than the control subjects; that some of them were better
than others; and that all subjects became better reporters with
increasing experience in the sleep laboratory.

The thematic-dimension results (Tables 2 and 3) and the formal-
quality results (Tables 4 and 5) present an interesting contrast: in
general, the thematic dimensions reflect the impact of the group
experience whereas the formal-quality scales assess more stable
individual differences among the subjects.

With regard to the questions raised earlier, the thematic and
formal ratings, taken together, provide evidence that: (1) while
there are stable individual dream styles, the focus-session experience clearly affected dream content; and (2) these effects resulted
from the focus-session experience and not from other factors associated with the study.

DISCUSSION

The results of the Group Therapy Study show that this particular presleep experience strongly influenced dream content. The
case studies show that the material aroused during the focus sessions was represented and worked over in the dreams according to
each subject's individual style. The *Incorporation* ratings show
that the central content of each dream was related to the material
discussed in the preceding group session. The other rating-scale
results parallel and complement the case studies. In the discussion
to follow, we will consider some of these results in more detail and
deal with certain critical questions. Additional general discussion is
reserved for the final chapter, following the presentation of the
Surgery Study.

The focus-session experience can be viewed as a personally
arousing "problem" that each subject had somehow to solve. What
he did in the group sessions, his behavior in the sleep laboratory,
his dreams, and other efforts, can all be viewed as part of his
efforts at solution. Considered in this light, the total performance
of each subject is all of a piece: his dream processes very much
parallel his waking actions. Hal, for instance, pulled himself together toward the end of his second focus session, declaring that he

"had no problems," and during the presleep preparation he repeatedly assured the experimenter of the same thing. In his subsequent dreams he eventually found himself in a position where everything was all right—there were no people around to threaten him and his need for "care" was magically met. His dreams thus paralleled the defensive solutions that he attempted in the group and presleep periods. Similarly, the rather rigid intellectual control that Jackie affected in order to deal with the focus-session experience was paralleled by the relative control and lack of emotion in her postgroup dreams. Her attempts to deal with the threat represented by the therapist-experimenter were also paralleled in the dreams that dealt with him. Roger reacted to the group at first with an attempt at intellectual control, with some projection, and later by showing his weaknesses. The first reaction was paralleled by his presleep efforts to "write refutations" to other group members and by dreams in which he was the "explainer or interpreter." The second reaction was paralleled in dreams representing his ineffectuality in the face of female-mother figures. Pam mastered the focus-session experience by confessing with a great deal of emotion. In a sense, she so overplayed the patient role that the group members and the therapist were largely neutralized. Her extragroup contact with Roger served a similar neutralizing function. Her dreams also display these themes, and such related matters as her indirect aggressiveness and her "phoniness" (i.e., playing false roles). There are, then, quite clear parallels between the material aroused in the focus sessions and the postsession dreams. The dreams seem to represent the subjects' more or less successful attempts to deal with the aroused material.

It is interesting to note the consistencies in some of the symbols used by different subjects. Water has a central position in several of Hal's dreams. In dream 1 it drips out of the swimming pool, leaving him damaged or bruised. In dream 8 an endless ocean supports him, and in dream 9 he watches water go by while feeling lonely, yet knowing his family is concerned and will care for him. Clearly, the symbol of water plays a part in the memory system dealing with dependency, with being taken care of and supported. Why "water" has this particular meaning for him is open to speculation. One would need a great deal of associational material to ascertain how it was acquired. It lends itself to the use he makes of it, of course—water can support you, as on a raft, or you can drown in it; it is associated with drinking, the earliest form of feeding. Perhaps it relates to some specific memories of being bathed by his mother. In any case, it illustrates how a particular symbol can have a certain meaning within a person's memory system.

A somewhat more general symbol runs through Pam's dreams, representing her "false front." In dream 1 a "great, big, thick glass" keeps her from getting close to people. This may symbolize an attitude toward herself: she is transparent (emotional, she confesses readily), yet keeps people at a distance and does not really reveal what is within her. In dream 2 her "reading glasses" (again glass as a symbol) blur vision rather than clarify it. They are "like a front . . . so that they [the other people] couldn't really see what I was like." In dream 3a the symbol is "make-up," and in dream 7 it is the "barriers" that people hide behind and that should be "let down." These closely related symbols all pertain to the idea that Pam, and others, are not what they seem on the surface. As we pointed out in her case study, her need for a false front stems from a core conflict concerning her own competitiveness and aggression. She uses an exaggerated "weakness" and femininity to control the direct expression of her aggression, but since it is a reaction formation she constantly feels that she is "not what she seems to be" on the surface.

Let us now consider some of the rating-scale results. The impact of the group experience was most evident on the thematic-dimension scales. The ratings of the control subjects all change in the direction of pleasanter interactions, more adequate-successful roles for both the dreamer and others, and more desirable dream outcomes. These findings were to be expected. They are consistent with the literature on the general effects of being a subject in the sleep laboratory and reflect a progressive lessening of anxiety with increasing experience. For the experimental subjects, all of the thematic ratings (except Hal's on *Quality of interactions*) either do not show this change or change in the opposite direction from the baseline to the postgroup condition. Roger's postgroup ratings show the largest changes in the directions of less pleasant interactions, less adequate roles taken by himself, and less desirable dream outcomes. This is consistent with his case analysis, from which it can be seen that the group experience opened up areas of conflict, weakened the effectiveness of his defenses of intellectualization and projection, and left him more overtly anxious and in conflict. The same effect is reflected in his scores on *Anxiety* (he shows the greatest increase from baseline to postgroup), increased *Cognitive disturbance* (reflecting the fragmented and confused reporting that is a result of the breakdown of intellectualization), and *Primitivity*, which reflects the breakthrough of impulses.

Hal's ratings change, in general, in the same direction as Roger's, although not to the same degree. His postgroup dreams have less pleasant outcomes and his own roles in these dreams are less adequate. Similarly, they increase in *Anxiety, Implausibility, Involvement,* and *Primitivity.* These findings show a general trend toward the breakthrough of conflict concurrent with the breakdown of defense that occurred in the group. The change in *Cognitive disturbance* is slight, reflecting, perhaps, his much smaller reliance on intellectualization as a defense. One change in the opposite direction occurs: in the *Quality of interactions*, his postgroup dreams are more pleasant. The direction of change on this scale reflects the fact that on both postgroup nights Hal's later dreams represented a defensive or magical attempt at resolution of the aroused conflicts.

Pam's thematic ratings are more difficult to interpret, as was her more complex reaction to the group. The scales show changes in the less pleasant, less adequate directions, but these changes are very small. Her scores on *Anxiety, Cognitive disturbance, Implausibility,* and *Primitivity* actually decrease from baseline to postgroup. These trends may represent the success with which she controlled the group by her cathartic performance and her sexual encounter with Roger.

Jackie's ratings are quite consistent with the material presented in her case study. She shows the least change on the thematic dimensions; *Quality of interactions* and *Outcome* are practically identical in the two conditions. *Anxiety, Cognitive disturbance, Implausibility,* and *Primitivity* also show little change from baseline to postgroup. Jackie was able to maintain her controlled, intellectualized (if you will, counterphobic) defensive stance throughout the focus sessions and this ability was, with the exception of one vivid dream segment, reflected in her postgroup dreams.

In general, we believe that the statistical findings are consistent with the case material. That is, it is possible to make sense out of the two taken together, though it should be kept in mind that the objective findings provide no unequivocal "proof" of the hypotheses put forth in the case studies.

The discussion to this point has stressed the commonalities in the dream and nondream reactions of the subjects. We will now consider those ways in which the dreams permit unique processing of the information aroused by the group experience. In general, dreaming allows the material aroused in the group to be represented or processed in a wider variety of ways than does waking thought. The fluidity of associative processes, the ease with which one symbol is substituted for another, one person for another, one affect-laden situation for another, permit a blending of currently aroused material with older, similar material. For Roger, his girlfriend, his mother, Pam, and an unknown female are all blended together in dreams which deal with the same general conflict (see dreams 3 and 7). For Hal, the negative affect aroused by being the focus of the group is blended with a different kind of being "special"—a situation in which he is the center of a group's adulation (dreams 4 and 5). We can speculate that this freedom in the use of symbols and symbolic substitutions, the availability of more memory material—including the "old solutions"—and the operation of a greater number of programs, all make dreams singularly well suited for the integration of aroused material. In this respect, the sequences of the dreams of each night are very interesting (see Trosman et al. [1960] for a similar discussion of this point). The sequences suggest a course in which the early dreams display the currently aroused information and later dreams work it over, bringing in more and more early memories, including earlier "solutions" and defenses. This course is clearest in Hal's dreams, although similar trends are discernible in the other subjects.

Some Critical Considerations

Let us now consider several uncontrolled factors that might have influenced the results. First, it is obvious that we are dealing with a small number of subjects who were essentially self-selected for the project. The fact that the four experimental subjects differ so much from one another indicates that we might find continuing variability if we extended the sample. There is no answer to this criticism, except what can be provided by additional research.

Second, the order of dream collection was not controlled: for all subjects the collection of baseline dreams preceded the collection of postgroup dreams. Previous research, however (confirmed by our findings for the control subjects), has shown that stress is highest on initial nights in the sleep laboratory. The order of collection, then, was working against the effects that were found: the ratings of the postgroup dreams of the experimental subjects changed in directions opposite to the normal or expected ones. This uncontrolled factor cannot, therefore, be considered an artifactual cause of the findings.

The order in which the four experimental subjects took their turns as focus of the group interaction was also uncontrolled. There is an obvious difference, for example, between Hal's experience as the first focus subject facing an unknown situation, and Jackie's experience as the fourth, facing a situation that she had just seen three others go through. The effects of these differing expectations on the subjects' performance, as well as on the dreams, can only be guessed. Our impression from the case material—and the reader is free to judge for himself—is that the subjects' consistent personal styles, defenses, and conflicts were not markedly affected by their differing expectations.

Finally, several related problems must be considered, having to do with a confounding of the group situation with the sleep-laboratory situation. First, the same person served as group therapist and as principle dream experimenter, creating an important psychological bridge between the two situations. Previous research (Whitman et al., 1962) has indicated that subjects in therapy tend to inhibit the reporting of negative dreams about the dream experimenter (reporting them instead to their therapists) and, conversely, to inhibit reporting negative dreams about their therapists to them (reporting them instead to the dream experimenter). Neither course was available to the subjects in the present study, and this may have inhibited the reporting of negative dreams to the therapist-experimenter (see, for example, Hal's dream 6, in which he defends mightily against saying anything negative about the therapist, reporting, ". . . the person that would get material through against me . . . the, the therapist, and I really did nothing to stop him. I like him because it seemed like he supported me . . ."). Perhaps of greater significance, the therapist-experimenter's dual role made him a powerful figure for the group members, as is revealed in a number of their dreams. Having the same person serve as therapist and dream experimenter intensified the impact of the experience, and accelerated transferencelike reactions that might ordinarily take longer to develop.

A further confounding factor poses the greatest difficulty with respect to interpreting the effects of the group experience on dream content. This is the fact that what the subjects were urged to discuss during their focus sessions was material that, in a certain sense, they would be likely to dream about anyway. That is, if we assume, with most writers on dreams, that people dream about their conflicts, problems, affect-laden experiences, etc., it is not surprising that our subjects dreamed about the central content discussed in the group. The related problem in correlating the material from the group sessions with subsequent dreams—namely, that so many topics and elements were touched on in the lengthy group discussions that on a purely random basis some of them would appear in the subjects' dreams—is not a serious one, since incorporations were scored only when a dominant theme or central conflict from a focus session appeared in a dream. It was, in fact, a central aspect of this study to take the very matters that people are likely to dream about and so to intensify them during the focus-session experience that they would stand out in the postgroup dreams. And that, by and large, is what did occur. There are large differences between the baseline and postgroup dreams that can unquestionably be attributed to the group experience. But the themes and particular individual concerns and styles of the subjects can also be recognized in the baseline dreams. While these themes and conflicts were made to stand out by the group experience, this very situation also posed a threat to defenses, and both the behavior of the subjects and their postgroup dreams show evidence of increased anxiety (seen most clearly in the dreams of Hal and Roger) and increased defensiveness (seen most clearly in the group behavior and dreams of Jackie). The trends that appear in all four thematic dimensions may be seen as results of the breakdown of defense and the emergence of conflict.

The problem of confounding nevertheless remains, and the effects of the group experience on dreams should be viewed as the intensification of a more or less natural process rather than as a manipulation of dream content by arbitrary experimental input.

Much of the value of the Group Therapy Study lies in the demonstration of the usefulness of certain techniques and procedures. The combination of case study with rating scales is one such useful technique. We might comment further on group therapy with individual focus sessions. When we originally contemplated this study we had many doubts about whether such a group could be put together without a great deal of artificiality resulting from its experimental character. If intense, realistic interactions were achieved, would the group members continue to participate? Would they be able to fall asleep and report dreams after what might be a very upsetting experience? We also entertained doubts about the ethicality of the procedure.

The results are certainly very encouraging with respect to these questions. All the group members stuck it out to the end of the project; the level of interaction and involvement was intense; and the quality of the interactions was as genuine as that of any therapy group with which we have had experience. In fact, it is our impression that greater intensity was obtained more rapidly than is usually the case. This could have been the result of the frequent meetings, the effects of being aware of their own dreams, the focus-session technique, or all three. We also suspect that a certain amount of luck was involved in the selection of these particular subjects, who turned out to be both cooperative and courageous.

Finally, with respect to the ethicality of the focus-session technique, we can only say that the therapist acted much as he would in any therapy group. He made no special effort to break down the subjects; on the contrary, he frequently found himself acting as a modulating influence on their interactions with one another. The subjects were fully informed about the procedures, no deception was employed, and the therapist and other therapeutic facilities of the Psychology Clinic were available should the subjects request them, as Jackie subsequently did.

5

THE SURGERY STUDY

The Surgery Study was an investigation of the effects of a real-life stress experience—a surgical operation—on dreams. A small number of subjects was studied intensively during the time preceding their operations and again after the operations. Before describing the methods and results, we will review the relevant literature on psychological reactions to surgery.

REVIEW OF THE LITERATURE

Facing a surgical operation is an experience of stress which extends over time, permitting the mobilization of a variety of individual psychological reactions. Before surgery the person is exposed to his own anticipations and fantasies and may engage in defensive activities against whatever fears are aroused in him. The stress is inherently psychological, and the nature of the person's response to the threat of surgery will depend on the particular fantasies and expectations aroused in him.

In this section we will review the literature on common psychological reactions to surgery, especially the type of conflict likely to be aroused and the kinds of defenses which are often mobilized.

Deutsch (1942) was one of the first to provide a theoretical model of psychological reactions to surgery. Working within a psychoanalytic framework, she postulates that the arousal of fear and anxiety is central, and that before the operation the patient undergoes a period of "inner preparation" in which he attempts to defend against this aroused anxiety.

Deutsch believes that to understand what the "inner assimilation" of anxiety means in the individual case it is necessary to know the nature of the person's fear. Objectively, surgery commonly confronts the patient with the double threat of bodily damage and possible death. However, each patient has many private conflicts which the threat of surgery may activate. The more "latent" and intense (i.e., neurotic) these activated conflicts, the more the level of aroused anxiety is likely to exceed the objective risk of the operation. For example, the objective fear of bodily damage and possible death can be greatly intensified by an underlying fear of punishment, or by the reactivation of an early fear of being separated from or abandoned by loved ones.

Deutsch's psychoanalytic model was a precursor to Janis's (1958) empirical study of psychological reactions to surgery. Janis investigated the impact of surgery on 22 patients in a general medical hospital, devoting the most systematic attention to their levels of fear and anger. The data were derived from structured preoperative and postoperative interviews, supplemented by behavioral observations on the wards. On the basis of this information the patients were classified into three categories of preoperative fear: high, moderate, and low. The major finding was that postoperative difficulties in adjustment were most likely to occur in patients with high and low amounts of preoperative fear, and least likely to occur in patients with moderate preoperative fear. Interestingly, postoperative reactions were found not to be related to the type or severity of the surgery performed.

The reactions of patients who showed a high degree of preoperative fear in Janis's study were "neurotic" in the sense described by Deutsch; that is, the anticipation of surgery apparently reactivated neurotic conflicts which generated a high degree of anxiety. This anxiety was not appreciably modified by reassurances from hospital authorities or by the actual passing of danger after the operation. Many of these patients were preoccupied with fantasies of punishment, mutilation, or death. The moderately fearful patients, on the other hand, appeared to be highly responsive to reassurances, and seemed to develop defenses which enabled them to cope effectively with the stress of the postoperative period. Janis suggests that a moderate degree of preoperative fear is adaptive because it initiates the "work of worrying," a process which effectively prepares the patient for the impact of surgery. Patients who displayed a relative absence of preoperative fear, on the other hand, were more likely to react with anger and intense resentment during convalescence. Janis suggests that, because of strong denial or inadequate preparatory communications, these patients were not prepared for the hardships of surgery and consequently developed feelings of victimization.

Several of Janis's findings about preoperative emotional arousal have not, however, been supported by the few other systematic studies of reactions to surgery that have been carried out. Opten (1966) attempted to replicate Janis's findings in a study of 54 patients who underwent major surgery. Although Opten used Janis's interview schedules, he found it very difficult to detect in his sample of patients the feelings and behaviors that Janis found in his. He rarely found the reactions of anger, hostility, or resistance which would have allowed him to look for the expected relationships between preoperative and postoperative adjustment.

Titchener and his co-workers (1957) studied 200 randomly selected patients going into major surgery; the data were primarily derived from psychiatric interviews, and concerned the personality of each patient, his reaction to illness, and his psychosocial adjustment before and after surgery. Their findings did not agree with Janis's: patients with a high level of preoperative "anxiety-fear" made good postoperative adjustments and generally improved in psychosocial adjustment as well. Patients with intermediate levels of preoperative anxiety-fear showed the worst postoperative adjustment. Patients with low fear emerged from surgery with good levels of hospital adjustment, but generally did not improve in psychosocial adjustment. Titchener et al. found that preoperative anxiety which served as a signal differed from the more intense anxiety which resulted from a traumatic degree of stress. Finally, they found that the personality trait most closely related to good or improved psychosocial adjustment was a substantial degree of psychological flexibility which permitted an effective mobilization of the patient's defenses to meet the stress. Many of the patients who were improved surgically, but had persisting psychosocial problems, demonstrated rigid and incapacitating defenses.

Titchener's study and others suggest that the kind of anxiety, as well as its intensity, can make an important difference in adaptation to surgery. Wright (1954) measured the effects of chronic versus situational anxiety with several tests of perceptual-cognitive performance before and after surgery. He found that situational anxiety, or a degree of anxiety commensurate with the impending surgery, "temporarily reduced a patient's capacity to respond to new challenges which require unhampered concentration or novel adjustments." Surgery patients who had chronically high levels of anxiety experienced similar perceptual-cognitive constriction, but their fundamental patterns of social response were interfered with as well. Price, Thaler, and Mason (1957), using a biochemical measure of stress on 24 male patients awaiting surgery, found that an elevation of certain corticosteroids was much more highly correlated with rated "emotional involvement" than with rated anxiety. They defined emotional involvement as a participation or investment of active feelings of any kind in the patients' interactions with those around him. Anxiety alone turned out to be rather poorly correlated with both steroid levels and several Rorschach indicators of emotional distress.

Titchener's, Opten's, and Price's findings differ from Janis's, particularly in regard to preoperative anxiety and subsequent indices of postoperative adjustment. The differences in these findings may be due to differences in the methods and criteria used to assess anxiety. For example, Janis employed semistructured interviews and independent behavioral observations, whereas Opten used only interviews, and Price et al. used several different psychological tests as well as an interview. Second, the timing of the interview may have had an important influence on the assessment of preoperative anxiety. For example, although both Janis and Opten conducted their interviews on the afternoon before the operation, Opten's interviews were usually obtained immediately after admission to the hospital, whereas Janis waited until the anxiety-arousing admission procedures were well behind the patient, giving him a chance to "settle down," before conducting the interview. Janis himself has suggested that the average patient may be more relaxed and open after the admission procedures are completed. (The other studies provide too little information about methods and procedures to permit an adequate evaluation and comparison with Janis's.) Finally, differences in hospitals might have made a difference in the psychological reactions of the patients. An overcrowded hospital may not give surgeons enough time to allay the patients' anxiety and prepare them properly for their operations.

Several of the above-mentioned investigators note that, in addition to fear and anxiety, two other emotional reactions—anger and dependency—are characteristically aroused by surgery. Exposure to the threat of bodily damage seems to result in a strong arousal of aggressive impulses and a concomitant need to block or control their expression. The arousal of dependency needs seems frequently to be associated with guilt about increased aggressive feelings, as well as with a reactivation of a childhood fear of being abandoned. The dependency is often expressed in a heightened need to be reassured about the continuing affection of loved ones.

The arousal of fear, anxiety, anger, and feelings of dependency occasions defensive reactions in the patients. Deutsch mentions the expected heightening of defenses but says little about their specific form. Price et al. (1957) note that defensive behavior during this period was highly individual. They were able to identify only three general patterns of defense: (1) assuring oneself of the surgeon's magical omnipotence, (2) avoiding any communication about the seriousness of the surgery to significant others, and (3) projecting fears and doubts and discussing them as if they belonged to someone else.

Janis (1958) has made the most intensive study of preoperative defensive reactions, which he calls "reassuring beliefs and activities." He found that his low-fear patients were most likely to adopt a joking or facetious attitude and to deny strongly the serious implications of their impending operations. They often developed "blanket reassurances" which prevented a sufficient amount of the "work of worrying" from taking place. His moderately fearful patients, who typically engaged most in "reflective fear," tended to adopt reassuring beliefs that were anchored in reality. They generally asked for and paid attention to information about the nature of their impending operations. Patients with high preoperative fear, on the other hand, were generally unable to mitigate their fears and disturbing thoughts, although they made repeated efforts to gain reassurance. It was as if they were unable to sustain a conception of themselves as being safe and physically intact. They were more likely than the others to engage in (1) distracting mental activities, (2) thoughts or fantasies about the personal gains that would ensue from undergoing the trials of surgery, and (3) thinking dominated by an attitude of resignation and fatalism.

In summary, these studies suggest that three important variables are involved in reactions to surgery: (1) the degree of preoperative fear or anxiety, (2) the nature of the aroused anxiety, and (3) the amount and type of psychological preparation. These variables are related, since the form of preparation is in part dependent on the nature of the anxiety. The studies indicate that thinking or fantasy stimulated by fear is necessary for the development of defenses which will enable the patient to cope with the eventual impact of surgery. If waking thought and fantasy play such a role, it is reasonable to assume that dreams may also. Dreams might be especially important in the case of surgery, since the patient's position prevents attempts at active mastery (the "good patient" is passive and does what his doctor tells him). With active mastery precluded, passive fantasy, including dreaming, might assume greater significance.

Theoretical considerations, then, lead us to postulate an important role for dreaming in the mastery of stress aroused by impending surgery. To date, no evidence bearing on this issue has been reported. The study that will now be presented was carried out to investigate the role of dreams in patients' psychological preparations for surgery.

METHOD

Five subjects scheduled to undergo major surgery were selected for intensive study by means of interviews, psychological tests, rating scales, and behavioral observation. Their dreams were collected by EEG-REM methods on four consecutive nights before their operations and during a relatively less stressful three-day postoperative period.

Subjects

The subjects were obtained by enlisting the cooperation of two surgeons who made the initial selection and then referred potential subjects to Dr. Lane. The only criteria were (1) that the subjects had voluntarily agreed to undergo major surgery; (2) that they were under 65 years of age; and (3) that they did not require heavy sedation either during the day or at night. The most vital consideration was, of course, their willingness to participate in a potentially stressful investigation. The surgeons gave 12 patients a brief explanation of the research and referred them to Dr. Lane for a detailed explanation. Five decided not to participate before the second interview. (Two claimed that they would not be able to sleep in a laboratory situation, one was on a moderate daytime dosage of tranquilizers and said he felt too concerned about the operation to participate, and two were not interested enough to be bothered.)

Of the seven who did agree to participate, two (both men) were dropped after three nights in the sleep laboratory because of their increasing resistance and hostility. The five subjects (identified by pseudonyms) who completed the study were:

(1) Al: a 64-year-old retired veteran who was hospitalized at Portland VA Hospital for vascular surgery on his leg. His major symptoms were coldness in his legs and feet, some cramping in his legs, and reduced mobility.

(2) Melvin: a 34-year-old part-time hairdresser and shipping clerk, hospitalized at the Portland VA Hospital for a vagotomy and gastric resection of an ulcerated stomach. His major symptoms were nausea and digestive trouble.

(3) Penny: an 18-year-old high-school senior who was to be hospitalized in Eugene, Oregon, for removal of her gall bladder. Her major symptoms were nausea and severe attacks of stomach cramping and pain.

(4) Paul: a 58-year-old logger, hospitalized at the Portland VA Hospital for the removal of a tumor in his colon. His major symptom was constipation.

(5) Mona: a 42-year-old housewife and mother of four children who was to be hospitalized in Eugene for exploratory surgery on her side. Her chief complaint was chronic soreness of the left side.

The Settings

The subjects were studied in two different settings. The three men were in a Veterans' Administration hospital during both pre- and postoperative periods of dream collection. They had all been in the hospital at least five days before their participation in the study, and all aspects of the study were carried out in the hospital. The two women were living at home during both pre- and post-operative periods, and came to the sleep laboratory of the University Psychology Clinic (the same one used in the Group Therapy Study) for the nightly dream collections. They entered a private hospital after the last night of preoperative dream collection.

The sleep laboratories were similar in the two places, consisting of two adjoining rooms, a "sleep room" and an "experimenter room." The sleep room contained a bed and some furniture and was partially light- and soundproof; an auditory intercommunication system enabled the experimenter to arouse the subject during REM periods. The adjoining experimenter room contained a tape recorder connected to a microphone in the sleep room, for recording the subject's dream reports, and an electroencephalograph to monitor EEGs and EOGs throughout the night.

Procedures in the Preoperative Period

Each subject spent four preoperative dream-collection nights in the sleep laboratory; one day intervened between the last night of dream collection and the operation. (It was possible to arrange an adaptation night in the laboratory for only two subjects.) As far as was possible, the schedule of research activities was standardized for all subjects. The subject usually arrived at the laboratory at about 9 P.M., and the period of time before sleep was devoted to collecting information from him. Personality data about the subjects was needed for two related purposes. First, we needed sufficient information about each person to formulate a case study. Second, we needed information about the meaning of the operation, the form of anxiety and types of defenses aroused, that would enable us to understand the dreams of each night in their appropriate psychological context. General personality information was obtained from a social-personal history interview, carried out the first preoperative night. This was supplemented by the results of four psychological tests: the Minnesota Multiphasic Personality Inventory; a sentence-completion test which contained many phrases related to health and bodily processes; the Thematic Apperception Test; and the Rorschach. One test was given on each preoperative night. (Representative responses of each subject to these tests are presented in Appendix C.) Information about the specific state of the subject in relation to his impending operation was obtained from a nightly informal interview which focused on the day's events.

In addition to the interviews and tests described above, several rating scales and more structured interviews were used, including one adopted from Janis (1958) and the Lorr-McNair Mood Scale. The latter scale has been shown to be a sensitive indicator of short-term fluctuations in mood (McNair and Lorr, 1964); it consists of separate scales for tension, anger, friendliness, confusion, fatigue, vigor, and depression. The subject rated his mood during the preceding day each night before going to sleep.

Procedures in the Postoperative Period

Each subject spent three postoperative nights in the sleep laboratory. The time that intervened between the pre- and postoperative periods of dream collection varied from one to five weeks, depending on how rapidly he recovered from surgery. As in the preoperative period, interview and rating-scale information was collected from each subject before he retired. The Lorr-McNair Mood Scale was also filled out by the subject on each postoperative night, providing a quantified index of daily emotional state which was subsequently used in a comparison of differences in emotional climate between the pre- and postoperative periods.

Dream Collection

In both preoperative and postoperative periods, the nightly rating scales and interviews were followed by preparation of the subject for EEG and EOG recording. The subject then retired and the sleep-dream cycle was monitored through the night. For the three male patients in the VA hospital, Dr. Lane carried out all the tasks and monitored sleep throughout the night. For the two subjects studied in the nonhospital setting, Dr. Lane was assisted during the initial preparation by a female student, and sleep was monitored in three shifts through the night in the same manner as in the Group Therapy Study.

The schedule of awakenings was the same one used in the Group Therapy Study (see Appendix A). The subject was aroused by calling his name over the intercom and the standard interview (see Appendix A) was used. The dream reports were tape-recorded and transcribed verbatim; the transcripts were used in all subsequent data analyses. As in the Group Therapy Study, the dream reports presented in the next section are edited versions of these transcripts.

In the 20 preoperative nights of dream collection, the five subjects produced 49 dream reports; in the 15 postoperative nights they produced 45.

Additional Information

Additional information was obtained from the doctors' and nurses' notes and comments about the subjects' behavior and adjustment in the hospital. These observations concerned sleep disturbances, manifestations of anxiety and tension, verbal complaints, overt resistance to medical treatment, and general behavior on the ward.

The nature of the situation was such that a good relationship was established with the experimenter and used by each patient as a source of psychological support. The patients were quite open in the interviews, and a good deal of information was obtained. The information from all sources—interviews, tests, rating scales, and hospital records—provided a full picture of each patient's personality and his particular reactions to surgery.

Control Subjects

The dreams of two control subjects (the same two that were used in the Group Therapy Study) were collected over a similar period of time with no intervening stress.

Data Analysis

The data were analyzed in two ways: (1) in a series of individual case studies, and (2) by means of dream-content rating scales. The five case studies are presented first. They are based on all the personality data—interviews, psychological tests, hospital behavior—and on the REM dream reports. Each case study will begin with a general description of the patient, followed by a discussion of the meaning of his operation to him and his particular attempts to cope with the stress of surgery. This is followed by a presentation and analysis of all his dreams from the preoperative period.

The dream-content rating-scale results will be presented in a subsequent section. These ratings allowed us to compare the differences in pre- and postoperative dreams for each subject and the dreams of the surgery patients with those of the two control subjects.

THE CASE STUDIES

AL

Al is a 64-year-old retired veteran who was hospitalized because of vascular blockages in his legs which were causing leg cramping at night, coldness in his feet, and reduced mobility. The latter was particularly important because Al had always led an extremely active life which he continued after retirement, engaging in fishing, prospecting, and related outdoor activities.

Al's assessment data reveals him to be a reasonably well-adjusted person who is very cooperative, compliant, and good-humored, and who actively seeks the attention and company of others. He creates the impression of being tough, experienced, and independent, and of having little room in his life for fear or weakness. A central, life-long conflict is the clash between this tough, assertive exterior and underlying passive-dependent ideas and feelings.

His early family history sheds some light on the origins of this conflict. Al was the oldest of eight children. His father is described as a punitive disciplinarian who had little love for children:

I had to mind him or he'd hit you . . . I never liked my father . . . He never gave an inch. Us kids were all scared to death of him . . . When I got older I was pretty well trained—I knew which way to jump. In high school I finally crossed him though . . . he was going to beat my brother up . . . and I vowed I'd beat him if he ever hit that kid, I said I'd kill him if he did. I left home then . . .

The conflict with his father led Al to an assertive, "tough" way of life, yet the underlying fear of authority remains. In potentially anxiety-arousing situations, Al typically expresses anger or attempts an active, assertive solution. At the same time, it is difficult for him to express this anger directly unless he has experienced a great deal of injustice. Instead, he develops physical complaints and expresses anger indirectly, complaining about past situations or about people other than those present.

Al described his mother as a "kind and generous woman" who satisfied his dependent needs. His memories of her centered on the way she nursed him through several bouts of childhood pneumonia. He identified with her kindness and nurturance, exemplified in the generous and big-hearted way in which he approaches people. Yet this generosity has frequently led to his being taken advantage of rather than winning him the acceptance and support that he would like.

When he left home, Al was determined to prove himself a man. He controlled his dependent wishes and developed an active, aggressive way of life, typified by his strong drive toward adventurous, physically demanding work. Some of his successful occupations were bush piloting in Alaska, train and tanker engineering, and logging.

Al's passive-dependent needs always dominated in intimate relationships, however, particularly with women. At 27 he married a "childhood sweetheart" and was divorced after 17 years of poor marital adjustment. He claimed that his wife dominated him and that their sexual adjustment was chronically inadequate. He blamed the latter on his wife's physical vulnerability to childbirth: "I knew that if I got her pregnant it might kill her." Nevertheless, they eventually had two children. Al summed up the marriage as the biggest failure in his life: "Her whole life was to make me over, to boss me . . . she wanted to henpeck me. I never did anything right with that woman." The only person in his family with whom he has stayed in close touch is his daughter; "She's the apple of my eye."

Al was scheduled for an aneuryectomy (an operation in which a damaged portion of a blood vessel is removed) to clear the vascular blockage in his leg. This followed a much more serious aortic aneuryectomy eight months before at the same hospital. In view of Al's personality, his past history, and information received in the preoperative interviews, it is clear that the main threat posed by the operation was the prospect of physical debility. This would mean giving up his role as the active, assertive achiever, with the concomitant danger of being in a dependent position.

Al dealt with this conflict by reasserting his toughness and lack of fear, and by acting in a very generous and nurturant way toward the other patients. He continually emphasized that the anticipated operation did not make him worried, fearful, or anxious in any way. While he did admit the possibility of "a little" pain, he never voiced any actual fear about it:

> Q: How much pain do you think you will experience during or after your operation?
> A: Experience pain? Oh, hell no . . . I never have before, never known about that in my life. I anticipate no trouble or no pain . . . Oh, I know there will be some soreness, but I don't think about those things . . . just think that I've got something to fix and I'll go in there and get it repaired and then come out.

Al also denied any unpleasant feelings or inconvenience connected with his hospitalization. On the contrary, he considered it quite enjoyable because he liked talking with people and making new friends. The nurses' observations of his ward behavior support this claim; they saw him as a very friendly, talkative person who derived genuine satisfaction from his social interactions with the other patients. In general, his consistent denial of any apprehensiveness about the impending surgery, his limited demands on the staff, and his ability to eat and sleep well without sedation qualify him as an almost classic example of Janis's (1958) "low-fear" surgery patient.

His behavior during the nightly interviews and sleep-laboratory sessions was similar. He carried out all the tasks demanded of him cooperatively, and often engaged in long, animated discussions of his past experiences. Nevertheless, the stress occasioned by the impending surgery, combined with the stress of participating in the dream project, did arouse considerable anger which he could only express indirectly. He complained a great deal about bodily aches and pains and frequently unleashed lengthy criticisms of various professional people he had known, though he never criticized Dr. Lane or the doctors involved in his operation. He expressed no direct anger about being a dream subject, but did complain about the hard work and made numerous depreciatory comments about his dreams: e.g., "The God-damned crazy things don't make any sense anyway." The indirect message seems clear: participating in the dream project subjected him to great physical hardship, but he could handle it and would "tough it out" as a gallant personal favor. In addition, an important motivation for being a dream subject was the special recognition and status it afforded him from both the staff and the patients on his ward.

Psychological preparation for the operation—what Janis calls "the work of worrying"—was largely absent in Al. Instead, he tended to deny or minimize the seriousness of the surgery, frequently comparing it to a routine repair job that one might perform on a mechanical object. He expressed his thoughts and feelings in concrete and colorful metaphors, which, along with his creative sense of humor, enabled him to cope with the stress. His position as a passive, relatively helpless hospital patient kept him from dealing with his anxiety in his typically active and assertive way. This restriction, along with his fear of antagonizing those powerful authorities, the doctors, led him to displace his anger onto remote targets and to make the most of his bodily complaints. On the other hand, active socialization, which included boasting about past accomplishments and fostering supportive relationships with those who openly feared their impending operations, allowed Al to cope with underlying fears of physical debility and old age. He made good use of social support in bolstering his self-image as an independent, adequate, and still potent man.

Al went through his operation quite successfully and made a rapid recovery for a man of 64 years. However, it was accompanied by the resistant, angry reactions which Janis typically found in his low-fear patients after surgery. Al's hospital records contained three incidents of openly resistant postoperative behavior. In addition, he complained of feeling unexplainably nervous and shaky for several weeks after surgery. This behavior was reflected in his mood ratings after the operation, which showed an increase in tension over the preoperative period (t = 3.04, p < .05).

The specific meaning of the operation to Al is nicely revealed by the following interview excerpt, which was part of the information that the raters used to score the dreams for incorporation.

> Q: How does your leg feel? How does it affect your leg? Does it hurt when you walk?
> A: Yeah . . . and my legs are cold . . . there's poor circulation . . . my feet are cold all the time . . . that thing is swole up there so damned big . . . I think it's getting longer all the time . . . it's just like tying a string around a hose, you know . . . you can't force it through there down to my feet . . . course I know what the penalty is if I, I don't happen to be around them [doctors] and that starts leaking and then it starts to drip, you know. Then pretty soon it burst . . . course if it burst you're dead . . .

Several aspects of the meaning of his condition are revealed in this quote, including coldness, blockage of fluid (specifically water), the mechanical analogy, the comparison of his operation to the mechanical repair job of fixing a hose, and his having to submit to the authorities or "pay the penalty."

Let us now examine how Al's understanding of his condition and his attempts to cope with it are manifested in his dreams. The first preoperative night contains striking evidence of direct and symbolic incorporations, probably because a patient whom Al had come to know on the ward had died in surgery the previous day.

The First Preoperative Dream Night

> *Dream 1:* Oh boy, I got into politics. I'm running for vice-president. Some of these people didn't like it you know, and of course, I was just taking it all as a joke but later I found out that it was serious and they said I was lucky you know. And seems like I was sawing some boards to make something. There was some of them tickled to death, patting me on the back and all that crap. They nominated me for vice-president of the United States. That's why I had to laugh you know. I guess somebody said, "Aw that lucky bastard. He always managed to stand in the right place so he can step to the right or left and he just seen that coming." I just stuck my head

down and went on sawing lumber. That's what made me laugh. I don't know whether I laughed out loud or not. There weren't very many people there, just maybe a dozen or 15 people around there. They was lined up over there talking about it and looking at me. I can remember them looking over here at me like they would like to cut my throat. Mostly it was these jealous people you know ... I didn't even saw, but I was in a position to saw. I was trying to cut a 45-degree angle and I was laying a pattern on top of another board. I never sawed but I was getting ready to. I do remember that there was a ledge around us, sort of like a circle. Well, it was like there was a picture of a group and we just took a pair of scissors and cut around amongst them and carved a circle.

Dream 2: My daughter was there but her mother was speaking you see. It seemed like she was there but she was speaking anyway. But my daughter and I was talking about a quarter of beef. You understand? ... Now ... the funny part of it is ... this quarter of beef had been delivered apparently and we were talking about cutting it up ... to preserve it you know. This ex-boss of mine she come in the picture. She discussed that with me and with the daughter too how this meat should be cut up. There was a kind of a heated argument there about how that meat was gonna be cut I think between me and my ex-wife ... we were, uh ... more or less, arguing which way it was going to be cut. But then it turned into a surgical rather than a hospital, it still turned into an operation, a surgical conversation, something like that. They were me and one of them guys in that room over there, it seemed like my ex-wife moved out of the picture but Jack and my daughter and I was discussing or talking about one of those guys that had a surgery over there and how they cut them, and then this pocketknife [laugh]. I had a pocketknife and was examining it to see if there was any blood on it, you see? And the blood was all cleaned off of it. The handle was left but all three blades fell out of it ... So then we discussed whether it was worth fixing or ... I remember which one of them said it was all they had to do was just ... just buy some more rivets for the blades and the handle and they'd be all right ... and that's funny too, there was only one half of the handle there ... it was brown like a bone handle, you know.

Dream 3: Well, it was somethin' about driving a car ... there was some people in the car and I was driving the darn thing ... When we come out of this place where I had it parked, it was icy, you know, icy. And as I came out of this place, there was quite a little hill and there was ice ... And I realized I wasn't gonna make it, so I didn't even try to. I just went up it a little ways and I just let the car back, back down and take a little run at it. It was just a little kind of a place ... uprise. But there was a lot of cars comin' and I couldn't do it. And that's as far as I got. It was in some city or some small town ... it was Christmastime and we was shopping. It was cold, awful cold, and it was just solid ice all across and at the bottom of this hill where you turned up, so many people had come down

with their cars that there was a big slush hole there that was all water
[laugh]. This damn place was kind of like a toboggan place. It was a crazy
day that's all I know. I don't mean when I speak of ice being the road was
icy. It looked like it was a couple of two feet thick which is an impossibil-
ity any place in a road where there is people driving cars over it . . .

Dream 4: We was working on a stove you know. Well it was a boy there
. . . and this stove, we got it all back together. You know we had it all
apart to clean it. We got the stove built in there but it wouldn't tighten up
. . . on this side. There was a bolt like on each side. So we took it out tryin'
to get the other side to fit. You see, we had tore it down . . . and then it
seemed like we remembered we had tore that stove down the year before,
quite some time before that and had the same trouble there. Then we
remembered that we . . . kinda hammered that hole in and we done that
and we got the screw back in and it seemed like we just picked up one
piece of the stove and just push it down in there. I don't know what the
heck we was going to do with it. We talked about this bolt in the stove.
There was laundry trays in there but I don't think it was a laundry room. I
think it was a kitchen . . . in a house. See, I was down on my knees picking
with my hands up through that door and they was putting this bolt down
through the top of it . . . but there was two of us working there. I can
remember walkin' away from it after we finished it and just picking up a
long kind of a wide piece of tin that was just for down in the door . . . just
stuck it down in the . . . you see it had a door on the side . . . When I
walked away from it, this piece about five feet long. Of course, it didn't
even have any cinch or any part of the stove. I just tossed it down there,
brushed my hands and walked away, and this thing was sticking up in the
air. The job was finished . . . I don't know why that thing was stuck up in
the air there. It was a round long stove like an oil burner.

Many of the elements and themes in these dreams clearly symbolize the threat of surgery as well as Al's strategy for coping with
it. Dream 1 contains several references to cutting, no doubt representing the act of surgery itself: Al is getting ready to cut a 45-
degree angle on a board, and people are looking at him "like they
would like to cut my throat." Dream 2 begins with an obvious
symbol of his surgery: cutting up a quarter of beef to preserve it.
Then the symbolism fades into a directly surgical theme, unusual
for Al, in which he is coming to grips with the fear of bodily
damage and death; a theme undoubtedly stimulated by the death
of his fellow patient. Whereas Al was "elected vice-president" in
the previous dream, here there are symbolic references to loss of
power, impotence, and physical vulnerability (e.g., his "bone"

pocketknife falls apart on the floor). It is interesting that Al is arguing with his ex-wife (ex-boss) about how to cut the meat. She might be a suitable stand-in for his surgeon since both stimulate feelings of dependency, helplessness, and consequent anger. Dream 3 contains an amplification of his feelings of helplessness (driving on ice) and fear of loss of power. The ice on the road that is "a couple of two feet thick" (note the odd word use) probably refers to Al's own two feet, which actually do become cold and numb from reduced circulation. In dream 4, Al seems to regain some control over the threat of surgery by actively involving himself in the repair of a defective stove. The mention of having "tore that stove down the year before . . . and had the same trouble there" refers to his operation of the previous year, performed in the same hospital. The "boy" with whom he works on the stove symbolizes his young doctor. By exaggerating the doctor's youth in the dream, the actual power relationship—the doctor in control and Al passive and helpless—is reversed, and Al appears more powerful because of his greater age and experience.

Being at the center of attention and actively taking charge occurs in all four dreams and illustrates one of Al's enduring characteristics. At the same time it arouses ideas of possible incompetence (e.g., the knife that he will use to cut the meat in dream 1 falls apart) and jealousy and criticism from others (e.g., the group of people in dream 1 who would like to cut his throat).

Representing surgery as a concrete job transfers it into a context with which Al is familiar and in which he is competent. In all four dreams parts of the body are represented as external objects (e.g., a board, a quarter of beef, a knife, a car, a stove). These objects are all defective and need work of a sort that Al himself can perform. His defective leg, which he cannot "repair," is symbolized by defective objects that he is capable of dealing with.

The Second Preoperative Dream Night

Al had a particularly difficult time on the second dream night. He complained of back and shoulder pains which necessitated a readjustment of his mattress in the middle of the night, and was unable to recall any dream content on the first two awakenings.

Dream 5: There was some people . . . we were trying to travel up a river bed or coming downstream every so often in the rocks. You know how the water is down and the rocks . . . they was up, out, dry . . . there was boulders about the size of your feet or something like that, round rocks . . . we was staggerin' along trying to look up into the clouds and stumblin' over these damn rocks . . . it seemed like there was a damn dog there too . . . a March day, kind of gusty wind and lots of clouds in the sky. It seemed like we were waiting for . . . something to happen, but every time it'd happen a bunch of clouds kept clouding the sun over. It seemed like . . . we were waiting for the sun to come out and we were going to do something . . . but it seemed like we just no more than get started when this damn wind would come up a little bit and blow black clouds all over and you couldn't see a thing. Aha! There was a goose . . . an emperor goose . . . that's what we were trying to see! This thing was flying up and down and everybody wanted to look at it but every time he'd go by . . . he'd be behind the clouds . . . It seemed like we made about three trips up and down there over a long period of time to get a sight of this damn emperor goose . . . I think there were two in a group, but it don't seem like anybody was with me. I was off to the edge of 'em and I was muttering to myself because them damn clouds kept coming over and obscuring this goose [laugh] . . . but I think the thing come from that picture I saw in the Alaskan . . . this goose was an empress goose . . . it had a nest there and I was interested in the feathers and markings on them, and the white on the head and down the back of their neck . . . beautiful checkered feathers on him . . . her nest was there in Alaska and it was along kind of the beach back from the water, you know . . . felt a feeling of disgust when I couldn't seem to expose this goose to the other people . . . We sat down and waited too . . . then somebody said, "There comes the sun," and we get up and seems like we had to walk. It was a crazy dream, like all dreams are.

Dream 6: I was dreamin' . . . something wrong with my bed and I was going to lay on another guy's bed and read you know . . . cuz he was always layin' on my bed and readin'. So this day I went over there and my bed was broke down and I was gonna lay down and read. We was layin' there talkin', readin' layin' on my back. After we went to dinner and I come back to finish the story why . . . he got burnt up cuz he said he was asleep and I woke him up in the middle of the day you know [laugh]. So I got back up off his bed and got out of there. Oh yeah, there was a nurse there . . . or a woman settin' in the chair readin' and she was mad at me too . . . It seemed like it was the custom to come over and visit, and we'd lay on the bed with our knees up and set there and tell lies and read. That's what I was doin'. Whoever heard of anybody going and crawling into someone else's bed sleepin' in the first place. Crazy dream . . . Well, I got mad and pouted like a tomcat and went back over to my own bed and sat down. You know . . . everybody else was mad too because that guy popped off. And the nurse, she give me the bad eye to get out of there and not disturb that old guy . . . Anyway, I was a little peeved and I just went back where I belonged.

These two dreams contain several elements related to the preoperative stress. In dream 5, the stumbling over exposed boulders ("about the size of your feet") in a half-dried riverbed symbolizes the reduced circulation in Al's leg and the threat of losing his mobility. In dream 6, he becomes the object of attention on a hospital ward when he tries to lie on another patient's bed. Both of these dreams contain wishes to be recognized, liked, and taken care of by others; wishes that he attempted to gratify during the day by his boasting and socializing on the ward. Part of his motivation for being a dream subject was probably the status and recognition it afforded him. These daytime efforts are symbolically paralleled in his frustrated attempts to expose the "beautiful emperor goose" to a group of people in dream 5. Both dreams symbolize his fears of reduced mobility, enforced dependency, and loneliness due to bodily debility and old age (e.g., stumbling over rocks, failure to expose the goose, black clouds blocking the sun, his broken hospital bed, and being rejected by a fellow patient). They also symbolize the manner in which the general threat of surgery aroused specific ideas relating to his masculinity. In dream 5 the goose keeps changing from "emperor" to "empress," symbolizing the idea that being female might bring more of the attention and power that he is losing as a male. In dream 6, he relates to another man much as a woman might, though the relationship is represented as "just fooling around."

The Third Preoperative Dream Night

Al seemed very tired and groggy on the third night, although he complained less about bodily aches and pains.

Dream 7: Well, there was a guy who went to school there . . . and he was showing me his false teeth . . . He had to have some new ones made but he wanted them six wide on each side [laugh] . . . shit . . . my mother-in-law was in it too. Oh, my mother-in-law said . . . "Why there ain't nobody could have a set of teeth . . . to be six teeth wide" . . . around that horseshoe, you know [laugh] . . . Christ. And I said, "There was too, because I knew the guy, I went to school with him." . . . We was all setting in the seat. I can't even see the car but I know we was riding in a car . . . I only know that we were going along moving along the road . . . and sitting. My boy and girl were there too. I think they were mine . . . 'cause I was asqueezin' and aholdin' them and they was agigglin' and atalkin' and atellin', they was talking to each other but they was laughing with me . . . I just had my arms around them and they was giggling and cutting up . . . little kids . . . actually he took out his plate and showed them to me . . . he said, "I've gotta have some new ones made." . . . The teeth were wide . . . they were rows of teeth like a shark's teeth . . . [laugh] . . . they were so big it was impossible for a human being to get them back in his mouth . . . shit, you couldn't put them in an alligator's mouth . . . but I didn't think anything about it because I got into an argument with my mother-in-law.

Dream 8: Well, it seems like . . . I went to hear a violin . . . I'm going to hear this guy play a violin but . . . [laugh] . . . he's sitting up in the top row of a football bleachers . . . so I sit down up there and talk to him . . . seems like somebody was repairing the, rebuilding the roof on the building because I could see the shingles was all off, you know, and . . . [laugh] . . . putting new shingles on. We was talking about this sheeting. You know what the sheeting is that goes on the rafters? Well, they was all bare, the shingles was off and . . . I can see the rafters between the sheeting, it ain't solid sheeting, you know, it ain't like we do now days . . . There was a guy who was kind of overseeing us . . . he was standing there waiting to hear this guy play this violin too . . . So then he disappears . . . I pick up some friends and it seems like we go along and the next thing you know we're to this church . . . Then a girl and her mother was sitting there and I knew them . . . and the little girl had a nice stole on . . . Seems like I knew how she saved her money up to buy it over a long period of time, you know . . . Well it seems like I sat down by them and . . . then I asked her something . . . and she wanted to show this stole off to me, so she got up like a peacock, stood up then, took ahold of her mother's arm, she just strutted away with that stole on . . . she didn't want to waste any of it on me . . . God damned, it was purple just like grape juice [laugh], crazy God-damned dreams . . . Then the violinist came into the picture again and he was outside up on a high bank . . . and he tucked the violin under his neck and . . . he dug the bow down across the strings, it was just beautiful, but that's all he done, seemed like that's all of it.

Dream 9: Seems like I had to look, you know where you push the clutch lever down and brake lever down in the car? If you were underneath you could see that part coming down through there? I don't know if it was on a car or truck. I had to get down and look underneath [laugh] . . . and I was in water up to my waist. Of all the crazy damn things . . . but the car is

setting on . . . there was no water under there . . . Somebody was pushing
that thing up and down cuz that's what I was looking for. They was doing
it to help me but I'm down on my hands and knees . . . I think there was a
woman in here, a good-looking woman, talking to me. Seems like there was
a little touch of romance in it, you know . . . It seemed like I was going to
take her someplace but ah . . . this God-damn car is sittin' out in the water
and first it's in the mud and then it's on a hill . . . I walked out there two
or three times to look at this thing. I know I was getting pretty damn tired
of doing that . . . I kept telling them I couldn't see nothing wrong with it
and they said, "Well, there was," and I just kept going out there to please
somebody else and . . . I was getting pretty burnt up. Evidently it was my
own rig . . . There was a good-looking girl standing there and I think that's
why I was mad because it seemed like I was going to take her someplace
. . . but that clutch wasn't going up and down like it was supposed to . . .
And I couldn't see . . . it looked like to me it was working all right . . . car
wasn't running or nothing, just somebody sitting there pushing down on
the brake . . . and the clutch.

All three dreams on this night contained elements symbolically
related to surgery. In dream 7 a high-school acquaintance is showing Al a huge set of false teeth which he is going to have remade.
In dream 8 a roof is repaired ("putting new shingles on"), and in
dream 9 Al, in water up to his waist, is examining a clutch which
doesn't work properly. The clutch seems to be a symbolic fusion
of his current leg problem with longstanding fears of an impotent
penis, e.g., he was going to take a good-looking girl somewhere but
"that clutch wasn't going up and down like it was supposed to."
Whereas he is a relatively passive observer in dreams 7 and 8,
dream 9 finds him back in his customary active role, the same sort
of reversal of roles that occurred in the dreams of the first night.
In all three dreams someone is showing off for other people or
entertaining them in some way (a man showing his "huge false
teeth" in dream 7, a man playing a violin and a girl showing off
her purple stole in dream 8, and Al's wish to court a good-looking
woman in dream 9). This theme seems to represent his compensatory solution for fears of dependency, physical and sexual impotence, and the loneliness threatened by advancing age and increased bodily debility (symbolized by false teeth to be remade in
dream 7; rafters which can't hold solid sheeting "like we do now
days . . ." and a young girl who walks away from him in dream 8;

and the car with a defective clutch which he is supposed to use for courting a girl in dream 9). All three dreams refer to an earlier period of his life, perhaps representing the wishful solution of once again being young and healthy.

The Fourth Preoperative Dream Night

On this night Al was given the preoperative interview (Janis, 1958) before retiring. He seemed in a good mood and flatly denied any concern about the impending surgery.

> *Dream 10:* It's just something about a baby sitting up in a highchair doing something. I think we'd been out and come in and she'd put him in there and give him some bread and milk. He was all through because he had crumbs and stuff all over his face ... She was giving the baby a clean-up and putting it to bed ... I was at home ... and there was a guest, a friend came to our house and ... it got late and I asked him to stay overnight ... mostly because a rainstorm came up and so he decided to stay overnight, ah ... got that all ironed out and the kids were put to bed you know ... and it rained and it rained and so everybody had gone to bed but me and this fellow and we're sitting out there talking and I said I kind of believe I'll start up a little heat around here and have it warm the house up a little. And so I did. He said ... I believe if this thing will heat up like it will, it will be plenty of heat, and he said I wouldn't want any heat in my room so I said okay, I just shut it off. And I went to bed, and I fixed up a table so I could read or I was fixing up something there on the table beside the bed. And that was about all of it.

> *Dream 11:* Well seems like it was a house ... wherever this guy went, the cat was ... I guess the cat liked him very well. And ... he went to the hospital. Well, he was in bed, it seemed like he was a patient, you know. This cat was there too. Which I know it couldn't possibly be around a hospital, but he was there just the same. He entertained everybody, you know ... he was kind of a sneaker he was, you wouldn't see him but pretty soon you'd see his claws come up around the edge of a bed or a chair ... everybody liked him. I can see that man's hand or the cat's tail coming around his pants leg on the floor when he's up awalking, but I never seen him ... that's all I can think of him ... think of this dream.

> *Dream 12:* We was working on a train ... a work train ... this Oregon crew had to come over on account of some washout or something on the Union Pacific ... they had to come across the Washington side. So we saw them come down to that last station and do some switching and we kept right on working because we knew they could see us. I mean, we figured

we'd get all we could before they cut . . . picked up and run you know, also they come across the bridge up there someplace and hooked over onto our railroad . . . We was all just standing there looking at this other engine and . . . we lined the switch, it seemed like the switch . . . it was a funny thing. They had to come off this private road onto ours and them switches weren't a standard switch, we had to dig some rocks out of the ground . . . and throw this switch over. And I was doing that, I was helping . . . I can't tell you what a switch is, instead of them just being flapped over and locked down to the padlock they was flapped over, the ends of two pipes together and there was a piece of this crooked zigzag piece of iron that was run first in one pipe and then the other so you couldn't lift the one out. But anyway, it was a complicated thing and so we got down there and was digging them things out of them pipes so we could throw the switch for them guys so they wouldn't have to stop . . . it took a little time and they hadn't used that switch it seemed like for years and naturally the sand and dust had blowed into these pipes and it was all rusty. It took quite a little while . . . then when I raised up and told them to come on, the switch was open, the train wasn't there, all it was was just an engine, there wasn't any train to it, it had turned to a square-corner thing, like a suitcase with stripes on it like a circus tent, it had windows in the damn thing that went clear through it. These guys all got in it and they came down through this switch . . . then it seemed like it wasn't going anyplace anyway, it just came over to go to the roundhouse. But you know what a roundhouse looks like. Well this damn thing was shaped just like a locomotive only a couple of inches bigger all around and they backed into there [laugh] . . . then we got into a row . . . a fight. This little kid . . . [laugh] . . . he didn't mind nobody and everybody was mad at him, he'd kicked somebody in the shins. By God, one guy got up and he hit that kid and that kid just reached up and kicked him and knocked him cold. So there was one other guy there and I think he came off this other train crew, and he walked over there and this guy asked him to do something about him knocking his friend down off of this other engine and he kicked that kid on the kneecap and that guy went down and then it seemed like there was a whole bunch of people and he just went around kicking them all in the kneecap . . . he was beating the hell out of a bunch of grown men and it seemed like he was about two feet high . . . a pygmy or something. The way he'd get you, he was an ornery little devil, he'd walk up and kick you right under the kneecap . . . kick your kneecap off, just like kicking a lid off a coffeepot. Some way or other everybody would go down . . . I, we, was all half scared of him or it seemed like. But then hell, I got mad . . . they wouldn't have nothing more to do with him and then I grabbed him from behind because he was looking right at me, but that's the way I guess I figured it out and . . . I grabbed him. I was giving him a bad time there but I didn't quite get a chance to kill him or whatever I was supposed to do because you woke me up . . . but he was just like a football you couldn't hold him after you got ahold of him, he just wiggled around. I was hitting on him with my hands and rolling him.

Dream 13: Well . . . these people, they lived out of town . . . and their septic tank plugged up, filled up, you know. And there was water everywhere out there. Out from the house. Seemed like I was visiting these young fellows, but . . . this trouble come up and they was all trying to fix it and there was no way they could fix it. They didn't have any way to pump it out, it was running over the surface. Then the next thing, we was hauling their hay in. And we hauled their hay in there for days and put it in the barn. We kept piling that hay in the barn till it . . . the barn some way or other the pressure of that hay in that barn began to squeeze the water out of the septic tank. So the water began to flow over and it flowed out in the chicken pens and then the chickens was out there laying and their nests were getting full of water. Well, kept monkeying around there and couldn't get none of that water and we couldn't use the toilets because the septic tank was full and . . . then it seemed like there was a new crop of hay come on right away. It must have been the same year because right while we were standing there worrying about it they started hauling more hay in. And I said, "Where you going to put the hay?" and they said, "In the barn." And I said, "Well, by God we had to quit hauling hay in there this morning because we couldn't get no more in it." "Oh," they said, "since that septic tank has got full and run over now we can put more in it." And I thought they was crazy so I went and looked and heck the barn wasn't even a fourth full [laugh] . . . Oh crap. We was going to go home and then there was . . . somebody else there was with me from then on and they come there and said we was wanted over home. So we started out and it seemed like we was dragging our coats. We was so darned mad at them guys because when we drug our coats behind us, we was in the sewage, this water [laugh] . . . It's bad enough to dream that, but I have to tell it, it's worse than ever. When it started out it was just in the residential area . . . just outside of a small town you know . . . but at last when they started cutting hay in this barn, and we was mad at the cesspool, we couldn't do nothing about it, everybody was running around there and muttering and cussing the tank and then the damn hay in the barn about a hundred yards away started squeezing the tank [laugh]. To me it was a mystery, I was mystified at the whole proceedings there, how it could work. It seemed like I was standing there with a sneer on my face watching them.

Dream 14: Well, I remember that this old man had two sons. One of them was a nice guy and the other was a tough guy . . . he thought he was tough, you know. He was too, pretty tough. But I got along pretty good with him because he had to have somebody. So when I got acquainted, I didn't know he was a wise guy or a tough guy and so I would do him a few favors but then later, it seems like he run away, he was gone. When he come back, I happened to be over there talking to the old man and the other boy. He come back all of a sudden, they didn't know where he was and they didn't know when he was going to be back, but he come back right by me and I stuck out my hand to shake hands with him, why he just brushed right by me and didn't shake hands. So the old man, we went in the house, he had a big house and the other boy, he went away too, so I was in there talking to the old man and pretty soon we heard an awful noise, not an awful noise but . . . kind of a clicking noise and . . . continuous noise . . . we knew what it was but . . . I can't say what it was. It seemed like . . . it was ruining that house you know . . . something . . . bumping on the house, but the old man says, "I'm afraid he's doing something, you know, I'm afraid he's adoing it again or he's going to ruin it this time." The old man had been downstairs but now when I'm talking to him he's an invalid, in his house, but first he was downstairs and I was down there and then when the rest of this come, the old man couldn't go down and that's the reason he said, "Will you go down and see what that son-of-a-bitch is doing now." . . . I walked down and out into the yard where this guy was and the other boy was there too, but he was standing by him, he was standing over a little ways and leaning on a fence . . . I just stood there a little bit, I thought I'd see what was going on and nobody said anything so I started to walk over to this mean brother and this other brother said, "Stay away from him." He said, "He's looking for trouble, stay away from him." And I said, "Well, I wasn't looking for no trouble but I wanted to know what was making that noise out here because his Dad wants to know." So I walk right over to him and I ask him and he wouldn't answer me, he just glared at me. And about that time you woke me up. It wasn't a clicking noise but he was doing something damaging . . . to the building. He was a troublemaker.

These five dreams reveal Al's characteristic symbols and his angry-assertive as well as dependent, support-seeking attempts at mastery. In dream 10, water—"a rainstorm came up"—and cold are the threat, and Al turns to a male friend for support. In dream 11, the "cat" on the ward entertains the patients much as Al himself does. In dream 12, the unusual railroad switch consists of clogged pipes which prevent locomotion, just as Al's clogged blood vessels interfere with his ability to locomote. Al himself takes a hand in cleaning out the pipes—he becomes active and assertive. Then the young doctor who will cut his legs open is symbolically represented as the "kid" who kicks the kneecaps off the "grown men." Al fights back and attempts to kill this threatening figure.

This theme is continued in dream 13 in which a defective fluid-transport system is again portrayed, and Al, again angry at the "young fellows," engages in attempts at repair. The symbol of the digestive system is very interesting—food (hay) goes in the top and comes out as feces (the overflowing septic tank) at the bottom, which permits more food to be put in the top. Concern about being able to eat and defecate may well have been aroused in Al in connection with the operation.

Angry action emerges as a characteristic way in which Al deals with potentially anxiety-arousing situations. Dream 14 vividly portrays three sides of Al—the old man whose house (body) is in danger of being ruined and the two brothers—one nice and sociable and the other tough and mean.

Summary: Effects of Stress on the Preoperative Dreams

Al's dreams represent the threat of surgery primarily in symbolic or indirect forms. Only three of the 14 preoperative dreams contained such elements as hospitals, patients, or operations. Blood, surgery, and death appeared in only one preoperative dream, and doctors or surgeons were never directly present. Nor did the vascular blockage in Al's leg ever directly appear as a dream element; rather, defective objects symbolized defective body parts. Eleven of the preoperative dreams contained such symbolic material, including such elements and themes as: loss of mobility, defective inanimate objects, water or fluid as a threat or discomfort, acts of cutting, the repair or reconstruction of objects, and the like. The dreams from this period also expressed a good deal of dependency and anger.

A comparison of the preoperative and postoperative dreams shows that the symbolic elements and themes described above are a result of the threat of surgery and do not represent persistent or typical features of Al's dreams. For example, eight of the preoperative dreams contained a major theme related to surgery, but none of the 10 postoperative dreams contained such a theme. The specific elements that symbolized surgery for Al appeared in 50.1% of the preoperative dreams versus 15.7% of the postoperative dreams. The preoperative intensification of Al's active and angry reactions is also apparent from a comparison of pre- and postoperative dreams, as illustrated by the number and type of Al's interactions as a dream character, ratings of emotion, and the amount of swearing and laughing in dream reports from the two periods. The number of interactions in which he participated as a dream character was much lower in the postoperative dreams (32 interactions in 14 preoperative versus four interactions in 10 post-operative dreams). He made friendly gestures and actively assisted and talked with other people in 19 of the 32 interactions in the preoperative dreams, whereas he talked with or assisted someone only twice in postoperative dream interactions. His preoperative dreams seem to reflect his heightened need for the attention and support of those around him. Perhaps in part these dream inter-actions represented his way of gaining sorely needed social support and recognition for his independence and lack of fear in the face of intensified threats of dependency, impotence, and bodily dam-age.

Expressed anger is probably an important indication of how much preoperative tension was aroused in Al. While there was no substantial difference between the percentages of pre- and post-operative dreams in which Al explicitly reported feeling emotion (79% to 70%), the over-all intensity of feeling was substantially lower in the postoperative dreams. For example, the predominant emotion of anger was rated as significantly lower in the post-operative dreams. In addition, Al swore during the reporting of 86% of his preoperative as opposed to only 20% of his postopera-tive dreams. The fact that he also laughed during the reporting of 71% of the pre- as against only 20% of the postoperative dreams may also indicate a heightened state of emotional arousal during the preoperative period.

All of the differences between the two periods are particularly striking in view of the fact that Al was still in the hospital and experiencing some bodily discomfort and reduced mobility when the postoperative dreams were collected.

In general, Al's waking conception of his operation and his modes of coping with the stress are quite strikingly paralleled in his preoperative dreams. In both waking thought and dream his physical problem is represented in the form of a defective "ma-chine" in need of repair, and in both Al deals with his fear and anger by assertive activity and attempts to find support from others. In the dreams, however, emotion and disturbing preoc-cupations with bodily damage are expressed more intensely than in the waking state, where Al attempted to minimize or deny them. At the same time, this more intense expression is masked by the symbolic or indirect form of expression that is characteristic of his dreams.

MELVIN

Melvin is a 34-year-old shipping clerk and part-time beautician with a long history of peptic ulcers. He has spent some time in the hospital for this condition every year for the past 14, has had two previous operations on his stomach and, at the time of the study, was about to undergo a vagotomy (severance of the vagus nerve to the stomach) and a possible gastric resection. His current symptoms were weakness, nausea, and digestive difficulty.

Melvin is a small, rather nice-looking man who appears to be very anxious and inhibited. He expressed a great deal of open fear about his operation and considered not going through with it. He had been extremely reluctant to undergo the two previous operations even though his stomach was hemorrhaging on one of those occasions. The hospital records contain many references to his anxiety during medical tests and routine physical examinations. A striking example occurred on the second preoperative day of the present hospitalization when he actually left the hospital without permission and went home. He did return to sleep in the laboratory that night, but was extremely agitated. He wept several times during the interview and tried to convince himself that the operation was unnecessary, the surgeons incompetent, and the whole thing a mistake. He regained his composure in the course of this interview, however, and seemed considerably reassured by the support of the experimenter.

Melvin's reaction is very much like that of the "high-fear" patient described by Janis (1958). Such patients overreact to the threat of bodily harm and physical suffering because the anticipation of surgery arouses a specific neurotic meaning in them. For Melvin, this centered on losing the support of those he depended on and a related fear of not being adequately "cared for" by his doctors.

His early history provides some interesting clues to his present concerns, as it is characterized by the loss of those who would normally have cared for him: his mother was killed in a fire when he was eight months old and he was raised by a grandmother who died when he was 15. He describes his grandmother as warm and giving; in his words, "just as good as a real mother." He saw little of his father during those early years and felt that "he didn't seem to care much about me." He went to live with his father after his grandmother died, but they still remained distant. Melvin describes his father in exaggerated terms that emphasize his own relative inferiority:

> I admired his ability to outtalk anybody . . . If he wanted something, he wasn't afraid to ask for it . . . I'm just the opposite . . . shy and meek . . . He was about two or three inches taller . . . weighed 195, maybe 200. He was broad-shouldered . . . big-brawned . . . and I'm just the opposite. I took after my mother. She was very small-boned and very small stature.

This description illustrates a characteristic way that Melvin developed to cope with the threatened loss of care, namely to adopt a position of exaggerated weakness and helplessness in an attempt to arouse the nurturance of others.

Melvin is married and has three children. His relationship with his wife further illustrates his dependent life style. He describes her as "a very loving person," a good mother who "has taken awfully good care of the kids and she's always taken good care of me." She has been Melvin's major source of nurturance since his grandmother died, and a central fear aroused by surgery was that of being without her love and support. When she failed to appear in the recovery room until 10 hours after the operation, Melvin became extremely agitated and lonely. Clearly, a large part of the neurotic meaning aroused by surgery stemmed from his hypersensitivity to loss and his strong fear of not being adequately cared for. The early losses he suffered seem to have left him with little internalized confidence in others, so that he must continually seek reassurance.

He also feared that the operation would cause some permanent physical weakness, particularly weight loss, as the following statement reveals: "It seems every time I have surgery it ages me and I get physically weaker. I don't have the power, strength, or stamina I once had." These concerns about weakness and losing weight are related to his dependent character style—they represent a further exaggeration of the helpless or "weak" position that he typically adopts.

Melvin's view of himself as a weak and inadequate person who can get his needs met only in a dependent relationship is closely tied to his shaky identification as a man. When he was younger he tended to withdraw from normal competitive activities and, later, he selected the feminine occupation of beautician. In this field he competes chiefly with women, effeminate men, and homosexuals, all of whom he resents. He has frequently tried to "put the make on my customers" as a means of demonstrating his masculinity.

Melvin's general conflicts are specifically symbolized by eating (and being fed), as seen in his primary somatic symptom, his concern about losing weight, and his specific fear of having to swallow a drainage tube after his operation. In a preoperative interview he said, "I think the biggest thing that scares me is putting that tube down my lungs. I seem to panic whenever they try to get that down me. I start fighting . . ."

In the hospital record, several doctors noted Melvin's extreme anxiety about any tests that required swallowing a tube. The specific meaning of swallowing the tube can only be guessed at: perhaps it symbolizes the "bad feeding" that stands for inadequate "care."

Melvin survived the operation quite well, although he did report having nightmarish dreams of "huge open incisions on a stomach" for several nights afterward. After several initial postoperative days of relief from tension accompanied by feelings of elation, he again developed anxiety symptoms connected with various routine postsurgical treatments. This reaction, too, is consistent with Janis's description of the "high-fear" patient after surgery.

In summary, the anticipation of surgery aroused strong fears of not being adequately cared for and of intensified weakness and helplessness. Melvin attempted to cope with these fears by continually seeking reassurance and support from doctors (he sought out a private physician in addition to his hospital surgeon), from his wife, whom he tried to have with him at every possible moment, and from others. Serving as a dream subject, and especially the interest shown by Dr. Lane, seemed great sources of security to him.

In addition to the general features of Melvin's reactions described above, the following quotation was used by the raters in scoring the dreams for incorporation:

I'm in here to have surgery on my stomach and to cut the vascular nerves. This decreases the flow of acid . . . There's an obstruction in the opening of the stomach into the intestine . . . This is from the excess of acid flowing through there which causes it to be irritated.

The First Preoperative Dream Night

Melvin was interviewed and accepted into the project on this night. His request for a specialist had been refused that day by his surgeon, and this refusal had increased his general anxiety. He eagerly accepted the idea of being a dream subject and slept without sedation in the laboratory even though he had requested sedatives almost every night on the ward.

Dream 1: I was on my way to catch a bus or walk, and my neighbor waved at me as he walked by. He wouldn't give me a ride . . . the first car went by, I thought it was him. The second car, which was a truck, it was him. I'm not sure who it was in the first one. I think it must have been his wife—and he didn't pick me up. He had turned the corner in about a half a block and then stopped. I didn't understand why he didn't pick me up. He works at the same place I do. I had a little book that I was thumbing through. It was one of those thick books that kids used to have—those comic stories. They were real thick, mostly pictures.

Dream 2: I was dreaming about, uh, lifting heavy boxes. I had my youngest boy with me, Mark, and he seemed to be always getting in the way of a truck that was being unloaded and had a heavy trunk. And we wanted it to be handled carefully, we didn't want it to be dropped from this high truck and they got it on top of this building, and this one big guy had given us a lift. He seemed pretty nice and seemed, well, like your Dr. A [Melvin's surgeon], he was straightforward and might say what he thought. He'd gotten on top of this building and was going to just drop the box. The owner told him no, he didn't want it dropped, he wanted it handled carefully. So he said he was going to open it and take it piece-by-piece down. The owner was stuttering and stammering about, uh—"Who told you you could open it. That stuff is mine and I don't want it opened." And, in the meantime I was trying to keep Mark from getting hurt and was trying to keep him sitting still, and trying to be of some help myself—trying to help 'em unload the truck. Pretty soon there's a bunch of other fellows from inside the plant come out. I don't remember ever gettin' that darn thing down. They had the truck pressed up against the building. One of those old-time trucks that had a low, very low flat-type bed on it. I guess you call them stakes along the edge of the truck. It was built low about hub-cap length or width or height . . . The wheels stuck up into the flat bed. I, uh, seemed to have lost my truck. And they asked me where I lived. I explained to them that I'd lost my truck and that I'd had problems, I'd called the wife and have her come and get me and he didn't have to take me home. There was another guy there that, uh, when they started unloading this truck he asked this one guy to give him a hand, and he seemed to be, uh, handicapped. Seemed like he only had one arm or something and he said, "Yes, yes sir, I'll do my best" when he was asked to give a hand. I had a feeling that this big guy that was driving the truck . . . he was big, husky, quite strong and strong-willed, seemingly, and I seem to envy or . . . possibly wish I were like him or something.

Dream 3: Dreaming about this very thing that I'm doing right now. I think I was dreaming that it was all over with, that you came in and asked me how I felt and if I slept comfortably. I was complaining about the bed being too soft. I think I said I could sleep better on the floor and you looked at me as if I were crazy or something. I said I think I felt better on a harder bed 'cause it didn't bother my back as much, the bed was different than this one. It was a low bed, a double bed. I felt like almost I shouldn't have said anything, because it wasn't really that bad. I think you said something about there was another bed in the other room and asked me if that would be all right. I said no I think this'll probably be all right for a veteran, I could sleep on the floor. I don't think the other bed was any different.

I had some apples, and I remember a friend of mine being in there and he was eating something too. But he had a large copper tray like you serve potato chips and dip, just full of apples. I was eating these apples and he was joking with somebody else. It was out in front of some building. Seemed like it was downtown someplace. And the person that he was talking to had put them down and was selling something . . . this guy was selling the apples. Some of the things they talked about was that he could buy, apparently some woman's panties and bra and undergarments here at the hospital for some reason . . . uh, where this other guy couldn't get them so he was going to buy them for this other guy. And here at the experiment it seems as though the time was up, you'd come through a door about where this window is. I mean you opened this sliding door and you asked me different questions, then I had comic books and it seems like I was reading a book, I was eating these apples.

In all three of these dreams Melvin or some symbolic figure is not treated fairly or is handled in a rough manner. In dream 1, a neighbor doesn't give him a ride, in dream 2, a trunk is not being handled with adequate care, and in dream 3, he is given an uncomfortable bed. The "trunk" in dream 2 rather clearly symbolizes Melvin's body and his fear that it will not be handled carefully (the man who looks like Dr. A. is going to take it "piece-by-piece down").

The appearance of the handicapped man, the danger of the trunk being dropped, and the loss of Melvin's truck all symbolize his fear of bodily damage and his feelings of physical inadequacy. Similarly, in dream 1 he is without a ride to work, and in the last dream his back is bothering him. All these situations put him in a helpless position in which he must depend on others for assistance, reflecting the ideas and feelings he expressed so persistently when awake. In the dreams he attempts to master these situations by enlisting the support or help of others (the neighbor, calling his wife for a ride, others lifting the trunk) much as he does during the day. The dreams also represent the regressive solution of providing himself with good things to eat (the apples in dream 3), becoming a child (reading comic books), and even a symbolic hint of becoming a woman (the double bed and woman's underwear in dream 3).

The Second Preoperative Dream Night

Melvin was probably most anxious during the day preceding this second dream night. He fled the hospital, sought out a social worker and private physician, and experienced intense anxiety during the presleep interview with Dr. Lane.

> Dream 4: It seems like I was dreaming about sending my boys to church or something like that, where they had a lot of construction and tall buildings. Seemed like there was a building there with tall spires . . . seems like I was arguing with the wife about the place is the same where we send the kids to church now. I was tellin' her that it was no different and showing her a map . . . She didn't seem to want to send the kids, she had an argument against sending them, that the kids might get lost . . . It seemed like while we were driving around I could see people I recognized from the hospital here. Yeah, walking to different places almost as if it was laid out like this hospital. It was almost as if I were going over a bridge,

and I could see patients in these blue outfits below me, and the only one I recognized was an old man that wears a hearing aid in this room 8 I'm in and carries a cane . . . He was just walking underneath this bridgelike thing . . . Something I was thinking about was that we were walking along the side of a driveway going to the garage, the car, and there was what looked like a dog eating, yet it was in different colors. Scraps of bone but in reds and blues or whites or greens or something like that.

Dream 5: I was on the roof trying to get some moths down, and it was raining and there were people concerned about some kind of moth that was on the roof and the wife had a ladder, it was extended, those extension ladders, it was extended up above the roof and the wind was blowing quite hard. She had her flowers tied to part of the ladder, and I wanted the ladder lowered so that the wind wouldn't catch it, and she wasn't too happy about my takin' it down so that her climbing flowers couldn't have a place to climb. Seemed like the moths were, um . . . wood-eaters or something like this . . . that would destroy trees, I was concerned too that they would damage the trees or something. I was on a ladder and the wife was holding the ladder and these people were down below telling me where they were and it was raining and I was hanging on to the house and brushing them off with my hand.

Dream 6: I was riding a bicycle when you woke me up . . . in the snowy weather. There was a friend of mine that was delivering mail in the snowy weather, I had an old stocking cap that keeps the ears warm. I let him borrow it, and I took his hat. This person that I let borrow the stocking cap was a postman in uniform but I couldn't tell you who he is . . . it's almost as if it was one of my boys . . . it was a mailman and I had borrowed his bicycle. Well, in riding this bike on the snowy ground I was applying the brakes and skidding and I was having trouble in keeping my balance and the rear wheel would fishtail and . . . in this keeping my balance there was some kinda feeling connected there but I couldn't tell you just what it is. Oh yeah, this one time we were getting the ball down out of the wires of the telephone pole and climbing the ladder and then picking the ball out with my hands . . . it seemed to be on a corner. These roomers were a young couple, they were renting the garage. The girl's husband was helping me carry the ladder along with a third man in the dream who I didn't recognize. Her husband and I were carrying the ladder and you know this other guy came along and he started carrying the ladder and somehow he was left-handed or something like this, and so he . . . when he grabbed the ladder it made it difficult and so he got up in front of me because they had told him so, and then I stumbled on his feet so I had to walk in step with him in order to carry the ladder . . . it seemed more like I was hanging on the ladder and he was pulling it . . . kinda strange feelings over the carrying of the ladder as if I wasn't, um . . . fit enough to carry it just with one person's help . . . as if I wasn't adequate enough . . . to carry it, that's the reason this other guy came into the picture.

Dream 7: We was eating chocolate corn syrup, or chocolate corn syrup over cornflakes and ice cream and I was talking to somebody but I don't remember anybody in the dream. I remember the syrup tasting real good and cold. Feelings of enjoyment, syrup, the chocolate syrup and there was just this one flake . . . which was a cornflake, that was all, there wasn't a bowl for it or anything like that.

Melvin's fear of losing support, the central fear aroused in him by surgery, is symbolized in these dreams as a loss of actual physical support. In dream 5 he is atop a shaky ladder, blown about by the wind, in dream 6 on a bicycle that skids about on snow, again atop a shaky ladder, and also stumbling as he tries to help carry the ladder. In each instance he must depend on others for support—his wife holds the ladder in dream 5 and the "girl's husband" carries the ladder in dream 6—but is uncertain that their support will be adequate—e.g., is his wife more concerned about her flowers than about him?

In both dreams 5 and 6 the job to be done seems to symbolize the surgery. In dream 5 he must remove the wood-eating moths that could destroy or damage trees, symbolizing the ulcerated condition of his stomach. Also: tree trunk = the trunk portion of the body = the trunk in dream 2, all referring to the part of his body that will be operated on.

In dream 6, removing the ball that is stuck in the telephone wires fuses the removal of his stomach obstruction with the vagotomy—i.e., fixing a nerve (electric wire) involved in the cause of the obstruction.

In the final dream of the night, as in the final dream on night 1, the wished-for "adequate care" is symbolized by the childish image of eating delicious food. It is interesting that Melvin, Penny (see below), and Hal, in the Group Therapy Study, use food and eating as symbolic dream solutions for dependency conflicts, and that they are the subjects with specific symptoms related to eating—stomach ulcer and obesity.

Several elements are carried over from the previous night, including: putting his son in his place as a patient in dream 4 (as in dream 2 on the first night); not being able to locomote, symbolized on the second night as skidding on the bike and stumbling with the ladder (and on the first night as not getting a ride and not having his own truck); and anxiety or danger symbolized by a high place—being high up on ladders in dreams 5 and 6, and the tall buildings of the hospital in dream 4 (the box up high in dream 2, the high and low beds in dream 3).

The Third Preoperative Dream Night

Melvin appeared much calmer on this night. He had called his personal doctor during the day and was reassured that his surgeons were highly qualified. He seemed relaxed before retiring and was apologetic about the trouble he had caused.

> *Dream 8:* I was dreaming about I was at a hospital . . . and I was trying to find the doctor . . . I was supposed to be having some kind of a tube and this tube had air in it . . . suction . . . and this other patient had the tube that he had taken with him plus one of these . . . blood-pressure arm bands . . . He was going to have his teeth taken out . . . and he was in a room with a whole mess of other patients and I was out in the hallway and he'd give me a prescription for some pills that I could take either by water or with beer. I think it was a completely different hospital . . . my bed along with other beds is out in the hallway and this window is where this air tube come from, it doesn't seem like it pumps my stomach, it does something else . . . It leads to the top half of this window and into the other room . . . where it goes I don't know. This is why I was after the doctor to try and find that tube, 'cause it had gone through that window. There was some buttons on the walls, uh . . . seemed like the doctor said something about this air tube had something to do with breathing . . . and, um . . . if I was to lose the tube or something, I was to push this button . . . there were some buttons along the wall, up very high almost like a doorbell button. There was a whole mess of patients waiting in line to have their teeth taken out . . . and they were sitting in chairs; the doctor that I was looking for was the one who was doing this . . . he was in charge of a whole mess of beds where these patients would go after having their teeth pulled. It seemed like I was in a narrow passageway where these patients were sitting down in these chairs . . . there was just enough room for a person to go between their legs and wall where they were sitting down, down the wall to where the doctor was. It seemed like I was afraid of something. It seemed like I was awake or something . . . like this dream was . . . well, like I was in this dream . . . like I was more real or something . . . like I was awake during the dream or something.

> *Dream 9:* I was in the hospital still and there was an older patient that would go with me. We would go to where my car is locked up in the

parking lot . . . and this location wasn't at the hospital, it was around where I grew up as a kid, and this one guy was chained to a bed where we kept our car and I was almost afraid to get into the car because I was afraid maybe this guy might catch hold of me or something . . . no, the car was chained not the patient, it seemed like I had to undo the chain before I could get the car . . . yeah, that was it. The patient was in bed and I guess he couldn't get up because he did grab ahold of me almost like it was a dog on a leash he was trying to get ahold of . . . anyway, as soon as I'd undone the car why we, ah . . . started the car and started driving off . . . well I had to pick up the other car behind me . . . there was another car in back of me that was parked so close that I couldn't get out so I had to, ah . . . picked it up by the rear wheels and dragged it off to, ah . . . another place where I could get my car out. I guess I was dreaming I had superstrength, that I could just lift the car and roll it over like it was a wheelbarrel or something and move it out of the way. As soon as we got my car out of there why, the man that was with me pulled out a gun . . . it seems like he had done this twice before . . . and I had always gotten the gun away from him . . . and I said something like "Oh, no, not again," and anyway I told him to hold off for a while, I had to take something back to another patient, it seemed like a pair of glasses to the patient. I guess I wasn't really paying too much attention to the gun because I had intentions of taking the gun away from him or something. I think I said something about "Sit down with the gun," or something like that, so that we could get out of the hospital . . . otherwise he'd have to stay here or something . . . seemed like I'd gotten the gun away from him after we'd gotten into the hospital and I'd laid it down on my workbench. It seems like this workbench was in the nurses' office, right here at this hospital.

Dream 10: I was dreaming about the city of Portland . . . seemed like I was in an airplane and we was going over the city of Portland and there was several locations on the map showing different parts and the one that drew my attention was Laurelhurst Park and that pond . . . seemed when it started out I was working at this place and I was working late . . . I was working on model airplanes . . . and they were using a large fan to dry the airplanes with and this one guy had it on high and it was blowing my plane apart before I could get it glued together . . . the feeling of being mad at the fan blowing my model apart . . . it had blown the small staircase or something like that off the model . . . so I had changed the direction of the fan and . . . somebody got upset because his fan was in front of it and he wanted to dry his paint . . . it was on his model . . . and I had emptied a wheelbarrel that I had used to clean up some junk around the house and I had emptied the wheelbarrel there in the garbage can at work . . . and the wife was giving me heck about something, seemed like I repeated three words . . . "Ding, ding, ding," or something . . .

Dream 11: Something to do with the hospital here . . . seems like I was in a woodworking shop of some kind . . . this patient and I . . . and there was a girl that I used to know quite well seemed to be working here . . . and it was time to close up the woodworking shop and put all the tools away and I was busy cleaning everything up and she was talking to this guy . . . and I think I was a little jealous . . . she wasn't talking to me instead . . . he's the patient who's in this room I'm in now, he wears glasses and he was telling her about his losing his house in this last October storm and she was quite sympathetic with him . . . and he was an older man . . . probably in his forties . . . and she was a girl only around nineteen . . . she'd also talked to me about her losing weight . . . she was taking exercises and things like that to lose weight . . . she's lost quite a bit of weight . . . she was quite proud of herself . . . she was still a little bit . . . kinda plump . . . you know, like . . . kinda hippy and heavy legs . . . heavy thighs . . . She was wearing a black dress . . . very neat . . . quite attractive . . . I was just busy getting everything cleaned up and put away and all the tools in the proper places and then I was heading for a shower . . . after working with the wood.

The first two dreams of this night contain direct references to the hospital, doctors, and specific fears connected with the operation, particularly his fear of having a tube inserted in his stomach. In dream 8 the relation of this fear to Melvin's concern about care, symbolized by "good and bad" feeding, is represented by references to pills taken with "water or beer" and having teeth pulled. Dream 9 again deals rather directly with his fear of surgery—his feeling of being trapped in the hospital (the patient "chained to a bed"), his attempts to cope with the situation by running away, and the related fear of what the doctors will do to him; his fear of punishment by authority for rebelliousness is fused with his fear of surgery. The hypothesis that being grabbed and threatened with a gun symbolizes these fears is partially validated by his statement that the patient in dream 9 "had done this twice before" and his comment, "Oh, no, not again," referring to his two previous operations.

Dreams 10 and 11 contain few direct references to the hospital or surgery, but they symbolize, in characteristic fashion, his thoughts and concerns. In both, he is involved in "woodworking" or is in a place where woodworking is done. In dream 11 it is clear that the woodworking shop and the hospital are the same place. In dream 10 his attempt to work with wood (build a model) is unsuccessful because a large fan is "on high and it was blowing my airplane apart before I could get it glued together." Melvin is capable only of cleaning up the refuse. Similarly, in dream 11, he is capable only of cleaning up the shop, and the relation of the other man and the attractive girl further hints at his inadequacy. The reference to the "October storm" (a windstorm that destroyed some houses and many trees in Oregon) and the girl's losing weight both relate to Melvin's concern about bodily damage and loss of power.

These two dreams contain several symbols and themes that appeared in earlier dreams. Wood, as in the model airplane and the woodworking shop, occurred in dream 5 as the wood-eating moths that Melvin attempts to remove. In both instances, when he attempts to solve the problem himself he is in a very anxiety-arousing and "shaky" position—being high up on a ladder blown by the wind in dream 5, flying in an airplane and the fan "on high" that blows the model apart in dream 10, and the October storm which blew a house away in dream 11. The "high" and "low" symbolism also occurs in other earlier dreams—lowering the trunk from the top of a building and the high and low trucks in dream 2, the high and low bed in dream 3, and the ladders in dreams 5 and 6. The context in which this recurrent symbol appears suggests that it refers to the relative power-dependency relationships in Melvin's life. Only by remaining "low"—subservient and dependent on others—is he safe. When he attempts to take on tasks himself—to rise up—he finds himself in very shaky and dangerous positions. This imagery seems tied to his view of himself as physically small in relation to his father and other men, and to his related fear that the surgery will make him even smaller and less powerful.

In all four dreams Melvin's freedom of movement or purpose is interfered with in some way by the actions or presence of other men (e.g., the constricted passageway in dream 8, the patient with a gun in dream 9, the man with the fan and the man who takes the girl's attention away in dreams 10 and 11).

Attempted solutions include escape (dream 9) and fantasies of superstrength and freedom—he moves a car by hand (dream 9) and flys over Portland (dream 10). But his freedom in flying is immediately transformed into anxiety-arousing punishment for attempting too much independence as the airplane becomes a model airplane that is "blown apart."

The Fourth Preoperative Dream Night

Melvin was given a pass to go home on this day. He attended a dance with his wife, enjoyed himself, and seemed quite relaxed when he returned to the sleep laboratory that night.

Dream 12: Seems almost like a wild Western or something of that sort ... either that or something that took place in Africa ... seemed like it had a lot of whoopin' and hollerin' ... seems like I was at the hospital yet ... and I was scheduled for surgery ... and I was telling people about it ... when I was telling people about the surgery it was right here in Portland ... it seemed like when I was doing the whoopin' and hollerin' ... it was out in the desert or someplace where it was hot. It was horse riding and seemed like there was a lot of fast moving.

Dream 13: I was dreaming about pumping my stomach. I was getting ready for surgery ... seemed like there was a woman being tested for something ... Oh ... she was tested for sex I think ... just how much acid would be flowing through the tubes I guess ... the doctor had asked us both questions ... similar to what you're doing, and after that, why then they had to pump my stomach to get a reading of how much acid was there ... and seemed like on this particular test what we had ... the girl was, oh ... kinda kidding me about having to, ah ... worked up such a sweat ... and it seems that the woman and I would have intercourse and then after our having intercourse ... they would take her in the other room and perform tests on her and then after they were through with her then I would go in there and get a tube and pump my stomach. An aide came up after the test. At the beginning of the test I think I was having to stay here ... here at the hospital and people where I was staying was here in this room ... it seemed more like a child's room with child's type of games, the room was bright ... colored and I would hear voices of people, it would sound like people were coming but I'd never see them ... it seemed like sometimes I would try and see ... take a look at how the tests were coming or something like that and then I'd hear people coming and they would never show up ... they'd never get there. Uh ... had feelings of when the people were coming ... the fear of being caught ... sneaking a look at the results ... of the test ... seems like I was doing some art ... some painting ... or something like that ... while I was confined to the room.

Dream 14: I was working in shrubs ... bark dust ... doing something I enjoyed ... Yeah, working in the garden spreading bark dust around the flowers ... rhododendrons and things of the sort. It seemed like it was a kinda gray cloudy day and there wasn't any sunshine ... 'cause it seemed cool. Seems like I was on my knees scraping bark dust off my hands ...

Dream 15: Dreaming about buying a new car I think . . . we went to a car dealer and we started looking for a car that I had . . . we had been given an invitation to drive a new Ford for two days without obligation . . . nothing to sign or anything . . . with the exception of a card for insurance purposes . . . the new-car dealers were out to sell you a car and I hate to go in because I felt like they would put the pressure on . . . and the guy was saying something about "Sure wish we could get you into a new car." . . . I said well, if he could throw it to me with everything on it for $3,995, why he's got himself a deal on it. Somebody walked by just about that time, I guess it was the manager . . . says, "Sounds like you just bought yourself a car," and then the wife repeated what I had said, 'cause we had priced them when they were around $4,700 and we had hoped to get into a new car before this had happened . . . and so then we went to look up in his book I guess about what this thing did cost . . . had a card that I had in my wallet . . . and I could have sworn I had that card in my wallet . . . and when I went in there I asked the guy to see if he could match what his prices could be and matching this that I had . . . matching this card . . . and I couldn't find this card in my wallet . . . and I took something out of my wallet, tore it apart and folded out and looking to see if I could find that card.

The first two dreams in this sequence incorporate material directly related to surgery. In dream 12, he is at the hospital telling people that he is scheduled for surgery, and in dream 13, his fear about swallowing a tube is again present. The symbolism in this dream represents the connection between his concern about masculine inadequacy and sexual impotence and his fear of the possible damage that may result from surgery. His stomach (e.g., acid level, "pumping") is associated with sexual performance in a very clear way. He tries to deal with the conflict by adopting a sexually virile role followed by a dependent, childish one. Sexual intercourse is, in fact, one important way in which he attempts to prove himself a man rather than a dependent child. Yet waiting for the doctors in a "child's room with child's type of games" again expresses the stronger wish for a childish, dependent relationship with an adequate male.

Dream 14 has him again working on wood (bark dust) in a "low," and hence relatively safe, position. In dream 15 the potentially positive outcome of the surgery is represented as buying a new car, which seems to symbolize his hope for a new body. Still, he needs his wife with him, and a positive outcome remains in doubt because the card he needs to close the deal is either missing or torn apart.

Summary: Effects of Stress on the Preoperative Dreams

Melvin's preoperative dreams contain elements and themes directly related to surgery and also symbolic representations of his thoughts and fears. Of the five subjects, his dreams contain the largest amount of direct surgery-related material, with frequent references to surgery, hospitals, patients, doctors, and medical instruments. A high proportion of dream characters, including Melvin himself, are physically handicapped, hurt, or inadequate.

A comparison of the pre- with the postoperative dreams shows that the elements and themes described above resulted from the threat of the impending operation. For example, 53% of the preoperative dreams contained elements directly related to surgery as against only 8% (one minor element) of the postoperative dreams. Bodily defects or inadequacies appeared in 53% of the preoperative dreams (versus 30% of the postoperative dreams), indicating his greater concern about actual bodily damage before surgery. Blockages or loss of mobility occurred in 53% of the preoperative dreams (versus 39% of the postoperative dreams); the narrow or constricted passage which frequently appeared probably symbolized the actual restriction of food passing through his gastrointestinal tract. Actual or threatened loss of a possession or person, which occurred in 47% of the preoperation dreams (versus only 8% of the postoperative dreams), seems to be related to his concern about loss of care, loss of masculinity and power, and loss of weight.

Attempts to remove an object occurred in 47% of the preoperative dreams (versus only 8% of the postoperative dreams) and seem to represent the goal of the surgery. Such acts included men trying to unload a heavy trunk from a truck (dream 1), Melvin trying to get the "wood-eating moths" out of his roof (dream 5), Melvin going to get a ball down from the telephone wires (dream 6), patients waiting in line to have their teeth taken out (dream 8), and a doctor pumping acid out of Melvin's stomach (dream 13). All of the differences cited above are particularly striking in view of the fact that Melvin was still in the hospital and experiencing considerable discomfort during the postoperative collection period eight days after surgery.

Of all subjects, Melvin's preoperative dreams were rated highest in anxiety, a finding that is consistent with his very high level of anxiety during the day. The most common anxiety-arousing dream situation was one of threatened injury to a person or damage to an object. Of the nine dream scenes in which he expressed definite anxiety (six from the pre- and three from the postoperative period), seven contained obvious threats of damage, illness, or injury. These references to injury and illness also seem closely related to lifelong concerns about inadequacy and dependency—his own smallness or "lowness" in relation to others, fear of inadequate care and support, and insecurity about his sexual potency.

The intensification of his characteristic dependency was symbolized by the relative physical position of the dream characters and objects. For example, 54% of the preoperative dreams (versus only 21% of the postoperative dreams) featured a person or object in a very high or low position relative to other dream characters. The themes in which these high-low symbols were embedded made it clear that they referred to Melvin's relative inferiority and weakness in relation to others, particularly men, and attempts at gaining a superior position.

Melvin's characteristic waking mode of coping with the stress of his impending operation was to seek nurturance and support from others. His dreams reflect this: 47% of the preoperative dreams involved him in a dependent position. While some dependent behavior did occur in the postoperative dreams (15%) it was more blandly expressed and more often involved dream characters other than Melvin.

A related defense is the wishful return to a childish position. Melvin was engaged in childish activities or was in a child's environment in 33% of the preoperative dreams (versus 15% of the postoperative dreams). Related elements, not counted in the above percentages, include eating very gratifying food (e.g., the chocolate corn syrup and cornflakes in dream 7) and changing places with his own children (dreams 2 and 4).

The high anxiety aroused in Melvin by threatened loss of support and his use of exaggerated weakness and dependency leave him in a very constricted position. His concern about this difficult position and his fantasied solutions appear in the dreams, particularly on the third preoperative night after he had made the final decision to put himself in the hands of the hospital surgeons. The dreams of that night represented his wish to escape, with dream figures, including himself, riding in or driving vehicles, escaping from the hospital or from the role of patient. Dream 9, with its image of the chained patient-chained car and Melvin's ability to move the car represents both the conflict and his wishful attempts at solution. Such escape themes occurred with even greater frequency in the postoperative dreams (54%, compared with 40% during the preoperative dreams), owing to his increasingly strong desire to go home. When the surgeon notified Melvin on the second postoperative day that he would have to remain in the hospital longer than was anticipated, Melvin became very upset. Four of his five dreams that night contained automobiles, including one dream in which he was attempting to escape from "bootleggers" who had captured him, and another in which he and his wife were helping relatives to move.

Another theme which appeared more frequently in the postoperative period was that of a dream character changing, or preparing to alter some aspect of his life (39% of the postoperative versus only one instance in the preoperative dreams—buying a new car in dream 15). Since Melvin felt that the operation was successful and would be his last, this theme probably symbolized his hope of renewed health and an improved life situation. One very clear expression of it in a postoperative dream was the image of a crippled patient from Melvin's ward who appeared completely healed and "building his own house."

In summary, Melvin's anticipation of surgery aroused fear of inadequate care, love, and support, and concern about his inadequacy as a man. His high anxiety stemmed from related memories, including his longstanding fear of loss (perhaps going back to the loss of both mother and grandmother), his characteristic exaggeration of his own weakness, and his tenuous masculine identification. His attempts at defense in his dreams included regression to a childish position, fantasies of escape, and fantasies of power and superiority. Parallels to all of these efforts were observable in his waking behavior and thoughts. Both his waking and dreaming attempts were relatively ineffective, however. As a result, Melvin's dreams were higher in anxiety, and contained more unpleasant threatening content, than those of any other subject.

PENNY

Penny is an 18-year-old high-school senior who was scheduled for exploratory surgery and possible removal of her gall bladder. She is a rather plain-looking girl, short and overweight, who appears to be slow, cautious, and old beyond her years. She describes her biggest problem as shyness, and she harbors a rather strong feeling of inferiority. She has always felt somewhat alienated from others because of her appearance, especially her obesity, and has yet to have her first date, "probably because of my weight." She tends to withdraw and to insulate herself emotionally as a way of coping with anticipated rejection, though she does have a few girlfriends to whom she is very close. While her withdrawal is not extreme, she is overinhibited and introspective, as well as lacking in the enthusiasm and buoyancy usually found in girls of her age.

Both parents have overprotected Penny, reinforcing her social isolation and feeling of inadequacy. She describes her father as a nervous person who is very protective, and her mother as characterized by a similar amount of controlling protectiveness. For example, her mother will not allow her to see movies other than "Walt Disney types."

While Penny was beginning to move toward independence at the time of the study, her shyness and insecurity, combined with her parents' overprotectiveness, make this move a particularly difficult problem for her. Her conflicts are evident in various fears concerning her future: fear of not being able to find a job, of not doing well in college—in short, of not succeeding in the world on her own.

Penny's previous experiences with surgery and hospitalization provide important background information about her present state of mind. She was born with an extra thumb, which was surgically removed when she was four. Though she can remember very little about this hospitalization, the stigma, along with her obesity and poor clothing, contributed to a sense of differentness and inferiority. At the age of 10 she was hospitalized for an emergency appendectomy, about which she has quite vivid memories. The hospitalization and operation were abrupt, allowing little or no time for psychological preparation, and she was extremely upset, cried a great deal, and felt intensely lonely.

Four weeks before the present study she had been hospitalized for 13 days because of acute stomach pains and nausea. During the first week she was lonely and homesick and lay awake at night crying, reacting very much as she had to the appendectomy eight years before. Her reaction on both these occasions seems to have been due to a fear of parental abandonment combined with her sense of separateness from others. However, during the second week of this hospitalization she was able to overcome her inhibitions and engage in social interactions with the other patients. To her surprise, she felt relaxed and was able to relate to strangers as she had never done before. Furthermore, she was forced to lose 30 pounds, which aroused hope for a new and attractive appearance. She described her recent hospitalization as follows:

> ... before I was always so scared of people ... but in the hospital people aren't too modest about anything ... or everybody is sick up there and everybody has to wear the same little nightgown you wear ... everyone is in the same boat.

Thus her recent experience in the hospital allowed her to work through certain fears. It also aroused hope that the forthcoming hospitalization and operation would change her life by allowing her to lose more weight, increase her attractiveness, and overcome her shyness with strangers. She seemed to view the entire experience as a way in which she would gain enough self-confidence to become independent of her parents.

Penny engaged in a good deal of preparatory activity. She obtained detailed information from a nurse about the operation and spent a good deal of time sewing dresses in anticipation of her new, slimmer figure. While her preoperative fear was low, some concern about abandonment and loss of affectionate support remained. She also harbored some fear of bodily damage—despite her predominant fantasy of an attractive new body—evidenced in a concern about the possibility of an unsightly scar.

Penny's unrealistic fantasies of sudden physical and social transformation set the stage for almost certain disappointment after the operation. Indeed, she reported "several unexpected things" postoperatively, despite a successful operation and a normal recovery. She felt that the nurses were not very friendly or attentive and that she was unable to overcome her inhibitions enough to feel much increased self-confidence. In addition, she had to retain a drainage bag, attached to her stomach by a tube, which was very unpleasant and increased her feeling of discomfort around other people. She finally "jerked the tube out by accident," and was so frightened and upset that she did not tell her surgeon for several days. This incident—the most unpleasant aspect of the entire operation for her—together with her disappointment and the loss of a part of her body (the gall bladder was removed), tended to increase the level of stress in the postoperative period over that of the preoperative period.

In rating Penny's dreams for incorporation, the judges were guided by the general features just described, and by the following statement: "I'm going in for exploratory gall-bladder surgery, and they'll probably take the gall bladder out if it's diseased or not working, and if not, they won't."

The First Preoperative Dream Night

Penny seemed to be in a complaining mood on this night. She did not like the hard bed she had to sleep on and criticized the tests she had to take. After a short discussion with the experimenter about her previous experiences in the hospital, she seemed more relaxed and was ready to retire.

Dream 1: I remember something about coming up here. I could just see people upstairs and downstairs . . . kind of a cross section of the house of where I would be.

Dream 2: I was thinking about a party, oh . . . the thing that impressed me most was that everybody was so happy. And . . . in today's world it was kinda unrealistic . . . I would say because the people were . . . everybody was happy . . . you know the big white house? Kinda the front of it was taken off so you could see all the rooms . . . but . . . the action was still going on in the rooms as if nothing was taken off . . . just the front part of it was removed . . . somebody was still cooking dinner in the kitchen . . . you know . . . just as if the wall was still there . . . and at the party nobody was dressed up at all but they all had nice-looking clothes on you might say . . . casual clothes . . . I don't know, they were just standing around in groups talking and laughing . . . I could pick out three or four of my friends that were there . . . I was going around talking to everybody and everybody was laughing and having such a good time . . . that's about all I could say I guess.

Dream 3: Well I was thinking, um . . . partly about the dream that I had earlier tonight and I thought a little bit about the one I had last night . . . were you here tonight when I had the one about the party? Well I was thinking about that one . . . time passed and it just ended and people got in their cars and went home . . . and um . . . I was thinking about the one I had last night . . . It was at a fair and . . . last night all I could remember was that it was just like a little stand out there by itself and so I thought that because of the way that the stand was constructed it would probably be a fair . . . but much smaller and there didn't seem to be as many people and the things spaced out a lot more . . . and the rides and stuff like that, they all seemed to be quiet . . . This big fat man kept trying to feed me Mexican food and I didn't want any and . . . I don't know whether I was inside . . . but somehow he had hold of me so that I couldn't go . . . he kept trying to get me to eat it but I wouldn't and then I woke up so I don't know what happened . . .

Dream 4: I think it was one of my aunts was supposed to get married and all the people were coming here and everybody was deciding what to wear and everything . . . and then I think at the last minute nobody turned up . . . uh . . . there was a phone call from South Dakota where my grandmother lives and there was some material sent from there to make my aunt a dress, but it was real old because ah . . . the styles had changed so much that she tried to be in style. She's already started to cut out the material for her dress but the, it was so way out from today's styles that they couldn't do anything from it, and then at the last we got a phone call from them saying they wouldn't be coming and so somebody asked what the styles were like back there and so they decided that they were going to start a fashion store back there because styles were so different today. All these people were trying to figure out how they were going to get this style of dress out of that piece of material. And um . . . there were about 15 people trying to figure out how to do this. I was probably in there someplace . . . the people know that you're there but they don't take the time to acknowledge that. I felt about in the middle of it but ah . . . I was watching too. I think I was kinda let down at the end because nobody came. Um . . . maybe a little bit annoyed because they said at first that they all would come and then right at the last minute there were a whole bunch of phone calls and everybody said that they couldn't come.

These dreams seem related to Penny's anticipation of personal and social transformation, and to her waking preoccupation with food, weight loss, and clothing as symbols of this transformation. There is less intense concern about bodily damage of the sort found in the preoperative dreams of Al and Melvin.

In dream 2, the absence of the front of the building (the "big white house" is a direct representation of the clinic where the sleep laboratory is situated) and the consequent revealing of the rooms inside may be a symbolic fusion of the experiment in which her dreams are revealed and the impending operation in which her stomach will be opened. The pleasant social interaction ("cooking dinner . . . as if the wall were still there") and the attractive clothing stem from her fantasy of what the hospitalization and operation will do to change her life.

Dream 3, which seems more like a non-REM "thinking" report, continues the same theme. But here the negative affect appears— the people leave and Penny is trapped with a "fat man" who tries to force food on her. This incident may symbolize both her fear of giving in to the temptation of eating forbidden food and the anxiety aroused about the sexuality implicit in her anticipated "new body" and social attractiveness.

Dream 4 contains both positive and negative elements related to the same theme. The attempt to make a new dress for a wedding from "real old" material fuses Penny's actual dressmaking activity with the operation (cutting her body to improve it) and her more general fears and concerns. Clothing is a recurrent symbol for her body in her dreams, as it is in her waking life—she blames her poor clothing, in part, for her social isolation, felt more comfortable with patients during the preceding hospitalization because "everybody has to wear the same little nightgown you wear," and prepares for her new life by making new dresses. In dream 4, being stuck with her problems and being out of style are expressed in the image of the old, out-of-style material. (Interestingly, during an interview she described her gall-bladder difficulty as a disease of the aged, and subsequently spoke of being out of step with her contemporaries.) Her hope for change is expressed as starting a fashion store at a place where the styles are outdated. Her fear that this anticipated new life may not come to pass is symbolized by the failure of people to appear for the wedding: ". . . at the last minute . . . everybody said that they couldn't come."

The Second Preoperative Dream Night

Penny was very friendly and talkative before retiring. She discussed her forthcoming operation, saying, "I can't wait to go in the hospital because it means a change for me."

Dream 5: It was about money and there was college kids in it. We needed to get some money for some reason and it was over $100 ... I can't remember why they needed the money but they were discussing it ... talking about how they couldn't get it ... they were in a room and somebody was sitting on a desk and another one was sitting on a bed I think. And ... somebody else was sitting in a chair. Kind of casuallike you know ... with their feet up on the desk ... they didn't seem to be too mad that they couldn't get it. Maybe they could write home to father and maybe he could send the money.

Dream 6: A lady was worried about what to fix her kids for lunch. I guess somebody from a TV commercial, you know. It was just in a modern-type kitchen and she was just sitting down like at her breakfast nook and wondering what she was going to feed her kids. I was thinking about something else before that ... I think it was more about those guys I dreamt about earlier except that they bought a restaurant with their money where a lot of teenage kids hang out and ... all their fathers gave them the money ... and then the parents came down to see what it was like and ... the mothers didn't like it. I could only see clearly one set of parents who were outside arguing that they didn't like the music that was being played ... there were card tables and some of the kids were dancing and they didn't like how the kids were dancing or anything about it ... the women thought that it was terrible ... I think it was out someplace where the business was just starting up ... there is still a lot of space between the businesses because it hasn't grown up that much ... and all the mothers seemed very well dressed and they all had gray hair ... you know, like they go to the beauty shop every week, and all the fathers had good clothes, I mean expensive clothes you know, and they sent the money to the boys when they ... wrote home for it ... Well, to me it seemed like the older women kind of all had henpecked husbands, it just seemed like they kind of nagged at them until they changed their minds. And at the end they didn't like the idea at all. I saw one couple discussing it and the woman got kind of mad, so finally the man just gave up ... I remember one girl running in ... she was married to one of them and she says, "Well at least it will be different from now on." I don't know what that had to do with it. And ... so they went into the restaurant business I guess.

Dream 7: Probably a continuation of the one I had the last time where a lady was trying to figure out what she was supposed to fix for lunch. She fixed her kids lunch and then sent them outside . . . it was kind of like a TV commercial . . . the lady was pretty and all the kids were, I would say, very well behaved at the table and the house was cleaned up and it was a great big kitchen and there was, I'd say, built-in appliances and stuff like that and . . . the lady just had on kind of a shirtwaist dress and I think she had high heels on and there were two boys and a girl I think and . . . they were kind of grubby from playing outside before. But they just had like jeans and a tee shirt on because it was in the summertime. I didn't even see myself in there so I must have been watching.

Dream 8: I remember there was a room like a dormitory or something. There were five Japanese sisters . . . I was supposed to be in a play dressed up in the traditional costume of Japan . . . Well, when they were in the dormitory at night, they were getting ready to go to bed, and they were just horsing around, and in the morning, one of them used up all one of the other sisters' hair spray, but she had short hair that was just straight and blunt-cut. And I don't know why she would use hair spray, but anyway she used it all up. And so that one sister got kind of mad at her so they were just horsing around then. And . . . they were in two separate rooms and that night they heard a strange noise and so the oldest one stayed in with the youngest one in one room and then the next to the oldest stayed with the two middle girls, but nothing ever happened. Uh . . . they ranged in ages from thirteen to nineteen or something, and at the end they were supposed to help me dress up in their traditional costume to be in a play for something.

I thought it would probably be like a girl's boarding school. I don't think they were university age but . . . kind of like teenagers . . . they were all kind of heavy and I said their hair was kind of cut like a Dutch boy's you know, and they had real round faces. But they were Japanese people and their coloring was darker than ours and they had kind of slanted eyes . . . And that night they decided the oldest would sleep with the youngest in the same room 'cause the youngest one was the most scared and . . . then in the morning I guess they forgot all about it. But then they started playing around again. At the end I was dressed up and in a kimono and I was up on a stage by myself and I was smiling. Well, I think a lady introduced us . . . so that they could dress me up like that at the end. I didn't see the lady or anything but they were called in you know, to advise the people on how things really looked. They all seemed to be smiling . . . maybe that was why I was smiling at the end . . . they had great big broad smiles I can remember. I saw part of the audience once. You know, looking out at them. It was just kind of dark, they had to shut down the lights and you could just kind of see the shadows of people's faces . . . it's just a mass of eyes looking at you or something like that.

The four dreams in this sequence all seem to deal with independence emerging from dependence—its possible satisfactions and attendant dangers. The dependence on parents appears in dreams 5 and 6 as taking money from a father, children being fed by their mother and again, in dream 7, as a mother fixing lunch for her children. The emerging independence is represented in dreams 5 and 6 as opening a restaurant "someplace where the business was just starting up." The "college kids" are probably derived from Penny's own plan to attend college, which was to be a move toward independence. Opening a restaurant (and the new, glamorous kitchen in dream 7) are interesting ways of symbolizing potential independence because they preserve a central symbol of the dependent relation—food.

The move toward independence arouses fears and concerns that are seen most clearly in the image of the disapproving mother figures in dream 6. Penny's own anxiety about sexuality again seems to be central to these fears, although she tends to represent it in the form of parental restrictions.

Consistent with her waking tendency toward passivity and withdrawal, in her dreams Penny herself is typically on the periphery while other characters are engaged in the central action. Moreover, several of her dream reports—e.g., dream 7, and dream 3 on the previous night—are more "thoughtlike" than dreamlike, consistent with her introspective style of life. In dream 8, she comes close to being the center of attention, appearing to derive satisfaction from an exhibition of herself in different clothes ("dressed up and in a kimono"—"on a stage by myself"—"smiling"). But potential disapproval is again present, this time as a "mass of eyes looking at you." Becoming Japanese may be a symbolic fusion of these two trends, since she can be noticed for her femininity and attractiveness and still be an obedient daughter and "dressed up in a traditional costume."

The Third Preoperative Dream Night

Penny brought her father, sister, and brother with her and showed them around the sleep laboratory. Before retiring she mentioned that her father had been "kidding" her about her participation in the study and had predicted some "dilly" dreams for that night.

Dream 9: I was thinking about what I was going to talk about because somebody woke me up and I couldn't talk . . . I couldn't say anything. Like I was up here and . . . tried to say something, but I couldn't. And somebody else was doing an experiment up here . . . there was also a man in the bed and he seemed to be very disgusted with what was going on and thought that it was a complete waste of time. He didn't like to fill out the sheets or anything like that. He got mad at doing that . . . and . . . I imagine that it took place here, but when he came here and he was happy and smiling . . . and then his whole attitude changed so that he was rude and cross and grouchy towards other people . . . One time the man, when he was all hooked up and everything . . . and he was in a bedroom someplace off by himself, he ripped all the electrodes out, not off his head but from the sockets over his bed, but nobody could tell this by looking at the machine . . . it didn't pick it up. It just went right on going . . . I was just thinking maybe he got mad when he found out what he was going to have to go through. I mean, you know, to sit and have the electrodes and then fill out the form. Maybe he didn't think about it as much when he consented to do this thing. He was kind of skinny and kind of tall and he had black hair and it was combed back from the front and it was kind of long, you know, just like you take a comb . . . like a girl tries to get it into a ponytail. You know how they comb it back from all the sides. I think he had kind of a big nose and he had circles under his eyes or his eyes were sunken in . . . and then he had kind of a small mouth . . . It was like he was in here and I might have been in the room on the other side of the stairway or something like that . . . but I was here and he was here but we were separated. I just got ready and went to sleep. I could see myself asleep with the electrodes on and by the time I did that, he was still ranting and raving about the questionnaire he had to fill out . . . I think it kind of made me mad because he shouldn't have said that he would do something and then quit as easy as he did. I'm pretty sure that this was the first night that the guy came to sleep here, but he just got mad, real mad.

Dream 10: I think somebody had named three different people that were missing from the dream thing. And before I told you that the guy could take out the electrodes, you know, and it didn't matter on the machine? Well, he took them off of his head while they were still in the socket, and I did the same thing and we went down to the corner west of this house and there was a little café there, so we had coffee and doughnuts and then we came back after a little while and nobody even noticed us. I can remember sneaking downstairs with this guy and then we got our coats on downstairs and then we went out the door over on the side of the house and we went down there. It was not like a café. It was more like the stand like I saw in the dream the other night. There were just the regular kind of stools to sit on, but it was kind of makeshift and I remember that he could close down anytime . . . like one of those desks with the round top, he could just pull the top down until it met the counter and that was the way he closed up and there was only about room for one person to move around in the back behind the counter, and so he was the only one that was back there . . . well he knew the guy behind the counter real well so he was talking to him and I was just kind of looking around a little bit because I had never been there before . . . I can't stand coffee and I can't have doughnuts . . . he was kind of fat and had kind of a belly on him and I remember he had greasy hands from making hamburgers and he had a dirty apron on and I didn't particularly like to go over there but this guy that I went with knew him real well and he said that it would be okay. So they just started talking and I think I was just scared that we were going to get caught so I was always looking around, you know. We didn't bother to get dressed. We were just sitting down there in our coats and pajamas. There was nobody else around, I don't think. I didn't see anybody walking along the sidewalk or anything and the café was kind of open, you know, so you could just pull the top over it. It was really kind of like a hot-dog stand except that it had three or four stools out front . . . so we just were sitting there kind of in the night air. I think the whole thing wasn't very sturdily built, kind of like . . . like not the hot-dog stands they have today. Those aren't built very well and they . . . were just makeshift stools . . . the whole thing was kind of rickety. It was poorly built and I didn't figure it could stand the Oregon weather and I don't even know why it was there . . . Then . . . right at the end, somebody named over a loudspeaker three names which . . . two of them fit us, and then there must have been somebody else that they found out was out of the house. I mean, that had done the same thing and they couldn't tell on the machine . . . so we just kind of took off and ran all the way back to the house and upstairs, and then the guys that were up here were waiting around kind of mad . . . but I think it was kind of fun because on the way back when we were running we were laughing about it . . . but I don't know how we got out of the electrodes . . . after you put that stuff on them . . . but they were still all in the sockets, you know, except that we just weren't there.

Dream 11: First, I was supposed to be in a soap-detergent test and we were supposed to wash clothes to see which ones turn out whiter. And that was someplace at a school. It was in a red brick school and they were doing it with some kind of stuff that worked in cold water. And, you know, there's a commercial on TV like that, that says, get all the stains out in cold water . . . so that it won't stain or something like that. Then after that happened there was a stack of clean clothes on the washer, kinda like towels and there was a pair of kid's jeans that proved the fact that you could wash it in cold water . . . and they turn out just as good or better than if you washed them in hot water. There were just six or eight washing machines and dryers, everybody else seemed to act just like it was a laundromat, and after they put their clothes in there, they just sat down someplace and read magazines until it was over . . . I went home and changed my clothes and then went to a place where they had a lot of food out, like fruit cake and cake and pie and all that kind of stuff . . . I think they were launching a charity campaign or something and there were going to be a whole bunch of people there and all the tables were set with silverware and napkins . . . I was helping do that and . . . just before you woke me up I was smiling. I don't know what for. It was a great big room and it had a picture window at one end, a great big window that covered most of the wall, a museum up in Portland has a room that's kinda like that upstairs in their building . . . except when we were up there . . . they were redoing some of the stuff . . . and . . . at the museum the drapes were kinda torn and stuff like that, but there they weren't . . . and it had a picture window at one end and I think it had chairs around the outside for people to sit . . . oh, the room was much bigger than it was at the museum . . . and, oh, they had real expensive drapes on 'em and stuff like that . . . it had a U-shaped table in the middle with all this food on it . . . like hot lunch, refreshment time for something . . . where you pick up your plate and fork and then just go along the line and pick out whatever you want . . . and ah . . . I was helping set the table, and . . . get the chairs along the outside, I mean . . . get 'em straight and everything before the other people came in and . . . before you woke me up, I was standing in the middle of the U with some other ladies . . . so that you could ask if anybody needed any help or anything . . . to help serve and stuff like that . . . there was a meeting going on in the next room with somebody that was heading it . . . well, at the end of this one . . . all the ladies that had come to help with me were standing inside the U . . . after we got all done we kinda heard the meeting break up and so we all just stood there, we didn't say anything at the end . . . I think I was nervous in that one because at the end there was supposed to be some important people in that meeting or influential . . . that had money . . . but I don't know who they were or anything.

Dream 12: I was watching TV and there was kind of a horror movie on . . . Oh it was this great big monster was chasing me . . . it wasn't like *Outer Limits*, it was more like *Dr. Jekyll and Mr. Hyde*, where they chased them through the woods and over the hills and all that kinda stuff, like this big hairy monster was doing . . . some of the people from the different shows were kinda in all one show together, and . . . maybe it was just at my house or something but anyway, Pam and I were playing real old records like some of the old stars on TV today where they were real young and they were there too . . . and some of the records were real old and they kept getting stuck and so finally we decided not to play and . . . the people that were on the records started arguing and . . . one girl had her purse and she kept hitting this guy over the head with it and . . . then we decided to quit . . . playing the records, but then, I think those people who came were the neighbors because from what I remember I was moved into a new house and there were two other new homes next to mine. So they all came over, but they were on records when they were little kids and so they brought those over too, and so we played the records that they brought over and some of them were terribly worn, it just seemed real old ones and the covers were kinda falling apart and everything on theirs. And when the records wouldn't go they started fighting back and forth, like they'd played that one so much that . . . you must be conceited if you like yourself that much, and things like that, and so then they started fighting . . . finally I think I gave them their records back and they both went home . . . there were more than two neighbors that came over . . . like a group of bachelors who live together, well it was kinda like . . . there were two different groups living in the two houses that were by mine. I, um . . . we were older and I bought this house and . . . we were kinda in a new development . . . it was kinda weird because the house next to me . . . the driveway of the house by it cut right through the back yard and my back door was right by where their two driveways ended . . . I was happy at the first . . . and right away the neighbors came over and . . . I was pleased because of that, but then after they started arguing I was kinda shocked . . . because two different groups of people would argue like that, you know, in front of somebody they didn't even know . . . then they all left at the end, so I guess I kinda felt relieved.

Dream 9 expresses Penny's anger at being in the restricted position of a dream subject though, characteristically, the anger must be projected onto another dream character. There is also some hint at the sexually arousing aspects of sleeping with a man (Dr. Lane) in an adjoining room. Anger about restrictions is continued in dream 10, where it blends into her more general resentment of the restrictions imposed by her diet and overcontrolled way of life. Her wish to break free from these restrictions, to rebel and become independent, is represented by her "sneaking" away to a restaurant where she indulges her forbidden desires for food (doughnuts, which her diet prohibits), for sexual involvement (she sneaks off with a man), and for exhibitions of herself (sitting outside in coat and pajamas). While all this is "kind of fun," the forbidden nature of these activities is suggested by the distasteful appearance of both men and her wariness for fear of being caught. Dream 10 also symbolizes her inability to achieve her aims with her present mode of life (eating greasy food) and her present body (the "poorly built," "rickety" hot-dog stand).

In dream 11 her hopes for a new body and a new mode of life are represented by several of the same symbols that appeared in previous dreams. The freshly washed clothes (in contrast to the dirty apron and greasy hands of dream 10), the remodeled banquet room, and the museum in which the old torn drapes are replaced, all represent the recurring new-for-old theme. Her wish for a new, "remodeled" body is represented by new clothes (as it was in dream 4 and others), and a new relationship to food and eating (as in the new restaurant in dream 6 and others). The unpleasant affect associated with the gratification of forbidden desires in dream 10 is absent here as she adopts the role of servant to the gratification of other people's desires. This reversal of roles is also symbolized in the contrast between the small, cheap, shabby, dirty restaurant of dream 10 and the large, expensive, respectable, and clean museum-restaurant of dream 11.

The theme of a new life is continued in dream 12 in which her wish for independence and freedom is symbolized as her own apartment in a "new housing development." Two general fears associated with independence and freedom are also represented. The potential sexual involvement (the bachelors next door whose driveway leads to her back door) seems to arouse a good deal of anxiety—the "big, hairy monster" who chases her. Independence means giving up dependence, and thus arouses her fear of abandonment and loss of attention. This theme is symbolized by the old phonograph records of forgotten childhood stars which she trys to play for her neighbors. The records which are worn, and their jackets which are falling off, symbolize Penny's bodily defects. The narcissistic investment of the neighbors in hearing themselves on records reflects Penny's own wish to exhibit herself and be noticed. She handles the threat of retaliation (the arguing and fighting) for such "conceit" by again adopting the relatively passive, unselfish role of hostess to the neighbors' desires. The context and wording indicate that this dream refers to her own fear about giving up the physical complaints and ugliness that have brought her nurturance and attention.

The Fourth Preoperative Dream Night

Penny seemed relaxed, and expressed no concern about the prospect of leaving for the hospital the next morning. She said that her bags had been packed and ready to go for several days.

Dream 13: At first I think I was in bed and at the end ... I was all dressed up but I was holding the rating scale that was cut out ... it just had ... like three different questions ... and then it was cut out so that they didn't have the regular sheet of paper, it was kinda odd-shaped ... I was real skinny and I had hair on top of my head ... all brought up instead of down and ... I had different clothes on ... I don't think I've ever been dressed up enough to wear three-inch heels ... they were real high ... there wasn't very much action at all and there was just two different scenes. The first was just in bed I guess, and at the end I was standing by the door downstairs and I was waiting for my dad or somebody to pick me up with the charts in my hand ... a chart, you know, that the machine makes and also a rating scale.

Dream 14: Something about the money that I was supposed to get at the end, when this is all over with ... Subjects are supposed to get some money for coming up here and everything ... I was still in bed here and I was dreaming about it and so I was still hooked up and everything ... I think my brother was getting ready to go someplace ... he was just running up and down the hall in our house with his shorts and shirt on and then he got his dress shirt over it and then at the end he was putting on a tie ... I think at the end he still didn't have any pants on. And I don't think he had any shoes on either. He was very happy because ... I think probably he was going to Pleasant Hill to see his girlfriend and he was hurrying so as not to pass up the chance of going ... I just thought it was kinda funny that he was running around without his pants on because usually that is the thing that he worries about most, or his shoes is what he worries about most. So usually those go on first and then his shirt.

Dream 15: I was talking to my brother before we went to Pleasant Hill and ... we were sitting in the car ready to go ... we were just talking about all different things ... I asked him if he was glad he was going to go and he said yes, and ... I was kinda glad that he was going to go see his girlfriend 'cause that's what he wants to do all the time. I think we were going to go visit some friends while he was visiting his girlfriend. I was sitting in the front seat and he was sitting in the back seat waiting for my mother and sister to get out to the car so that we could leave ... and I think we were also talking something about school, or how he was doing in school, which is a very touchy subject to him normally.

Dream 16: Most of the time I think I was thinking about other dreams that I'd had before. I was thinking about the one I had tonight, that it was kind of odd that I'd be talking to my brother . . . and there was one last night that I had . . . it was kinda unusual too . . . there was supposed to be a man dreamer up here and he took the electrodes off of his head without it showing on the machine . . . the machine just kept working as if he still had 'em on. So we got up and left and went down to a café that was supposed to be on the corner and we both had coffee and doughnuts and . . . I can't stand coffee and I can't have doughnuts so . . . I dunno what I was doing there.

Dream 17: I was just thinking about getting up . . . and I was just thinking about different things, like an argument my girlfriend had with her dad . . . there was another time that I was thinking about another dream that I had the other night. I think I was thinking just about leaving home . . . well most of the stuff that I have I got with my money, my clothes and stuff like that, and so if I had enough money to get an apartment then I could just leave home, but I think my mother is kind of overprotective and she wouldn't hear of this at all even though I don't have the money, but she ran away from home when she was fifteen.

The central themes of emerging independence and a new life are continued on this night, and many of the same symbols, such as clothes and money, appear again. Leaving is a central feature of all five dreams, probably because of Penny's scheduled departure for the hospital the next day.

In dream 13, Penny is waiting for her father to pick her up from the sleep laboratory. She is holding a rating scale that is "cut out" in an odd shape, symbolizing her body after surgery. This dream is dominated by her "new look" in body imagery, e.g., she is "skinny" and dressed up in new clothes, expressing her fantasy of sudden personal transformation after surgery. In dreams 14 and 15, the theme of leaving is prominent, but is largely projected onto her brother, who is leaving for "Pleasant Hill" to see his girlfriend. The associated elements are: "the new"—money—clothes—independence—sex (brother without pants on, boy-girl relation)—positive affect ("Pleasant Hill"). This projection permits simultaneous expression of her wish for an exciting new life and her fear of giving up her protected position and the related fear of parental disapproval. That is, her sexual desires, including the wish to exhibit herself, are expressed via the brother, and she is left in the relatively safe position of onlooker.

In the rather thoughtlike dreams 16 and 17, leaving and potential independence are again central themes. Dream 17 presents the
conflict between her wish to be independent ("my money"; "my
clothes"; "get an apartment") and her parents' overprotectiveness
("argument my girlfriend had with her dad"; "mother is kind of
overprotective").

Penny's impending departure for the hospital apparently aroused
her general concern about leaving and associated material, including her previous hospital experiences and her fear of abandonment. Interestingly, the members of her family appear in all the
dreams of this night, whereas there had been no direct reference to
them in the dreams of the previous three nights. It seems likely
that the immediate prospect of separation intensified her wish to
have them close.

Summary: Effects of Stress on the Preoperative Dreams

Penny's thoughts about her impending surgery were dominated
by her hopes and fantasies that it would lead to a new life. These
were in part realistic, in view of her recent positive experience in
the hospital, and in part unrealistic, since her hope for psychological and social change far outran anything that might result
from the operation. Thus her anticipations of surgery were relatively positive and nonanxious; the inflated nature of her expectations, however, prepared the way for an unpleasant postoperative
experience. These trends are clearly seen in her pre- and postoperative dreams.

In general, neither her pre- nor postoperative dreams directly
incorporated material related to surgery. Concern about surgery
was reflected, however, in symbols of defective or damaged objects and in references to cutting. Defective or damaged objects
appeared in 38% of the preoperative dreams (versus 15% of the
postoperative dreams), seemingly as symbols of her own body. She
maintained some protective distance, however, by projecting this
damage onto other people's possessions. Some of the defective
objects were a house with the front removed, a piece of cut cloth,
a rating scale cut into an odd shape, worn-out phonograph records,
and a poorly built, "rickety" hot-dog stand. Some mention of the

word "cut," or an object that had been cut, appeared in 25% of the preoperative dreams but in none of the postoperative dreams. Cutting is a symbolic element that appears in the preoperative dreams of all the subjects to some degree, and seems to refer to the act of surgery itself.

Food and eating were other symbols that appeared in Penny's dreams more frequently before surgery than after (38% versus 8%). They could have been related to her malfunctioning gall bladder, which did cause digestive difficulties. But food and eating were also very clearly connected with her feeling of dependence and inadequacy and her wish to move toward independence and adequacy (physical attractiveness). The way in which food and restaurants appeared in the dreams indicates that this latter meaning was the dominant one.

The themes of bodily changes, emerging independence, leaving and being abandoned, and her particular modes of coping with these issues dominate Penny's dreams. Her feeling of inadequacy and her fear of being unloved and abandoned were represented in several ways, including acts of departing. These occurred frequently: in 56% of the pre- and 23% of the postoperative dreams. On the last preoperative night, four dreams centrally concerned leaving. Several of Penny's dreams involved attempts to escape from confinement or restrictions. In some instances it was clear that the restrictions represented her parents' overprotectiveness and her dependence on them. These dreams also represented fear of inadequacy and rejection, anxiety about sexual encounters, and desire to remain in a safe, dependent position. Penny's struggle with independence is a characteristic one for late adolescence, in her case intensified by hospitalization and the anticipation of surgery.

Hopes and fantasies of compensatory gain from surgery were prominent during the preoperative period, and in her dreams were expressed in themes in which the dream characters were seeking or undergoing significant changes in their lives. Contrasts between old or traditional styles and new or innovative ones appeared in 38% of the pre- versus 15% of the postoperative dreams. Clothing was the most frequently used symbol in the preoperative dreams (75%, versus 38% of the postoperative dreams), and was clearly of central importance as a symbol for her body and self. This symbolic use of clothing parallels the central role played by clothes in her waking preparatory activity (e.g., sewing new dresses for her anticipated "new" body) and her tendency to project her own sense of inadequacy onto inadequate clothes. In three dreams she appeared as slim and wearing the sort of tight-fitting clothes she hoped to wear after the operation—an expression of her mildly sexual, exhibitionistic wish to be recognized and looked at.

Her hope for a new social life was represented by social interaction that she or other dream characters engaged in (38% of the pre-, 23% of the postoperative dreams). The low-anxiety dreams in which this theme appeared expressed Penny's fantasies of improving her appearance and becoming accepted as a full-fledged member of her peer group. In these social interactions she or other people were usually depicted as optimistic and happy.

The unrealistic nature of her hopes led to moderate disappointment after surgery, when she was faced with herself as essentially unchanged in appearance and social accomplishments. In addition, she had to cope with the loss of a part of her body and an unexpected medical procedure—the insertion of a drainage tube and the attached disposal bag. This burdensome and unsightly apparatus reinforced her image of herself as physically different from her contemporaries. As a result of these circumstances, her postoperative dreams expressed more anxiety, hostility, and emotional involvement, and incorporated more material related to the stress of surgery, than did the preoperative dreams. Moreover, 30% of the postoperative versus 0% of the preoperative dreams contained references to an actual or threatened loss of some person or possession, perhaps reflecting her reaction to the loss of her gall bladder as well as the loss of her hope for sudden personal change. Such losses are typically followed by some degree of grief or mourning, particularly in people who experience actual bodily damage from surgery (Janis and Leventhal, 1965). Two of the postoperative dreams rated highest in anxiety contained elements symbolically related to her disturbing experience with the drainage tube. This was one of the few stress stimuli to be centrally incorporated in her dreams.

In summary, the main effect of the preoperative stress was to arouse hopes and fantasies of becoming more attractive and independent. Along with these went a slight intensification of the existing conflict about giving up her dependent position. The dreams of the postoperative period revealed a preoccupation with loss and the specific idea of getting rid of something. This preoccupation was associated with increased anxiety and a mild grief reaction to the loss of a part of her body and to the loss of her hope of dramatic personal change.

PAUL

Paul is a 56-year-old logger who was scheduled for the surgical removal of an advanced tumor in the colon. Despite the seriousness of the operation, which would involve a colostomy, he claimed to be free of all but a slight degree of worry. His main attitude was, "It's just one of those things that has to be done . . . that's all there is to it." He did voice some concern about losing his old job as a "faller and bucker" because of the colostomy, but quickly qualified this by saying that "It is all to the good because it will be getting rid of the tumor." In general, Paul was calm and optimistic throughout the preoperative period. He never expressed annoyance or complained in any way about either the hospital procedures or the inconvenience of serving in the dream project. The nurses reported that he was a "model patient," always did what he was told, and frequently tried to reassure other patients who expressed concern about their impending operations.

Paul seemed to be the least emotionally aroused of the five subjects during the preoperative period. He appeared to be very calm, deliberate in manner, and, above all, very emotionally controlled. His responses during the interviews and to psychological tests were quite short and colorless, and frequently vague. For example, his 20-response Rorschach contained no human-movement and only four animal-movement responses, indicating a constriction or inhibition of fantasy. Although quite intelligent, he is a person who tends to avoid fantasy and even imaginative thinking, concentrating instead on obvious, practical matters. While he rather persistently denied the serious nature of his condition, the assessment revealed a moderate degree of depression, indicating that his massive efforts at defense by denial were not entirely successful.

There was little indication of psychological preparation in Paul's preoperative behavior, although he enjoyed frequent visits with the other patients on his ward. On the last preoperative night, he reported feeling quite prepared for the surgery and did not seem to have any unrealistic expectations about the pain or risks that would be involved. Paul came through the operation well, but recovered quite slowly. Nevertheless, he was very optimistic and his emotional control appeared to be just as strong as it had been before the operation. The only disturbing event occurred soon after the operation, when the nurse tried to insert a drainage tube into his lungs. He reported that he had not expected this procedure, and that it had disturbed him so much that "the nurse had to tie my arms down by the side of the bed to keep me from resisting her . . . against putting that tube down my throat." Apparently this was the only incident in his hospital experience for which Paul was completely unprepared. Because of its unexpectedness, he came close to losing control of his emotions for the only time.

The Preoperative Dream Period

The major effect of impending surgery was a severe disturbance in dream recall and, apparently, in dreaming itself. Of nine REM awakenings during the preoperative period he was able to report only one fragment of a dream (". . . I thought I was talking with my wife"). Furthermore, during three of the five REM periods on each preoperative night the degree of eye-movement activity was so low that he may not have been experiencing anything like a continuous dream at these times. The major effect of the preoperative stress was, therefore, to increase his tendency to control fantasy by interference with the dreaming itself during REM periods and by an inability to recall the dreams that did occur.

Paul's failure to produce any dream reports during the preoperative period of course prevents the type of analysis carried out for Al, Melvin, and Penny, and we are forced to focus on the dreams from the postoperative period.

From nine awakenings in the postoperative period, Paul was able to recall three reasonably complete dreams and one fragment. The density of his eye movements also appeared to have increased, though he still seemed to be "skipping" at least one REM period every night. In both pre- and postoperative periods he had no trouble falling asleep, and slept quite soundly between awakenings.

We will present here the three adequately recalled dreams from the postoperative period.

The First Postoperative Dream Night

Dream 1: . . . thinking about an alcoholic when I come to . . . this fellow was scared of the stuff but he couldn't leave it alone . . . it was just like you and I were reversed and I was in your place and you were in mine; see, I was the alcoholic and you were the, I was even afraid to look at an empty bottle I was so bad . . . you were afraid to even let me look at an empty bottle, there was several empty bottles and you tried your best to even keep those stashed away from me so I wouldn't see them . . . apparently, every time I see the bottle I got perturbed.

The Second Postoperative Dream Night

Dream 2: I was just thinking I was back in the woods again, and I was looking at a spring, it was made out of block or two-inch timbers, two-inch planks . . . and I thought they was men working around me but I hadn't contacted them yet . . . Oh, I was just looking at the location plates to find out what section it was, there was a location mark on the side of this springbox . . . Well the last I was more or less very much interested to see where I was at what section, range and township, etc., I was just looking at this old, ah, it had been scratched on an old gallon tin-can cover we had put on this springbox, apparently many years before . . . This particular one [springbox], it had a pipe going in and a pipe out and the pipes had plugged, two-inch plank and probably, oh, twelve inches width, probably the box was four foot square . . . possibly it had been used sometime for supply of water, you know, for steam donkeys in the past. Apparently it was an old burn and it had been logged before but they had left quite a few logs and we were going along, you know, picking out the best, now apparently this was a way back because I didn't have any power saw yet, just an axe, you know, the regular crosscut saw . . . and yet I was talking to one of the supervisors we have now. I asked him if he could see the other men, then up against some hills you could see fresh timber coming, and they were cutting fresh timber apparently, while I was bucking windfalls or picking up salvage, more or less on my own just like I used to do years and years ago . . . looking for logs to salvage, you know, to buck off the ends. Wait a minute, there was a set of fallers, they had lowered a power saw and a man down to cut a tree down over a ledge, but I can't recall if I knew the set of fallers or not . . . apparently quite rugged country . . .

Dream 3: There was a light piece of tubing like they use for taking blood samples and things like that . . . I remember there was an attendant or a doctor, I think they were just getting ready to do something when I come out of it. I seen this tube, you know, something similar to what they use to take blood transfusions or take, take blood from you, or something on that sort of order . . . I was laying in bed . . . it seemed like there was quite a few, at least clustered around my bed and just the time you woke me up one of them touched me or appeared to have . . . it seemed like this piece of tubing was either laying there or one of them had it in his hand.

The symbolism in dream 1 is not entirely clear. A plausible hypothesis is that it refers to Paul's inability to recall dreams, to see what is potentially very disturbing to him. Being awakened and not being able to report anything was, of course, his dominant experience in the sleep laboratory.

Dream 2 seems to symbolize his operation, the disruption of his life, and his wishful attempt to master this disruption. "Looking for logs to salvage . . . to buck off the ends" in a region that had "been logged before" probably symbolizes his desire to recover from the operation and salvage what is left of his body. The old springbox containing the plugged pipes may refer to his bowels, which had been "shut off" by the colostomy, and the men around him "cutting fresh timber" may symbolize the surgeons who were operating on the other ward patients while Paul was convalescing. In general, the dream expresses a desire to be young and healthy, perhaps even to the extent of re-establishing contact with his earlier life. In this connection, it is interesting that Paul is a Rosicrucian, and that he believes in reincarnation. He had discussed this matter with Dr. Lane on the day before having this dream, and had mentioned that he would like to "come back as a forest ranger." "Cutting," a frequent symbol in the preoperative dreams of all subjects, occurs in this postoperative dream, as does a reversal of roles—that is, Paul does the cutting rather than having it done to him, just as he reverses roles with Dr. Lane in Dream 1.

Dream 3, obtained at the next REM awakening, deals more directly with surgery, and supports the hypothesis that dream 2 is concerned with the same topic. The "piece of tubing" is rather clearly related to his strong fear at the insertion of the drainage tube. He had "worried about . . . every few minutes they would come around with that tube again . . ." In this dream the tubing may symbolize the general threat embodied in the surgeons, with their life-and-death power: ". . . what they use to take blood transfusions or take, take blood from you."

In summary, the major effect of the stress was a striking inhibition of dream recall and, perhaps, even of experiencing dreams at all. This is consistent with Paul's general tendency to overcontrol fantasy and affectively arousing material. The nature of the operation may have been another influence, since Paul's life was seriously in danger, and even successful surgery would cause permanent bodily damage. In addition, dreams had a special significance for Paul: he professed great interest in them because he believed they prophesied the future, and he often wrote them down. Although he claimed he was not afraid of knowing about his dreams before surgery, it is possible that his underlying anticipation of bodily mutilation and death reinforced an avoidance of dreaming and dream recall. In this connection he reported that three months before his hospitalization he had had two or three dreams a night which he described as very vivid and "close to nightmares." He "forgot" to write these dreams down and could not remember having had any since.

MONA

Mona is a 42-year-old housewife and mother of four children who had complained for a number of years of acute pains in her side. She believed that the pains kept her from "accomplishing the amount of work around home I felt I ought to be doing." She had postponed doing anything about the pain, ostensibly because of a post-partum psychosis that had followed the birth of her last child. Ever since, she had been afraid that a major operation would trigger a similar reaction. However, five months before the current hospitalization she was forced to undergo a hemorrhoidectomy which she survived with little difficulty, and this experience prompted her to "get my side fixed too." She was scheduled for an exploratory operation for a suspected hernia.

The principal threat posed by surgery for Mona was the possibility of another psychotic breakdown. As she put it in a preoperative interview:

> Q: What are you most concerned about when you think about the upcoming surgery?
> A: Well . . . you'd probably never understand what experience, what I've experienced . . . but I'm not afraid of death. I'd hate to leave my children but I don't think there's much risk or I wouldn't even consider it [surgery] . . . But there's a lot of things worse than death in this life and I think mental illness is one of them, especially if a person never recovers . . . but I really have no fear. I think it's the childbearing that brought it on me.

Related to her fear of another breakdown is the threat of losing the support and nurturance of her husband and children. This seems rooted in a childhood fear of being abandoned by her mother. For example, when she was asked about this topic in an interview, she burst into tears and said:

> My mother used to threaten to leave us, used to threaten suicide too. But I have a great respect for her because I realize it was her health . . . she occasionally packed up and would leave . . . I know she felt stress . . . As we grew older we really got calloused about it . . . to protect ourselves [crys]. She went into a neurosis for three years in which she never got up and did anything. My oldest sister really took a hold and took care of the younger ones . . . [crys].

Her characteristic defensive efforts are also related to her mother. Mona overreacts to any possibility that she might be neglectful, and compulsively plays the role of the hardworking, dedicated mother to her own children. Thoughts of or wishes to escape from the hard work and responsibilities of motherhood are not tolerated, even in fantasy. Instead, she copes with such wishes by ever more compulsive housework. Physical symptoms provide the one acceptable excuse (see her description of her own mother) and the pain in her side has therefore served an important function. Periodically during the day the pain forces her to rest, providing a legitimate excuse for relaxation as well as a minor punishment. Since her symptom was centrally involved in a basic life conflict, it is possible that surgical treatment of the pain threatened to interfere with an important defense. It is also possible that her anticipation of being without the needed symptom was the major source of her fear that the operation might lead to a psychotic breakdown.

During the preoperative period, Mona both denied any fear about the operation itself and displayed a moderate to high degree of emotional arousal. She was very tense in the sleep laboratory and had a good deal of difficulty falling asleep. She appeared to be trying hard to maintain tight control over herself: rather than engaging in mental rehearsal or psychological preparation for the operation, she avoided thinking about it and kept busy with her work. Her focus seemed to be on the fear of losing control of her feelings and having another breakdown.

As might be expected, Mona's postoperative adjustment was rather poor. She weathered the surgery and short hospitalization (three days) quite well, but recovered slowly. The surgeon reported that no hernia was found, only some fatty tissue that "might have caused some irritation." He also reported that there was some question about whether the symptom was completely of organic origin, and that her recovery was "slower than expected." Six weeks after surgery, she was finally ambulatory and comfortable enough to begin the three-day postoperative dream-collection period. During this time, Mona appeared to be generally less tense in the laboratory situation and slept better than she had before surgery.

The Preoperative Dream Period

The main effect on Mona of the preoperative stress was an interference with her ability to recall or report dreams when awakened from REM sleep. Only two out of the 12 awakenings during the preoperative period produced full reports; two others produced brief fragments, and on the remaining eight she could report little or nothing. Even counting the brief reports, her recall during the preoperative period was only 25%, compared with 90% (nine reports from 10 awakenings) during the postoperative period. As in the case of Paul, Mona's difficulty in recalling or reporting dreams is consistent with her characteristically repressive mode of coping with the potential threat of surgery.

We will present the four preoperative dream reports that were obtained and such analysis as is possible on so small a sample.

The First Preoperative Dream Night

> Dream 1: . . . I had a thought of a swinging bridge . . . Just one of those bridges across the river . . . we used to have one across the river Umpqua in southern Oregon years and years ago . . . a swinging bridge . . . they're kind of anchored on either side and they give a lot in the . . . if they're walked on . . . there's give to the bridge . . .

The Third Preoperative Dream Night

> Dream 2: . . . Well, I was concerned because I found myself standing before this chest of drawers . . . with this stuff up on my head. I was a little concerned I might unhook them and pull . . . I was in the bedroom sitting at the head of the bed and then I was standing in the bed . . . I was still hooked up here with these wires and I was drinking the rest of the chocolate milk, and then it dawned on me I was hooked up and might loosen these on my head, I don't know how I thought I could be doing that and fastened to these [laugh].

The Fourth Preoperative Dream Night

> Dream 3: It seems I have some spoons on a tray, ah, sometimes instead of drying silverware at home I'll put it on a tray and put it in the oven, you know . . . and a couple spoons dropped through the railing to the lower floor, it was very humorous for the children, but for me it wasn't because I had company I was trying to serve . . . trying to get the spoons, you know, ready . . . my husband and a group that he belongs to and we entertain occasionally in each other's homes and have an evening together and the company were there, and here I was with the tray with the silver it was all slipped off, ah, the two pieces fell through the railing, then I proceeded to walk down the stairs and some of the adults were standing near the bottom and as I went on down, it seemed like the whole thing slipped, the whole tray full of silver just seemed to slip . . . it just seemed like I was on the bottom of the whole pile as it slipped, but it didn't seem to bother me any because this particular group that we have has quite a sense of humor.
>
> Before I was up on the upper floor with the tray, I had been up where the children were, and, well, just played with them, it seemed like I was with them for some time. I was listening what was going on downstairs, to the group talk, it seems to me like, that I knew I was supposed to be with them. My husband's the group leader of the group so I take the responsibility to make arrangements for the next time. Here I was entertaining but I

had a feeling I should have been there, because I might have to volunteer again, see. I knew I shouldn't be up there, I should be down with the group. It seemed like I waited until I just had to go down too [laugh].

Dream 4: Thinking about a possible line of work I might eventually get into. We have a good friend for the last twenty years and I was explaining to them that I thought possibly I would take a little additional office training, bookkeeping and this sort of thing, so I might be more valuable for instance. Now this really happened yesterday, the little one I have home, she had some temperature so I took her over to ah, doctor's office and he examined her and ordered a bottle of penicillin for her. I picked up a prescription of it and we gave it to her by mouth and then I left her with my husband and when I came back she said, "Look," and she'd broken out, down, ah, in little welts and she was just breaking out all over and so I just put her right in the car and went back over to the doctor's office. Well in my dream I was explaining all this. I thought possibly that if I got into the doctor's office, I went up to the window and explained to the girl there she had had a penicillin reaction, and of course doctors are always busy, you know, and I mean I was anxious that he see her before it commenced to fade—the reaction. I was so surprised that they would be so disinterested when I, she was right in the middle of all this breaking up and they just didn't realize, you know, that it was important that he see it as it was. And I tried to get across the fact that I think that this'll fade and I wanted to see it when it's really just little bubbles and they just didn't seem to realize that it was important, and I was explaining this to my friends in the dream why I thought that I would be a little more valuable maybe in an office this way, and as I was explaining to them I stepped around them because there was some glass like a windowpane, I just stepped all over this and made a cut, a couple of cuts in the bottom of my feet and the blood was spurting out and he was down there holding on to it, there was a good-sized vein there sticking out and he was holding it to keep the bl . . . blood from pumping out. I guess it was a . . . because you could just see the blood just shooting out of the vein. I seem to be standing in a place that was a rectangular place, possibly a three-by-three, he was standing up quite a bit higher than I was and as I was trying to talk to him, here I was walking on this glass, it looked like broken windowpanes that were evenly broken across you know, they just jutted up but I looked down and found that I had stepped in another place and cut again [laugh]. Isn't that a silly dream?

Dreams 1 and 2 both make reference to standing in an unstable place, i.e., the swinging bridge that gives a lot if walked on, and standing on the bed. Dream 2 also makes reference to a fear that she might "loosen these [the electrodes] on my head." These images may symbolize her mental and emotional instability and fear of losing her mind.

Unstable footing recurs as a symbol for her general instability in dreams 3 and 4. In dream 3, slipping and falling rather clearly symbolize her fear of slipping socially and exposing her inadequacies. Since Mona viewed her "mental illness" as a lasting social stigma, social slipping and mental breakdown are related. Throughout the period of dream collection, she repeatedly talked about her psychotic breakdown as if it were a disgrace which she would never live down. Several times she also expressed a great concern about the possible social repercussions it might have on her children. In this dream her wish to remain with the children rather than joining the adults quite clearly refers to her central conflict about assuming the responsibilities of motherhood.

In dream 4, her conflict about the housewife-mother role continues to be the theme: getting an office job represents an escape, but leads to guilt about being a bad mother—her child gets worse instead of better from her "care"—and subsequent punishment in the form of cut feet. This conflict is fused with her fear that doctors won't treat her correctly (which they did not, in a sense) and that the operation might lead to a breakdown. (Thus, the daughter who is "in the middle of all this breaking up.") The doctor's lack of interest in her daughter's symptoms may symbolize her feeling that the surgeons were not getting the correct message about her own symptoms. (Two doctors had previously refused to operate on Mona because, she thought, "they were probably afraid to operate on a woman who has had my trouble.") She may also be expressing some fear that the surgeon would not find anything physically wrong with her (e.g., "I tried to get across the fact . . . that this will fade . . .").

The "little welts," the daughter at the doctor's office, and the gushing blood are all suggestive of pregnancy and childbirth. These symbols tie her concern about her daughter to the fear of breakdown: her guilt about being a "bad mother" was central to her psychosis (she developed delusions that she had mistreated the baby and was not competent to take care of it). As she put it in an interview, "When I look back on it, it really seemed like a terrific effort to care for, to keep, to get up at night and care for the baby. It seemed like I really didn't have the strength."

The threat of mental breakdown, so prominent in the preoperative dreams that Mona was able to report, was almost totally absent from the postoperative dreams: in nine postoperative dreams only one symbolic element was scored as an incorporation. On the other hand, the conflict between being an adequate mother and being free of responsibility, being nurtured, or simply having fun continued to appear with great frequency.

RATING-SCALE RESULTS

One hundred and sixty dream reports were obtained from the five surgery and the two control subjects during the pre- and postoperative periods. Each dream report was rated for incorporation and on two of the thematic-dimension and the six formal-quality scales previously described. In addition, each dream report was rated on three scales directly related to surgery. The majority of the dream reports were rated by Dr. Lane and a second judge who had no direct contact with the subjects and did not know from which period, pre- or postsurgery, the reports came. The final scores in each case were based on the pooled ratings of the two judges.

The tables to follow present the mean ratings of the surgery and control subjects, and of each surgery subject (except Paul, who produced too few dreams), on the various scales. As in the Group Therapy Study, the comparison of dreams from two periods allows us to see what effects are due specifically to the stress of surgery, and the comparison of the surgery and control subjects (and of the surgery subjects with one another) allows us to examine individual differences. The statistical significance of the results was determined by two analysis of variance tests (the same as in the Group Therapy Study) on each dimension or scale. One tested the differences between the surgery and control groups and the other the differences between the surgery subjects. In the presentation to follow, we have simply noted those findings that were significant. The reader interested in a more detailed description, including the complete analysis of variance tables, can refer to the original study (Lane, 1966).

Incorporation. Incorporation of elements related to the stress of surgery was rated on two scales: *Direct incorporation* and *Symbolic incorporation.* Elements obviously related to surgery—doctors, patients, a hospital setting, medical examinations or equipment, operations—were scored as *Direct incorporations. Symbolic incorporations* included defective objects, blockages, etc. In scoring for *Symbolic incorporation*, the judges knew the nature of the operation and had available a statement from the subject that expressed his idiosyncratic view of his condition and impending surgery. For both *Direct* and *Symbolic incorporations* the dreams were scored 1 (one element present); 2 (more than one element present); or 3 (major theme dominated by incorporated material).

Table 6 presents the incorporation ratings of the surgery and control groups. Since the control subjects had no contact with surgery and knew nothing about the nature of the study, one would not expect them to incorporate surgery-related material in their dreams. Nevertheless, the comparison is useful because the scoring of *Symbolic incorporation* involves inferences about the meaning of certain symbols. If the symbols are not related to surgery but occur in the dreams of the general population, one would expect to find them in the dreams of the control subjects. Table 6 shows that both *Direct* and *Symbolic incorporations* occur much more frequently in the dreams of the surgery subjects (both differences are significant, $p < .01$).

Table 7 presents the mean incorporation ratings for the four surgery subjects. On *Direct incorporation*, three of the four subjects show a decrease whereas one (Penny) shows a slight increase.

TABLE 6

MEAN RATINGS OF SURGERY AND CONTROL GROUPS ON
TWO SCALES OF INCORPORATION

Groups	Direct Incorporation		Symbolic Incorporation	
	Preoperative	Postoperative	Preoperative	Postoperative
Surgery (N=4)	.42	.13	.80	.53
Control (N=2)	0	0	.16	.25

TABLE 7

MEAN RATINGS OF FOUR SURGERY SUBJECTS ON
TWO SCALES OF INCORPORATION

Subjects	Direct Incorporation		Symbolic Incorporation	
	Preoperative	Postoperative	Preoperative	Postoperative
Al	.29	.10	1.64	.80
Melvin	.93	.15	.40	.42
Penny	.00	.23	.47	.77
Mona	.63	.00	.63	.05

The pre- to postoperative conditions differences and the subject x condition interaction are both significant ($p < .05$). *Symbolic incorporation* is significantly different between subjects ($p < .01$), primarily because of the higher scores of Al. The pre-post differences are not significant.

The ratings of the individual subjects are consistent with the reactions described in the case studies. Penny's dreams show increases in both kinds of incorporation after her operation which, for her, was the more stressful period; the other subjects all show decreases. Al incorporated the stress-related material primarily in an indirect or symbolic fashion, consistent with his outward denial of concern. Melvin, who was more openly fearful, incorporated in both modes, but was rated highest on *Direct incorporation* in the preoperative period.

Thematic Dimensions and Formal Qualities. The dream reports were rated on two thematic dimensions (*Quality of interactions* and *Roles of dreamer*) and on six formal quality scales (*Anxiety, Cognitive disturbance, Implausibility, Involvement, Primitivity,* and *Recall*). The reliabilities and scoring procedures for these dimensions and scales have been presented in Chapter 3.

Tables 8 and 9 present the mean ratings on the two thematic dimensions for the surgery and control groups and for the individual surgery subjects. There are no significant differences between the groups or the subjects on these dimensions. The *Quality of interactions* becomes more pleasant in the postoperative period for both groups ($p < .05$), In general, the stress of surgery is not reflected in the thematic dimensions.

TABLE 8

MEAN RATINGS OF SURGERY AND CONTROL GROUPS
ON THEMATIC DIMENSIONS

Groups	Quality of Interactions		Roles of Dreamer	
	Preoperative	Postoperative	Preoperative	Postoperative
Surgery (N=4)	2.28	2.14	2.14	2.13
Control (N=2)	2.20	1.84	2.00	2.17

TABLE 9

MEAN RATINGS OF FOUR SURGERY SUBJECTS ON THEMATIC DIMENSIONS

Subjects	Quality of Interactions		Roles of Dreamer	
	Preoperative	Postoperative	Preoperative	Postoperative
Al	2.09	2.27	1.93	2.00
Melvin	2.50	2.08	2.47	2.31
Penny	2.21	2.09	1.88	2.08
Mona	2.47	2.15	2.75	2.11

Table 10 presents the mean ratings of the surgery and control groups on the six formal-quality scales. The surgery group was rated significantly higher on *Anxiety* ($p < .05$); *Cognitive disturbance* ($p < .01$); *Implausibility* ($p < .05$); and *Involvement* ($p < .01$). The subject-by-subject findings for the experimental group are presented in Table 11. The only significant differences occurred on the *Involvement* and *Recall* scales. The subjects differed significantly on *Involvement* ($p < .05$), owing to the higher scores of Al and Melvin. Significant differences on *Recall* between subjects, as well as between the pre- and postoperative periods, indicate that some subjects were better dream reporters than others

TABLE 10

MEAN RATINGS OF SURGERY AND CONTROL GROUPS ON FORMAL-QUALITY SCALES

Groups	Anxiety		Cognitive Disturbance		Implausibility		Involvement		Primitivity		Recall	
	Pre	Post	Pre	Post	Pre	Post	Pre	Post	Pre	Post	Pre	Post
Surgery (N=4)	2.24	2.17	2.05	2.03	2.58	2.44	2.97	2.81	2.39	2.40	2.74	3.00
Control (N=2)	1.69	1.94	1.46	1.77	2.01	2.10	2.27	2.40	2.16	2.19	2.37	3.15

(Paul and Mona being the poorest) and that almost all subjects tended to improve with increased experience.

Surgery-Related Scales. Three scales not employed in the Group Therapy Study were used because we anticipated that they would be particularly sensitive to the impact of surgery-related stress on dreams. Two of these scales (*Body imagery* and *Castration*) assess concern with damage to the body; the third (*Hostility*) assesses an affect that other investigators have commonly found to be associated with preoperative stress. The *Body imagery* scale reflects the degree of health and well-being of all human and animal characters and the degree of physical integrity of inanimate objects. On an eight-point scale, supranormal body imagery, such as a man with Herculean strength, would receive a low score, noncritical illnesses and injuries an intermediate score, and distorted or bizarre body imagery a high score. Interrater reliability of two judges was .51. The *Castration* scale is a combination of Hall and Van de Castle's (1966) two scales of "castration anxiety" and "castration wish." It is very similar to the *Body imagery* scale except that, instead of scoring all elements of bodily illness, injury, and distortion, it scores only for specific parts of the character's body (five-point scale). For example, a dream character being shot and killed would not be rated as castration, but someone being shot in the arm would be. According to Deutsch (1942), the anticipation of surgery very frequently arouses a strong fear of castration in males. For this reason, it was expected that the preoperative stress would affect the dreams of at least the male subjects in this way. Interrater reliability of two judges was .67 on this scale. The *Hostility* scale measured both the emotional and behavioral expression of hostility on a 10-point scale (1 = no hostility; 10 = extreme hostility). Unlike the other rating scales, the *Hostility* scale contains 10 levels or subcategories of hostility expression. This means that a dream can be rated for more than one manifestation of hostility, and the total hostility rating is a sum of these ratings. A dream could be rated as high as 55. The actual range in this study was 0-31. Interrater reliability of two judges was .82.

Table 12 presents the mean ratings of the surgery and control groups on the three surgery-related scales. The ratings of the sur-

TABLE 11

MEAN RATINGS OF FOUR SURGERY SUBJECTS ON FORMAL-QUALITY SCALES

Subjects	Anxiety		Cognitive Disturbance		Implausibility		Involvement		Primitivity		Recall	
	Pre	Post	Pre	Post	Pre	Post	Pre	Post	Pre	Post	Pre	Post
Al	2.16	1.83	2.16	2.15	3.14	2.40	3.43	2.75	2.43	2.38	2.87	2.60
Melvin	2.50	2.23	1.75	2.17	2.62	2.54	3.28	2.96	2.72	2.59	3.39	3.45
Penny	1.92	2.48	1.67	1.81	2.28	2.37	2.36	2.90	2.16	2.27	3.27	3.56
Mona	2.88	2.00	2.43	2.07	1.69	2.44	2.75	2.50	2.00	2.33	2.15	3.10

TABLE 12

MEAN RATINGS OF SURGERY AND CONTROL GROUPS ON
SURGERY-RELATED SCALES

Groups	Body Imagery		Castration		Hostility	
	Pre	Post	Pre	Post	Pre	Post
Surgery (N=4)	3.96	3.18	.88	.36	5.85	4.24
Control (N=2)	1.60	2.33	.04	.41	2.97	1.96

gery group were significantly higher on all three scales (*Body imagery*, $p < .01$; *Castration*, $p < .05$; and *Hostility*, $p < .05$). Table 13 presents the subject-by-subject mean ratings on these same scales. The subjects differed significantly on *Castration* and *Hostility* (both $p < .01$). The dreams of the male subjects contained the greater number of castration elements, consistent with psychoanalytic theory and with the findings of Hall and Van de Castle (1965). *Castration* ratings are lower in the postoperative period ($p < .01$), due to the absence of the specific threat of physical damage from surgery. *Body imagery*, which assesses more general concern with body function, does not decrease postoperatively, probably because the subjects were still experiencing physical discomfort. The difference between subjects on *Hostility* is due primarily to the greater number of hostile elements in the dreams of Al and Melvin.

In summary, the rating-scale results show, in several ways, the strong impact of surgery-related stress on dream content. First, when we compare the surgery and control groups on all 13 rating scales (two measures of *incorporation*, two *thematic dimensions*, six *formal-quality* scales and three *surgery-related* scales), we find that the surgery group was rated significantly higher on nine of the 13. It could be argued that these differences are due to factors other than the anticipation of surgery, since the surgery subjects differed from the controls in a number of ways: e.g., they were older, more disturbed, and in poorer physical health. The pattern of differences, however, indicates that the anticipation of surgery

TABLE 13

MEAN RATINGS OF FOUR SURGERY SUBJECTS ON
SURGERY-RELATED SCALES

Subjects	Body Imagery		Castration		Hostility	
	Pre	Post	Pre	Post	Pre	Post
Al	5.57	3.40	1.36	.80	10.32	6.45
Melvin	3.73	3.77	1.13	.46	4.80	5.75
Penny	2.94	3.54	.37	.15	3.53	3.50
Mona	3.25	1.56	.25	.00	3.38	.67

was the crucial factor: on all nine scales the differences between the two groups were larger in the pre- than in the postoperative period. The surgery group was in fact rated higher on all 13 scales, and 12 of the differences in ratings were greater before surgery than after. Another way of looking at these findings is to compare the pre- and postoperative periods. Here we find that the dreams of the surgery group were rated lower on 11 of the 13 scales after surgery: i.e., less *Anxiety*, less *Involvement*, less *Castration*, etc. The dreams of the control group, however, were rated lower on only two scales in the postoperative period, and were actually rated somewhat higher on 10 others.

The rating-scale findings provide an objective and controlled assessment of the impact of preoperative stress on dream content that complements the findings presented in the case studies. The general effects of stress are an increase in dream anxiety, fragmentation, and bizarreness (*Anxiety*, *Cognitive disturbance*, and *Implausibility* scales), involvement of the dream characters, and hostility. Concern about the integrity and health of the body was heightened for all subjects and concern about specific injury was heightened for the men. The individual styles of the different subjects in coping with the threat of their impending operations were reflected in the high hostility scores of Al, the greater dream involvement of Al and Melvin, and the poor dream recall of Paul and Mona, who defended against danger with constriction and inhibition of thought and fantasy.

DISCUSSION

A consideration of both the case studies and the rating-scale results indicates that the threat of surgery strongly influenced dream content. This influence took different forms, depending on the individual meaning of surgery to each subject and his characteristic manner of dealing with stress. In the discussion to follow, some of these individual ways of dealing with the threat will be explored in greater detail. We will begin with a consideration of Al, Melvin, and Penny because they produced the greatest number of dreams. Following the discussion of these three subjects, we will consider some general findings relating to dream symbolism and the role of dreaming in adaptation to stress.

For Al, the impending operation represented the threat of reduced mobility and surrender to his desire to be taken care of. In his dreams these threats were symbolized by objects or people whose mobility was obstructed, and by themes which expressed conflict about being dependent on others. In Penny's case, the prospect of hospitalization and surgery aroused some fear of parental abandonment, and intensified her conflict about becoming independent. Accordingly, over half of her preoperative dreams depicted the main character in the act of leaving. In Melvin, the anticipation of surgery aroused neurotic fears of losing his strength, his masculinity, and his sources of nurturant support; and over half of his preoperative dreams contained references to losses—including the danger of objects or people losing their physical support and falling—and to bodily defects and inadequacies.

The fears and conflicts symbolized in the dreams rarely appeared without an attempt to resolve or cope with them in some way. Each subject's attempts at defense in his dreams were consistent with his waking style. Attempts at solution were represented most clearly in the subject's interactions and roles as a dream character. For example, Al's role in the hospital and his role as a dream character both represented an attempt to prove that he was still strong, potent, and able to take care of himself. Melvin, on the other hand, coped with his fear and weakness by openly communicating them, in order to enlist the support of others. Similarly, as a dream character he frequently took the role of a child seeking the help of some more adequate person. Penny's waking strategy led her to dwell on fantasies of improved social attractiveness. Her dreams reflected her hopes in a preoccupation with clothes and social activities. In general, this congruence between the defensive strategies in waking and dreaming suggests that the subject's attempts to resolve his problems in his dreams issue from the same characterological sources as his waking behavior.

The consistency with which each subject represented his fears and conflicts is seen in the recurrence of specific dream elements. Al's dreams contained high frequencies of defective objects, threats of blockage, water as a threat or discomfort, repair and construction, references to legs and feet, and acts of cutting. Melvin's dreams contained bodily defects and inadequacies, blockages, lost objects, acts of removing objects, and references to food and eating. Penny's dreams made reference to defective objects, lost objects, acts of leaving, cutting, and references to food and eating. In all three subjects, the incorporation of these elements was more frequent in the preoperative period when the specific threat of surgery was greatest.

One of the most striking ways in which the preoperative stress seems to have affected dream content was in the repetition of elements and themes. The great majority of incorporated elements for the three subjects were repeated in a higher percentage of the pre- than of the postoperative dreams. Interestingly, this was true not only of stress-related incorporations, but of almost all the elements and themes in the preoperative dreams. The narrow range of symbols and themes had the general effect of constricting dream content. For example, four times during the preoperative period Penny had a dream which not only contained the same basic content as an immediately preceding one, but was actually a continuation of its activities and events. Such a sequence occurred only once in her postoperative dreams. This repetition and constriction of dreams when the dreamer is under stress is similar to the repetitive, frightening dreams reported by soldiers in battle conditions. It was just this kind of data that led Freud to the ideas of the repetition compulsion and the role of dreams in attempts at mastery of threatening experiences.

A comparison of the dreams of the two high-fear or overtly anxious subjects (Melvin and Mona) with those of the low-fear or

relatively nonanxious subjects (Al and Penny) is of interest. Melvin
and Mona had the greatest number of dreams containing direct,
stress-related incorporations, with relatively fewer symbolic incorporations. This state of affairs was reversed for Al and Penny,
who had a large number of symbolic incorporations and relatively
fewer direct ones. It seems clear that the subjects who were openly
anxious about surgery had dreams which represented their concern
in more direct ways, and that these dreams were experienced as
anxiety-arousing and unpleasant. There is a parallel between style
and success of solution during waking and dreaming. Al and
Penny, who were able to transform the threat of surgery into a
form with which they could cope—fixing mechanical objects and
preparing for a new social life—continued these forms of coping in
their dreams. Melvin and Mona experienced a great deal of difficulty in the waking preoperative period and this is reflected in
their dreams. Lack of "disguise" does not seem to be the central
cause of increased anxiety, since few of the dreams included an
actual representation of surgery and some of the most frightening
dreams were the most disguised. Rather, anxiety level seems related to the subject's ability to transform the stress into a symbolic form with which he could deal.

Particular dream symbols or themes were consistently used by
certain subjects to represent their core concerns. For Al, there
were many instances of repairing mechanical objects—a theme tied
to his lifelong identity as a rough and ready workman and, during
the present period of stress, to his conception of his body and its
need for "repair." Melvin's dreams contained a number of references to "high" and "low" which represent his rising to a position
of greater independence and power and the attendant dangers of
doing so. This theme stems from his conception of himself as weak
and small in comparison to other men (such as his father) and his
characteristic usage of this "weakness" as a means of obtaining
nurturance. The danger of departing from his "weak," "small," or
"low" position is represented in his dreams as the dangers of being
up "high." For example, he is high up on a ladder, in danger of
falling, or flying in an airplane which becomes a model airplane
"blown apart" by a fan "on high." Mona's dreams represent her
"shaky" psychological and social position literally—she is standing
in shaky places (a bed, a swaying bridge) or slipping down a flight

of stairs. These examples are similar to those reported in the Group Therapy Study, where we noted some of the individual symbols and themes of the different subjects.

In addition to the individualized representation of surgery and the characteristic individual symbols and themes, some common elements appeared in the dreams of most of the subjects, no doubt because of their common predicament. Defective objects appeared with some regularity, symbolizing the subject's fear of bodily damage. The representation of his defective body took a different form in each subject, appropriate to his condition. Al's blocked artery and Melvin's blocked digestive tract were symbolized in their dreams by defective objects which blocked the movement of something. In Penny's case, the defective object frequently had a missing or detached part, representing her expectation of losing her gall bladder.

An act of cutting or references to cutting, cut-out objects, etc., appeared with some regularity in the dreams of many of the subjects. These were obviously related to the act of surgery itself.

Finally, new objects, innovations, or changes seemed frequently to symbolize the subject's hope of recovery and improved health. The construction of some inanimate object was a particularly popular symbol in this category.

SUMMARY

The main findings of the Surgery Study can be summarized as follows: (a) the preoperative dreams of the surgery subjects incorporated stress-related material both directly and symbolically; (b) the degree of incorporation was quite marked when the personal meaning of surgery and the individual modes of preparation were taken into account; and (c) the content of the dreams was more repetitious and constricted before than after surgery. These findings strongly suggest that the dream content was significantly affected by the preoperative stress.

Incorporation and constriction alone, however, are not convincing evidence that the dreams had an adaptive function. It might be argued, for instance, that during the preoperative period the daytime thoughts of the subjects were dominated by matters related to their impending operations, and that their dreams reflected their preoccupations merely as a kind of epiphenomenon. Several findings suggest, however, that the dreams did not statically reflect waking experience. First, most of the subjects rated themselves as thinking very little about their operations during the day, particularly those like Al with strong tendencies toward repression. Nevertheless, a substantial proportion of dream content, particularly Al's, dealt with topics related to the stress. Penny, on the other hand, who rated herself as somewhat more preoccupied with surgery-related thoughts than the others, showed a relatively low level of incorporation in her preoperative dreams. In general, the findings suggest that the amount of incorporation was related more to the level of emotional arousal than to the degree of preoccupation with surgery during the day: the dreams, rather than simply reflecting waking experience, seem to have dealt with unassimilated emotionally arousing information. For example, three subjects—Melvin, Penny, and Paul—had stressful experiences with drainage tubes for which they were not psychologically prepared. In each case the experience seems to have stimulated dreams which incorporated and dealt with the incident in a central way.

In the dreams of all the subjects, the individual fears and conflicts are expressed in altered form. That is, the stress-related stimuli appear to be recoded, symbolized, displaced, or condensed so that their expression is at least one step removed from the primary source of stress. It is interesting, for example, that none of the subjects dreamt directly about surgery itself, and that there were generally more symbolic than direct incorporations.

This recoding or transformation is central to the adaptive function of dreams. The thoughts and feelings aroused by surgery are integrated with, or assimilated into, an organized network of memories. This process of assimilation not only transforms the stress stimuli into forms which are familiar to the dreamer, but opens up psychological means of coping with the threat. For example, in his dreams Al tackled the job of repairing damaged objects on his own, rather than having to depend helplessly on the skill of a surgeon to restore his mobility. Melvin, in his dreams, was able to depend on the help of stronger and more adequate people rather than face the emasculating threat of surgery alone. Penny dreamt that she was slim and socially desirable rather than facing her actual fear that she might be abandoned to the hospital and forgotten. The stress experience was expressed in a symbolic form which incorporated characteristic defensive efforts.

The question of whether the defensive efforts of dreams went beyond what was achieved during the waking state remains open. Surgery is a peculiar experience, in which active participation of the person, so frequently useful in stressful situations, is blocked. In a real way, the surgery patient is helpless in the hands of his doctor. Moreover, the experience is typically an unfamiliar one. Both of these factors may promote regression, and they certainly force the subject to rely more heavily on fantasy than active mastery. The data also reveal that aroused concerns which were not psychologically coped with during the day tended to be dreamed about. Al is a good example of a subject who was emotionally aroused by the stress but could not consciously accept it as a problem. In the waking state he engaged in very little adaptive worry, mental rehearsal, or other direct problem-solving activities; his dreams, on the other hand, dealt with the preoperative stress in a conspicuous fashion. Such findings are consistent with the view, outlined in Chapter 1, that dreams function to assimilate emotionally aroused information.

6

DISCUSSION AND CONCLUSIONS

The dreams gathered in these two studies represent a creative-symbolic effort on the part of each subject to come to grips with himself—his fears and hopes, his strengths and weaknesses—in the midst of a crisis. Each subject views himself and his situation differently; each has his own dream language with its private symbols; and each uses this language to represent his world in a way that is personally meaningful. Like a novel or play, the dreams speak for themselves. One can empathize with the dreamer or feel more or less certain about the meaning of particular symbols; that is, one can interpret or analyze them much as a critic interprets a work of fiction. But to do so imposes one's own view of things—one's own language as a dream interpreter—on the dreams. For this reason we have felt a certain trepidation about our discussions of the subjects' dreams. Do we really say any more about their meaning than they communicate themselves?

Given these reservations, let us now, as investigators and theoreticians, impose our "dream"—our own particular set of meanings—on the results of these two studies. We will first consider the findings in relation to other studies which have attempted to influence dream content, and then consider them in relation to the theoretical ideas put forth at the beginning of this monograph.

THE EFFECTS OF PRESLEEP EXPERIENCE ON DREAM CONTENT

Previous investigations of the effects of presleep experience on dream content have been of two types: studies of the impact of a more or less standardized experience, such as viewing a film or being deprived of fluids, and studies dealing with the relation of dreams to personality, for example, the dreams of patients in psychotherapy. The first type of study has tended to rely on group statistical analyses of data; the second type has largely taken the form of case studies. (The work of Witkin [1969a, 1969b] and his co-workers is an exception since it relies, like the present work, on several levels of data analysis.) By and large, only minimal effects of presleep experience have been reported in these studies as compared with the rather large effects we found in both the Group Therapy and Surgery Studies. How can these differences be explained?

Two factors seem to be involved: (a) the realistic and intensely involving nature of both the focus-session experience and the pre-surgery periods, and (b) the individualized nature of the data analysis.

The subjects' behavior in the group situation leaves little doubt about the intensity of their arousal. Hal's anxiety and agitation, Roger's difficulty in falling asleep and preoccupation with writing down "refutations" for the group, Pam's extragroup contact with Roger as well as her emotional displays, and Jackie's subsequent crying and somatic reactions all attest to the degree of the situation's impact. In large part, we were able to achieve this intense arousal by using a technique which was, by its very nature, tailored to the individual subject. The focus session can be viewed as a self-correcting feedback system in which the subject expresses himself and, depending on how he does so, stimulates the group to a differential reaction aimed at further self-exploration and emotional arousal. The group reacted in one way to Hal's naïve presentation—interpreting his denial of problems; in another way to Jackie's—expressing anger at her extreme control and lack of overt emotion; and in still another way to Pam's cathartic display, which they tended to accept and support. While we can view the focus session as generally "the same" presleep experience for all subjects in its demand for self-exposure, it was obviously a very different experience for each person.

The surgery situation was similar. Here the anticipation of an operation had very different meanings for the different subjects, ranging from Penny's hopeful expectations of personal and social transformation to Al's bravado covering fear of physical debility and loss of independence to Mona's fear of a psychotic break-down. What is eminently clear is that both the focus-session experience and the anticipation of surgery had emotionally arousing effects that were intense and persistent. The persistence of these effects beyond the immediate time of arousal is an important way in which our studies differ from previous ones, in which presleep events, even when intense, have typically been short-lived.

Both situations, then, had more of a real-life character than most experimental situations, which, simply by being categorized in the subject's mind as "experimental," are of rather low intensity. In our view, the intensity, persistence, and realistic nature of the presleep experiences account for their impact on dream content. Our findings support the hypothesis that it is affect-related or emotionally arousing information of personal relevance that one dreams about.

Being a focus subject in a psychotherapy group or anticipating a surgical operation are arousing situations for subjects because they concern *themselves*—their feelings, thoughts, and ways of relating to others, or the integrity of their own bodies—in an all but inescapable way. The meanings imposed on such experiences are personal, so it is crucial to determine the manner in which each subject encodes the experience before attempting to analyze his dreams.

The fact that subjects do vary widely in their reactions to arousing or stressful stimuli brings us to our next point: the way our data analysis differs from that of previous studies. Research on psychological stress (see Lazarus, 1966, for a review) has established that subjects react in widely different—and sometimes even opposite—ways to stimuli which are, objectively, "the same." The viewing of a stressful film may result in increased heart rate in one subject; decreased heart rate but increased GSR in another; and no particular reaction in a third. To assess accurately the effects of such an experience one must take these individual reaction patterns into account. If one does not (i.e., if subjects are treated as a homogeneous group), the results are likely to cancel each other out. The same thing applies to dream content viewed as an outcome of some arousal experience. Subjects react in differing ways to the input experience and their dreams, in turn, are differently affected.

In our data analysis we took individual differences into account by combining case study (in which the meaning of the arousal experience for each subject was coordinated with postarousal dreams) with a more general rating-scale analysis, and within the rating scales we used analysis of varience techniques that permitted subject-by-subject comparisons and the detection of interactions. These techniques allowed us to demonstrate the impact of the presleep experience in an objective fashion while still capturing important individual differences in response.

THEORETICAL IMPLICATIONS

Let us now discuss the findings in terms of the theoretical considerations set forth in Chapter 1. To recapitulate briefly, we conceive of a set of interrelated memory systems whose organization has developed over the course of a person's life so that he meets his needs in certain characteristic ways. It is the basic structuring of the memory systems which gives direction to perception, fantasy, thought, and action. We account for the way human needs are mediated over the long period of development in terms of two general conceptions: (a) the potentiating effects of emotional feedback, and (b) the persistence of patterns laid down during early experience, particularly the early relationships within the family. Through the course of his life, a person works out adaptive solutions within all the areas of central need. He becomes a person who loves others in certain ways, finds enjoyment in certain activities but not in others, expresses or does not express his anger in particular situations, and so forth. These personality characteristics are embodied in his memory systems and determine perception (they impose order on sensory input); guide the internal transformations of perceived input (i.e., determine the particular course of fantasy, thought, and dreams); and guide action and interchange with the environment.

Ordinarily, a great deal of this memory material is unavailable; that is, only a limited number of programs are used in reality-oriented functioning. But in certain special states, the utilization of other programs favors an opening up of the memory systems—states such as the hypnotic trance, free association, the state induced by such drugs as LSD, and the REM state during which dreaming is likely to occur. A person's productions during one of these states can provide us with information about the organization and content of his memory systems that is not usually available. This additional information allows us to draw inferences about the particular structure of the person's memory systems. It is for these reasons that dreams have been so fruitful in shaping the major theories of personality; or, in Freud's terms, why "dreams are the royal road to the unconscious."

Dreams are guided, in part, by programs that were more prominent during earlier phases of development—programs that are more "primary-processlike." Dreams thus provide the possibility of integrating contemporary material into the adaptive "solutions" worked out in the past. This idea is central to our hypothesis concerning the integrative function of dreams. Consider, for example, the patterns of relating to other people that become established within the family. These patterns, together with their very important emotional effects, persist, and guide later relations with other people. In Loevinger's phrase (1969), "interpersonal schemas become intrapersonal schemas." It is not surprising that what our subjects dream about is themselves in relationships with those others, past and present, that they feel strongly about.

The group-therapy and surgery situations were selected for study because strong feelings toward oneself and other people would almost certainly be aroused. In the Group Therapy Study, the subject's perception of and reaction to the other group members provide one source of information about his memory-system structure. In the dreams that follow the focus sessions the aroused material is reworked under the guidance of additional programs, including those of a "primary-process" nature. We find a related reworking of material for the Surgery Study subjects during the preoperative period. Here, it is the subject's body and life that are threatened, and the assimilation of this threat is facilitated by the operation of dream programs and the availability of earlier solutions. A consideration of the dream process in specific cases will prepare the way for a discussion of the relationship of defense to the dream-assimilation process.

Defensiveness, as we usually think of it, is manifested in the *form* taken by social—usually verbal—communications. For example, the person may forget what he was saying (repression), or attribute acts and intentions to others (projection), or surround his communications in a web of intellectualizations, rationalizations, or denials, and so forth. Dreams, however, are private, visual experiences rather than social, verbal communications and therefore defense cannot have exactly the same meaning in the two conditions. A clarification of the differences will be useful.

Let us begin by distinguishing between dreams and dream reports. It should be obvious that we never directly observe another person's dreams but gain access to them only via his report of them. This report is a social communication, so that whatever occurred during the dream is subjected to processing by the programs involved in the verbal communication of an experience from one person to another. This process is reality oriented and is influenced by such factors as verbal fluency and skill, experience, desire to communicate, and so forth. It is probable that dreams are subjected to a certain amount of critical processing as they are transformed into dream reports, during which process inconsistencies are dropped or modified, bizarre elements are toned down or amplified or changed, and qualifications introduced. For instance, when Hal, in dream 3, says, ". . . I'm usually not that way with other people," he is introducing a qualification in the process of turning a dream into a dream report. When Jackie reports in dream 3 that "It was scary but I wasn't scared," we cannot tell if not being scared was something she experiences in the dream or is introducing in the process of reporting. We have found that this kind of reworking is less common when subjects are awakened during REM periods (in some instances their reports sound very much like free associations) than when they report their dreams the following day. Nevertheless, a certain amount of it must always go on.

How is the defensiveness of social communication manifested in the dream reports of our subjects? Paul and Mona either cannot dream or cannot translate their private dreams into public communications. They show the form of repression that Freud described in his early cases of hysteria. The other subjects can remember and report their dreams but defensiveness is apparent in the way in which their reports are made. Hal's dream reports, for example, are characterized by a naïve detachment—as if the productions he is describing are interesting but not really his own. Al's reports are characterized by a similar detachment. Roger's reports, on the other hand, are characterized by an abstract intellectuality which, when he is most under stress, becomes highly fragmented. Similar consistencies characterize the reports of the other subjects.

A constant feature of the defensiveness of these different modes of reporting (or not reporting) dreams is that the subject attempts to disown or dissociate his productions from himself. Either he does not "remember" that anything happened, or he speaks as if he is describing something that *happened to* him rather than something that he did himself. Such disowning or dissociating is the common feature of all forms of defensiveness. It occurs so frequently in dream reports because dreams, more than any other psychological phenomena, are experienced as unwilled—as happening to the passive dreamer. Dreams are experienced in this way because of the particular features of the REM sleep state; the lack of muscle tonus usually associated with voluntary action, the resulting passive state of the dreamer, the intrinsically private, non-reality-oriented nature of the state, and so forth. Since dreams occur in this state, one need not postulate any special defensive process during dreaming (e.g., the "dream censor"), though defensive disowning becomes apparent in the process of translating the dream into a dream report. Rather than defensiveness or censorship during dreaming, we may speak of the private, nonreality-oriented, assimilative process. It is this assimilative process that facilitates the integration of strongly felt information into the solutions made available by the dream or primary-process programs.

Strongly felt information may be assimilated in a variety of more or less creative ways. Dream symbols, like jokes, puns, and slips of the tongue, have an economy which permits the efficient expression of several things at once. They are also more or less aesthetically pleasing, depending on the talent of the dreamer. The economical and aesthetic qualities of dreams stem, in part, from their unwilled nature. That is to say, the creativity of the symbolism flows from that state when the person is not "trying" in any reality-oriented, willed, or conscious way, but is simply letting his dreams come to him. Such lack of reality-oriented, conscious effort is associated with the use of those early, primary-process programs which facilitate creative fantasy. The process is similar to the phase of inspiration in artistic creation.

But such assimilation, no matter how creative, will have no effect if dreams remain private; if they are not integrated into the person's waking conception of himself. In Piaget's terms, dreaming is "pure assimilation," which means it plays no role in adaptation to the world, since adaptation must always involve a balance between assimilation and accommodation. In psychoanalytic terms, we can speak of dreams as "pure regression," making essentially the same point as Piaget. Both pure assimilation and pure regression imply that something more must be done with dreams if they are to have an effect on the person's life. As dissociated fantasies which "come to the person" they may be interesting but they remain essentially foreign intruders on the mind.

Our experience with the subjects in both of the present studies confirms this view. Without work directed at integrating the dreams—at breaking down the dissociations that are present both in the dreaming and the reporting—the subjects do not learn anything about themselves. Just as one must work hard in the real world to transform a creative inspiration into a poem, a painting, or a piece of music or literature, so one must work hard at making individual sense of one's dreams if they are to be more than fleeting, uninformative glimpses of what is within.

APPENDICES

The schedule of awakenings was intended to maximize the likelihood of good dream recall while allowing the dream to proceed for as long as possible. The following schedule was used throughout the study and is based on the average length of successive REMPs throughout the night. Additional considerations in constructing this schedule were the findings that dream recall is greatest when the REMP is interrupted before its natural termination and that body movements during REMPs often signify the termination of a particular dream episode or an entire dream period.

SCHEDULE OF AWAKENINGS

1. All subjects will spend exactly 8 hours per evening in the dream room (from "lights out" to final awakening).
2. A REM period must continue for 3 minutes before any awakening is attempted. If it ends before 3 minutes are up, do not count it as a dream. If *any* REM period stops spontaneously after 3 minutes, awaken subject.
3. If a REM period continues for 3 consecutive minutes, it will be counted as a dream period and will require an awakening. The time of awakening will depend upon which REM period of the night is involved.
   a. First REM period: Awaken subject after 7 minutes of continuous REM or immediately following the first body movement after 3 continuous minutes of REM, whichever occurs first.
   b. Second REM period: Awaken subject after 17 minutes of continuous REM or immediately following the first body movement after 8 continuous minutes of REM, whichever occurs first.

    c. Third REM period: Awaken subject after 22 minutes of continuous REM or immediately following the first body movement after 11 continuous minutes of REM, whichever occurs first.

    d. Fourth REM period: Awaken subject after 26 minutes of continuous REM or immediately following the first body movement after 13 continuous minutes of REM, whichever occurs first.

    e. Fifth REM period: Awaken subject after 32 minutes of continuous REM or immediately following the first body movement after 16 continuous minutes of REM, whichever occurs first.

DREAM REPORT INTERVIEW SCHEDULE

Dream reports were collected according to a semistandardized procedure which was intended to permit comparisons among subjects while allowing each subject maximum freedom to describe spontaneously the dream experience in his own terms. The interview guide was as follows:

1. Use name to arouse.
2. Say, "Tell me what was going through your mind."
3. Use at least two general prompts: "Tell me everything about it"; "Anything else?"; "Tell me more about that."
4. Inquire into each separate element that is not reported in detail.
5. Inquire about:
    a. People
    b. Feelings
    c. Locations
    d. Subject's role in dream
    e. Subjective experience of clarity and completeness
6. In cases of confused protocol, ask for a recapitulation—a summary.

APPENDIX B
DREAM CONTENT RATING SCALES

UNITS FOR SCORING

It is assumed that each single dream is a unit unless otherwise indicated. Some dreams seem clearly to consist of separate sub-dreams, and these should be scored separately. A dream is separated into subdreams if it clearly consists of separate interaction sequences. An interaction sequence is defined in terms of:

1. Continuity of location (scene).
2. Continuity of action of central character or linkages of actions which follow naturally, one after the other.
3. Continuity of object (person or inanimate object) with whom the central character is interacting.
4. Strong conviction on part of dreamer that dream sequences unconnected in any of the above ways do, nevertheless, go together.

When all four of these criteria are lacking, a second interaction sequence is defined.

ANXIETY

Complete absence of anxiety	Somewhat anxiety-provoking	Moderately anxiety-provoking	Quite anxiety-provoking	Extremely anxiety-provoking
1	2	3	4	5

The term anxiety is used here in a broad sense. It includes extreme emotional manifestations (such as feeling panicky, frantic, and/or hysterical), more moderate feelings (feeling anxious, worried, guilty, troubled, disturbed, nervous, upset, agitated), and realistic states of fear, including terror, horror, and dread.

1. *Complete absence of anxiety* is scored when there is not any anxiety reported by the dreamer, and when there is no manifestation in the dream of anxious feelings, and when there is no obvious content which might produce anxiety.

2. *Somewhat anxiety-provoking* is scored when the dreamer does not report feeling particularly anxious, but an anxious response to an event or object in the dream would be appropriate; the dreamer may have been an observer of the event rather than a participant.

3. *Moderately anxiety-provoking* is scored when the dreamer reports feelings of anxiety, or if anxiety is *quite* predictable as a result of some threatening object or event, or if a central character (other than the dreamer) in the dream expresses definite anxiety.

4. *Quite anxiety-provoking* is scored when the dreamer spontaneously expresses anxiety either as a character in the dream or in response to having the dream, *and* if the source of the anxiety in the dream is clear.

5. *Extremely anxiety-provoking* is scored when the dreamer spontaneously expresses strong anxiety both as a character in the dream and in response to having the dream, *and* if the source of the anxiety is obvious; the dream may be disturbing enough to awaken the dreamer.

COGNITIVE DISTURBANCE

None	Slight	Moderate	High	Very high
1	2	3	4	5

This scale refers to three things: (1) the degree of *confusion* evidenced or reported by the dreamer about the dream contents, or in the actual reporting of it; (2) the degree of *fragmentation* of the dream episodes, including disturbances in time and space; (3) the degree of confusion about the intent, motivation, feelings, or behavior of the dream characters or the interactions and events that take place. This may manifest itself most clearly in *contradictions and inconsistencies* in the content of the dream which make it difficult to understand what took place.

This scale does *not* refer to the completeness or adequacy of *recall*, nor to the degree of implausibility, symbolism, or distortion of the dream content. Some overlap with the *Recall* and *Implausi-*

bility scales is inevitable, however. Implausibility, for example, naturally results if the temporal and spatial dimensions of a dream are highly fragmented.

Rate cognitive disturbance *None* when the dreamer, without confusion or perplexity, reports a clear, unfragmented dream with a consistent, coherent theme throughout, and without contradictions or inconsistencies.

Rate cognitive disturbance as *Moderate* if the dreamer shows some confusion or perplexity about the dream; if some disorganization occurs in the reporting of it; if the dream is somewhat fragmented (resulting in spatial or temporal gaps); if the theme shifts several times (resulting in some incoherence); or if some contradictions and inconsistencies appear.

Rate cognitive disturbance as *Very high* if the dreamer indicates marked confusion about the dream; if there is considerable disorganization in the description and reporting of it; if there are a number of brief, fragmentary episodes which result in no consistent, coherent theme; and if a number of contradictions and inconsistencies appear in the dream content.

IMPLAUSIBILITY

Quite plausible	Plausible	Somewhat plausible	Implausible	Bizarre
1	2	3	4	5

1. *Quite plausible:* Something that could well happen to the dreamer.
2. *Plausible:* Something that conceivably could occur in the dreamer's life or is possible in the future.
3. *Somewhat plausible:* Something that is *possible* but very unlikely to occur to the dreamer in real life or in the near future.
4. *Implausible:* Something most unlikely ever to occur in real life to anyone.
5. *Bizarre:* Something so extremely unreal or fantastic as to be unusual even in a dream report.

INVOLVEMENT

Strong involvement	No involvement	Some involvement	Moderate involvement	Intense involvement
1	2	3	4	5

Involvement refers mainly to the degree of the *dreamer's* emotional and behavioral participation in the dream, and secondarily to the participation of other characters.

Involvement consists of three things: (1) the amount of interaction, particularly emotionally charged interaction, among the dream characters; (2) the degree of affect experienced in the dream; and (3) the degree of kinetic activity of the characters.

Rate *No involvement* when the dreamer is not a participant in the dream and experiences no feelings about it; also, other characters experience no affect and are only minimally involved behaviorally.

Rate *Some involvement* when the dreamer is not a very active participant in the dream, and experiences no particular feelings about it; however, the *other* dream characters may experience definite affect and be actively involved behaviorally.

Rate *Moderate involvement* when the dreamer is an active participant in the dream, having several interpersonal interactions and experiencing some affective involvement; also, other dream characters may be very actively involved emotionally and behaviorally.

Rate *Strong involvement* when the dreamer clearly experiences feelings as an active participant in the dream and is behaviorally active, with several emotionally involved interactions with other characters; also, other characters may be very emotionally and behaviorally involved.

Rate *Intense involvement* when the dreamer experiences strong affect, is very active throughout the dream, and has many emotionally charged interactions with other characters; other characters may also be very actively involved emotionally.

PRIMITIVITY

1	2	3	4	5

1. *Extremely socialized expression of impulses:* Mere conversation, intellectual activity, analyzing, cooperating in some activity, helping or assisting someone.
2. *Mostly socialized expression of impulses:* Competing, dating, holding hands, dominating in a benign way, eating, smoking, playing games, crying, drinking, painting.
3. *Somewhat primitive or unsocialized expression of impulses:* Necking, verbal aggression, exploitive domination, immature dependent behavior, hypocritical behavior, lying, cheating, damaging possessions of others, injury by impersonal forces.
4. *Mostly primitive or unsocialized expression of impulses:* Naked or indecent exposure in public, physical fighting, intercourse, stealing, injuring or harming self or others, destroying possessions of others, death by impersonal forces. (Self-aggrandizement; withdrawal.)
5. *Extremely primitive or unsocialized expression of impulses:* Murder, rape, intercourse or sexual activity with family members, homosexual activity, sucking on breast, suicide.

RECALL

Night dream reports obtained during or immediately after the conclusion of a REM period are scored for recall on the following scale. Scoring is done from typescript and tape recording. The scale attempts to get at the repression that operates when subject is awakened and the visual, *inner* dream process must be translated into verbal, externally oriented, or interpersonal communications. Since we do not have access to the inner dream experience, repression must be inferred from the *subject's* mode of reporting.

1. No report; complete blocking.
2. A single fragment or several fragments; not in any way articulated.

3. Somewhat unclear. Dream is reported, but it is clearly incomplete. Unrelated episodes or clearly incomplete episodes.
4. Average, fairly well recalled dream. Subjective experience: slight cloudiness in some parts, but the main features are clearly recalled and coherent.
5. Dream of exceptional completeness and clarity. No loose fragments and no cloudiness; subjective experience of extreme clarity and complete recall.

APPENDIX C
PERSONALITY ASSESSMENT DATA
FROM THE SURGERY STUDY

AL

MMPI Scales: L   F   K   Hs   D   Hy   Pd   Mf   Pa   Pt   Sc   Ma
T-scores: 51 50 51 61   78 64   60   69   52   48   46   48
(K-corrected)

SCT items: No. 5. *My body is:* still healthy and strong. No. 14. *My greatest longing:* is for continued good health. No. 24. *When I think about myself, I am most happy when:* working.

Rorschach (N = 22): *Card I.* (3) A Kodiac bear hide—big and ragged—the front legs are off and the tail is down here. (4) A sailor with a uniform on with leggins—but he has no head (location: D_1). *Card II.* (1) Two elephants fighting. Their trunks are up in the air and their front legs are together. They are either kissing or fighting. *Card IX.* (1) A jellyfish.

TAT: Card 8 BM. I see a gun there. That boy shot somebody and he's there where these doctors are going to try and save his father's life. But he's got a look on his face like he was real forced. He don't seem to be too broke up over it. He's got his back turned—he won't look. Well, he's only a boy and I imagine he'll learn a hell of a lesson. His father will live and make a hell of a good man out of him.

MELVIN

MMPI Scales: L   F   K   Hs   D   Hy   Pd   Mf   Pa   Pt   Sc   Ma
T-scores: 40 66 48 85   97 65   60   61   68   67   55   50
(K-corrected)

SCT items: No. 5. *My body is:* small, weak, and fragile. No. 7. *When I look at myself in a mirror, I:* see a skinny, weak individual. No. 17. *When I think about myself, I am afraid:* of this horrible surgery. No. 32. *Death:* sometimes I feel this surgery will be it.

Rorschach (N = 18): *Card I.* (2) A beetle I had seen in Japan all washed out and flat . . . frightful-looking thing. *Card IV.* (1) Something with awfully big feet and a little head and a long heavy tail and awfully small arms. He is kicking his feet out and standing on his tail. *Card VII.* (1) A couple of bunny rabbits that do the bunny hop . . . maybe they have shooting irons and they're going to pace off and shoot each other.

TAT: Card 8 BM. Somebody is going to have surgery. Looks like he was shot. Somebody's holding a light for him, maybe he's had his surgery and he's already out, unconscious. Either that or this could be a dream that the boy is having . . . or it could be that the boy shot the man. I don't know about the outcome of the operation. Outcome could be the man died from the surgery or from the bullet . . . that he was shot with.

PENNY

MMPI Scales: L   F   K   Hs   D   Hy   Pd   Mf   Pa   Pt   Sc   Ma   Si
T-scores: 43 55 53 53   55 45   62   41   33   67   52   48   77
(K-corrected)

SCT items: No. 5. *My body is:* smaller than it used to be. No. 9. *I suffer:* from underconfidence and shyness around people. No. 26. *I envy:* fashion models. No. 29. *My chief worry:* is about the future. No. 28. *My looks:* aren't much to shout about.

Rorschach (N = 42): *Card I.* (2) A person here . . . he's in a mirror . . . he's standing with the mirror in the middle of him so he can see the same half of him on both sides. He's . . . looking up at the sky casting a spell. *Card II.* (1) A rooster looking into a mirror. *Card VII.* (1) Two girls with ponytails heading for each other . . . a head-on collision . . . a girl could be kissing herself in a mirror. *Card IX.* (2) A fancy dress from the neck down and it has two different tiers or layers.

TAT: Card 7 GF. This girl's mother has just gone to the hospital to have a baby and already she's resentful toward it, because her room has been fixed up for it and it has new clothes, and a baby-sitter is trying to get the little girl's mind off the little baby by reading her a story, but it doesn't work . . . pretty soon, if the lady doesn't quit reading . . . she will get up and throw the doll across the room and run to her room crying.

PAUL

MMPI Scales: L   F   K   Hs   D   Hy   Pd   Mf   Pa   Pt   Sc   Ma
T-scores: 50   48   51   70   80   55   55   69   47   54   48   38
(K-corrected)

SCT items: No. 5. *My body is:* composed of the elements of the earth. No. 18. *My greatest trouble:* being too cautious. No. 30. *My health:* other than trouble I soon hope to be over with is good, I would say. No. 12. *My mind:* is at ease.

Rorschach (N = 20): *Card III.* (1) The center red could be a butterfly or flying insect . . . lacking is the head and antennas. *Card VII.* (1) Harbor in the South Sea Islands . . . aerial picture. *Card IX.* (2) . . . a tropical tree . . . brilliant red flower on the top.

TAT: Card 13 MF. I would say it was a tragedy of some sort. The lady is very sick and the man seems to be grief-stricken. I can't say much more than that . . . they're pretty hard circumstances. Possibly, that's why he is grief-stricken.

MONA

MMPI Scales: L   F   K   Hs   D   Hy   Pd   Mf   Pa   Pt   Sc   Ma
T-scores: 63   50   72   55   54   68   60   60   56   60   58   43
(K-corrected)

SCT items: No. 5. *My body is:* the earthly tabernacle of my spirit. No. 9. *I suffer:* no more than most mortals on this earth. It looks to me most of them enjoy life. No. 29. *My chief worry:* I think we sometimes use the word worry when we mean concerned. Worry has to be controlled as it makes us ineffective.

Rorschach (N = 26): *Card I.* (4) A little deal in between looks like a glutious maximus (location: d_5). *Card II.* (1) The center section looks like the canal . . . a little hole through the vertebrae where the nerves go. *Card III.* (2) That wouldn't even make a decent girl . . . she is reclining and got a sea-lion head (location: D_2).

TAT: Card 13 MF. I wouldn't know what to think about that . . . I mean this picture doesn't give me any thoughts period. *Card 18 GF.* Good grief! Looks like a person trying to choke somebody, doesn't it to you? I can't give you a story.

BIBLIOGRAPHY

Bartlett, F. C. (1932), *Remembering: A Study in Experimental and Social Psychology.* Cambridge: Cambridge University Press.

Berger, R. J. (1963), Experimental Modification of Dream Content by Meaningful Verbal Stimuli. *Brit. J. Psychiat.*, 109:722-740.

Bertini, M., Lewis, H. B., & Witkin, H. A. (1964), Some Preliminary Observations with an Experimental Procedure for the Study of Hypnagogic and Related Phenomena. *Arch. Psicol. Neurol. Psichiat.*, 6:488-534.

Bokert, E. (1967), The Effects of Thirst and a Related Auditory Stimulus on Dream Reports. Unpublished Doctoral Dissertation, New York University.

Bonime, W. (1962), *The Clinical Use of Dreams.* New York: Basic Books.

Breger, L. (1967), Function of Dreams. *J. Abnorm. Psychol. Monogr.* 72(No. 5, Whole No. 641).

Cartwright, R. D. (1966), Dream and Drug-Induced Fantasy Behavior. *Arch. Gen. Psychiat.*, 15:7-15.

_____& Monroe, L. J. (1968), The Relation of Dreaming and REM Sleep: The Effects of REM Deprivation under Two Conditions. *J. Pers. Soc. Psychol.*, 10:69-74.

_____ _____& Palmer, C. (1967), Individual Differences in Response to REM Deprivation. *Arch. Gen. Psychiat.*, 16:297-303.

Castaldo, V., & Holzman, P. S. (1967), The Effects of Hearing One's Own Voice on Sleep Mentation. *J. Nerv. Ment. Dis.*, 144:2-13.

_____ _____ (1968), The Effects of One's Own Voice on Dream Content. Paper read at the meeting of the Association for the Psychophysiological Study of Sleep, Denver.

Collins, G., Davison, L. A., & Breger, L. (1967), Dream Function in Adaptation to Threat: A Preliminary Study. Paper read at the 7th annual meeting of the Association for the Psychophysiological Study of Sleep, Santa Monica.

Dement, W. C. (1960), The Effect of Dream Deprivation. *Science*, 131:1705-1707.

_____Kahn, E., & Roffwarg, H. P. (1965), The Influence of the Laboratory Situation on the Dreams of the Experimental Subject. *J. Nerv. Ment. Dis.*, 140:119-131.

_____& Wolpert, E. A. (1958), The Relation of Eye Movements, Body Motility, and External Stimuli to Dream Content. *J. Exp. Psychol.*, 55:543-553.

Deutsch, H. (1942), Some Psychoanalytic Observations in Surgery. *Psychosom. Med.*, 4:105-115.

Dewan, E. M. (1967), Sleep and REM as a Programming Process: The P Hypothesis for REM. Paper read at the 7th annual meeting of the Association for the Psychophysiological Study of Sleep, Santa Monica.

Domhoff, B., & Kamiya, J. (1964), Problems in Dream Content Study with Objective Indicators: II. Appearance of Experimental Situation in Laboratory Dream Narratives. *Arch. Gen. Psychiat.*, 11:525-528.

Erikson, E. H. (1954), The Dream Specimen of Psychoanalysis. *J. Amer. Psychoanal. Assn.*, 2:5-56.

Fisher, C. (1966), Dreaming and Sexuality. In *Psychoanalysis—A General Psychology*, ed. R. M. Loewenstein, L. M. Newman, M. Shur, & A. J. Solnit. New York: International Universities Press, pp. 537-569.

———Gross, J., & Zuch, J. (1965), Cycle of Penile Erection Synchronous with Dreaming (REM) Sleep. *Arch. Gen. Psychiat.*, 12:29-45.

Fiss, H., et al. (1968), Changes in Dream Content as a Function of Prolonged REM Sleep Interruption. Paper read at the 8th annual meeting of the Association for the Psychophysiological Study of Sleep, Denver.

———& Ellman, S. J. (1967), The Effects of REM Sleep Interruption on the Sleep Cycle. Paper read at the 7th annual meeting of the Association for the Psychophysiological Study of Sleep, Santa Monica.

———Klein, G. S., & Bokert, E. (1966), Waking Fantasies following Interruption of Two Types of Sleep. *Arch. Gen. Psychiat.*, 14:543-551.

Foulkes, D. (1962), Dream Reports from Different Stages of Sleep. *J. Abnorm. Soc. Psychol.*, 65:14-25.

———(1966), *The Psychology of Sleep.* New York: Scribner.

———et al. (1967), Dreams of the Male Child: An EEG Study. *J. Abnorm. Psychol.*, 72:457-467.

———& Rechtschaffen, A. (1964), Presleep Determinants of Dream Content: Effects of Two Films. *Percept. Motor Skills*, 19:983-1005.

———Swanson, E. M., & Larson, J. D. (1968), Dreams of the Preschool Child: An EEG Study. Paper read at the 8th annual meeting of the Association for the Psychophysiological Study of Sleep, Denver.

———& Vogel, G. (1965), Mental Activity at Sleep Onset. *J. Abnorm. Psychol.*, 70:231-243.

French, T. M., & Fromm, E. (1964), *Dream Interpretation: A New Approach.* New York: Basic Books.

Freud, S. (1900), The Interpretation of Dreams. *Standard Edition*, Vols. 4 & 5. London: Hogarth Press, 1953.

———(1920), Beyond the Pleasure Principle. *Standard Edition*, 18:7-64. London: Hogarth Press, 1955.

———(1933), New Introductory Lectures on Psycho-Analysis. *Standard Edition*, 22:5-182. London: Hogarth Press, 1964.

Goodenough, D. R., et al. (1959), A Comparison of "Dreamers" and "Nondreamers": Eye Movements, Electroencephalograms, and the Recall of Dreams. *J. Abnorm. Soc. Psychol.*, 59:295-302.

Hall, C. S. (1967), Representation of the Laboratory Setting in Dreams. *J. Nerv. Ment. Dis.*, 144:198-206.

———& Van de Castle, R. L. (1965), An Empirical Investigation of the Castration Complex in Dreams. *J. Pers.*, 33:20-29.

——— ———(1966), *The Content Analysis of Dreams.* New York: Appleton-Century-Crofts.

Hauri, P. (1967), Effects of Evening Activity on Subsequent Sleep and Dreams. Unpublished Doctoral Dissertation, University of Chicago.

Holt, R. R. (1965), A Review of Some of Freud's Biological Assumptions and Their Influence on His Theories. In *Psychoanalysis and Current Biological Thought*, ed. N. S. Greenfield & W. C. Lewis. Madison: University of Wisconsin Press, pp. 93-124.

———ed. (1967a), Motives and Thought: Psychoanalytic Essays in Honor of David Rapaport. *Psychol. Issues*, Monogr. 18/19. New York: International Universities Press.

———(1967b), The Development of the Primary Process: A Structural View. In Motives and Thought: Psychoanalytic Essays in Honor of David Rapaport, ed. R. R. Holt. *Psychol. Issues*, Monogr. 18/19:345-383. New York: International Universities Press.

Hunter, I. (1966), The Effect of Presleep Group Therapy upon Subsequent Dream Content. Unpublished Doctoral Dissertation, University of Oregon.

Janis, I. L. (1958), *Psychological Stress.* New York: Wiley.

——& Leventhal, H. (1965), Psychological Aspects of Physical Illness and Hospital Care. In *Handbook of Clinical Psychology*, ed. B. Wolman. New York: McGraw-Hill, pp. 1360-1377.

Jones, R. M. (1968), The Psychoanalytic Theory of Dreaming—1968. *J. Nerv. Ment. Dis.*, 147:587-604.

Kales, A., et al. (1964), Dream Deprivation: An Experimental Reappraisal. *Nature*, 204:1337-1338.

Klein, G. S. (1967), Peremptory Ideation: Structure and Force in Motivated Ideas. In Motives and Thought: Psychoanalytic Essays in Honor of David Rapaport, ed. R. R. Holt. *Psychol. Issues*, Monogr. 18/19:80-130. New York: International Universities Press.

——(in preparation), *Psychoanalytic Theory: An Exploration of Essentials.*

Kramer, M., et al. (1968), Drugs and Dreams III: The Effects of Imipramine on the Dreams of Depressed Patients. *Amer. J. Psychiat.*, 124:1385-1392.

Kuhn, T. S. (1962), *The Structure of Scientific Revolutions.* Chicago: University of Chicago Press.

Lane, R. W. (1966), The Effect of Preoperative Stress on Dreams. Unpublished Doctoral Dissertation, University of Oregon.

Lazarus, R. S. (1966), *Psychological Stress and the Coping Process.* New York: McGraw-Hill.

Loevinger, J. (1969), Theories of Ego Development. In *Clinical-Cognitive Psychology*, ed. L. Breger. Englewood Cliffs, N. J.: Prentice-Hall, pp. 83-135.

McNair, D. M., & Lorr, M. (1964), An Analysis of Mood in Neurotics. *J. Abnorm. Soc. Psychol.*, 69:620-627.

Money, J. (1960), Phantom Orgasm in Dreams of Paraplegic Men and Women. *Arch. Gen. Psychiat.*, 3:373-383.

Opten, E. (1966), Psychological Stress and Coping Methods in Surgical Patients: A Preliminary Report. Unpublished manuscript.

Piaget, J. (1945), *Play, Dreams and Imitation in Childhood.* New York: Norton, 1962.

——& Inhelder, B. (1969), *The Psychology of the Child.* New York: Basic Books.

Pivik, T., & Foulkes, D. (1966), "Dream Deprivation": Effects on Dream Content. *Science*, 153:1282-1284.

Price, D. B., Thaler, M., & Mason, J. W. (1957), Preoperative Emotional States and Adrenal Cortical Activity: Studies on Cardiac and Pulmonary Surgery Patients. *A. M. A. Arch. Neurol. Psychiat.*, 77:646-656.

Rechtschaffen. A., & Foulkes, D. (1965), Effect of Visual Stimuli on Dream Content. *Precept. Motor Skills*, 20:1149-1160.

——Verdone, P., & Wheaton, J. (1963), Reports on Mental Activity during Sleep. *Canad. Psychiat. Assn. J.*, 8:409-414.

Roffwarg, H. P., Muzio, J. N., & Dement, W. C. (1966), Ontogenetic Development of the Human Sleep-Dream Cycle. *Science*, 152:604-619.

Sampson, H. (1965), Deprivation of Dreaming Sleep by Two Methods. *Arch. Gen. Psychiat.*, 13:79-86.

Shapiro, A. (1967), Dreaming and the Physiology of Sleep. A Critical Review of Some Empirical Data and a Proposal for a Theoretical Model of Sleep and Dreaming. *Experimental Neurology*, Supplement 4, pp. 56-81.

Singer, J. L. (1966), *Daydreaming: An Introduction to the Experimental Study of Inner Experience.* New York: Random House.

Stoyva, J. M. (1965), Posthypnotically Suggested Dreams and the Sleep Cycle. *Arch. Gen. Psychiat.*, 12:287-294.

Tart, C. T. (1963), Effects of Posthypnotic Suggestion on the Process of Dreaming. Unpublished Doctoral Dissertation, University of North Carolina.

Titchener, J. L., et al. (1957), Consequences of Surgical Illness and Treatment. *A. M. A. Arch. Neurol. Psychiat.*, 77:623-634.

Trosman, H., et al. (1960), Studies in Psychophysiology of Dreams: IV. Relations among Dreams in Sequence. *Arch. Gen. Psychiat.*, 3:602-607.

Verdone, P. (1965), Temporal Reference of Manifest Dream Content. *Percept. Motor Skills*, 20:1253-1268.

White, R. W. (1963), Ego and Reality in Psychoanalytic Theory. *Psychol. Issues*, Monogr. 11. New York: International Universities Press.

Whitman, R., et al. (1962), The Dreams of the Experimental Subject. *J. Nerv. Ment. Dis.*, 134:431-439.

Witkin, H. A. (1969a), Influencing Dream Content. In *Dream Psychology and the New Biology of Dreaming*, ed. M. Kramer. Springfield: Charles C Thomas, pp. 285-359.

———(1969b), Presleep Experience and Dreams. In The Meaning of Dreams: Recent Insights from the Laboratory, ed. J. Fisher & L. Breger. *Calif. Mental Health Research Symposium*, No. 3:1-37.

Wolff, P. H. (1967), Cognitive Considerations for a Psychoanalytic Theory of Language Acquisition. In Motives and Thought: Psychoanalytic Essays in Honor of David Rapaport, ed. R. R. Holt. *Psychol. Issues*, Monogr. 18/19:300-343. New York: International Universities Press.

Wood, P. (1962), Dreaming and Social Isolation. Unpublished Doctoral Dissertation, University of North Carolina.

Wright, M. W. (1954), A Study of Anxiety in a General Hospital Setting. *Canad. J. Psychol.*, 8:195-203.

INDEX

Affects, 12, 13, 19-20

Al
  assessment of, 106-110, 203
  dreams of, 110-121; analysis of, 112-113,
    115, 117-118, 121-123, 171, 172, 176-
    183, 190

Anxiety
  preoperative, 96-101, 179-180
  see also Rating scales, formal qualities

Bartlett, F. C., 16
Berger, R. J., 27, 28
Bertini, M., 13
Body imagery; *see* Rating scales, surgery-
  related
Bokert, E., 24, 25, 29, 30, 36
Bonime, W., 7
Breger, L., 7, 10, 25, 30

Cartwright, R. D., 13, 31
Case studies; *see* Al; Hal; Jackie; Melvin;
  Mona; Pam; Paul; Penny; Roger
Castaldo, V., 28
Castration; *see* Rating scales, surgery-re-
  lated
Cognitive disturbance; *see* Rating scales,
  formal qualities
Collins, G., 25, 30

Davison, L. A., 25, 30
Day residues, 8, 13
Defenses, waking versus dream manifestations of, 189-190
Dement, W. C., 18, 23-25, 27-30
Deutsch, H., 96, 97, 100, 174
Dewan, E. M., 11
Domhoff, B., 24
Dreams
  anxiety, 8, 10
  censorship in, 14, 20
  cognitive information-processing model
    of, 7, 10-22
  content of, 32, 93, 184-186
  defenses in, 189-190
  deprivation or interruption of, 30-31
  dream report interview schedule, 196
  drugs and, 31-32

  effects of group therapy on, 48, 51-53,
    56, 59-60, 65-66, 69-71, 74-75, 78-80,
    87-94, 185
  effects of preoperative stress on, 122-123,
    138-140, 156-160, 163, 165, 178-183
  experimental situation and, 23-24, 34
  hypnotic suggestion and, 27
  individualized analysis of, 3-5, 185-187
  integrative function of, 22, 37, 91, 181-
    184, 188, 190, 191
  interpersonal interactions in; *see* Rating
    scales, thematic dimensions
  manifest and latent content in, 20-21
  mastery of experience in, 10, 179-180
  outcome of; *see* Rating scales, thematic
    dimensions
  presleep stimuli and, 24-27
  primary-process mode of thought in, 8,
    14-15
  psychoanalytic theory of, 7-10, 13-21
  repetition of elements and themes in,
    179-181
  reporting of, 34-37, 189-190
  roles of dreamer and others in; *see* Rating
    scales, thematic dimensions
  as the royal road to the unconscious,
    21-22, 188
  schedule of awakenings, 195-196
  sequences of, 37, 91
  similarity to waking thought of, 13
  sleep-protecting function of, 7-9, 18-19
  stimuli applied during sleep and, 27-30
  symbolic transformations in, 20
  symbols in, 179-182, 190-191
  unsocialized nature of, 13-14, 18, 189
  unwilled character of, 18, 28, 190-191
  verbal report of, 20, 34, 189-190
  see also Sleep, REM
Dream work, 9

Ellman, S. J., 31
Erikson, E. H., 7, 10, 20

Fisher, C., 29
Fiss, H., 30-32, 36
Foulkes, D., 13, 25, 28-30, 32
French, T. M., 7, 10

211

ABOUT THE AUTHORS

LOUIS BREGER received his Ph.D. in psychology from the Ohio State University in 1961. From then until 1966 he was on the faculty of the University of Oregon, serving as Director of the Psychology Clinic during the last two of those years. He joined the staff of the Langley Porter Neuropsychiatric Institute in 1966, and was a Visiting Professor at the University of California, Berkeley, during 1969-70. At the present time, he is Associate Professor of Psychology at the California Institute of Technology.

IAN HUNTER received his Ph.D. in psychology from the University of Oregon in 1966. After a postdoctoral year at the Mt. Zion Hospital in San Francisco, he joined the faculty at U.C.L.A. Since 1969 he has been Institute Psychologist at the California Institute of Technology.

RON W. LANE received his Ph.D. in psychology at the University of Oregon in 1966. From 1966 to 1968 he was a postdoctoral fellow at the Mt. Sinai Hospital in Los Angeles. At the present time, he is on the staff of the counseling center and on the faculty of Muir College at the University of California, San Diego.